SKIING WITH DE

LIFE, LIMBS AND LAN

SKIING WITH DEMONS III

LIFE, LIMBS AND LAND ROVERS

CHRIS TOMLINSON

www.skiingwithdemons.com

"Skiing is a dance, and the mountain always leads"
(Unknown skier)

"It's not leaking oil - it's sweating power"
(Unknown Defender owner)

YouCaxton Publications
Oxford & Shrewsbury

Dedications & Thanks

To Debbie: my friend, my life, my confidante, my wife.

I am grateful once again, to Carol Hardcastle, Dawn Roberts (proof readers) and Bob Fowke (editor), for translating the original manuscript into English. I'm also grateful to Dan House for creating the cover illustration and I'm especially grateful to Land Rover for turning owners into mechanics since 1947.

CONTENTS

AUTHOR'S NOTES

Good things come in threes. Things that come in threes are inherently more humorous, satisfying and effective than any other number of things, according to Confucius and his modern day equivalent, Wikipedia.

So it seemed logical for me to produce a third book to complete my trilogy. However, with only two seasons of the Chalet Project under my skis since the last narrative ended, there seemed nothing much to write about. The Après Aliens and the other Agents of Entropy had mostly been dormant. I hadn't been prepared to poke them with my usual life choices either, simply to create material for a third book.

Then on Wednesday the 24th January 2018 at around 11:30am the forces of entropy struck and handed me a narrative. In a freak skiing accident my right leg was partially severed, disconnecting my foot from my brain. I was plucked off the mountain by a helicopter and a world of pain, fear and emotional turmoil ensued – a perfect grow bag for humour.

Many skiers find themselves on crutches, usually after knee injuries and fractures. Most survive and return to skiing. Some don't (ski again that is) but skiing had become the central tenet of my life and, being a drama queen, that life seemed in jeopardy.

If *Skiing With Demons 1* was about a midlife crisis and 2 was about an existential one, then 3 would be about an anatomical crisis – trying to gain control of my foot and use it to ski again. Then another crisis presented itself and *Skiing With Demons 3* was on a roll. Assuming I skied again, did I actually want to be a geriatric ski bum? Was it time to end the Chalet Project?

Recovering from injury was an interesting, if unwelcome, experience and an untimely one too. Only ten months after the helicopter took off, I had to prove to the Ski Club of Great Britain (SCGB) that I could still ski well enough to continue being one of its leaders.

Meanwhile three summers had also passed since the last narrative ended. Even the most dedicated ski bum, still has twelve months in their year, no matter how much they wish they hadn't and some of them will be snowless. So I have included a couple of chapters about my summer passion, fell walking, to round things off. They provide a useful comparison, between skiing and walking that I hope any mountain lover (which I assume you are) should find amusing.

So this book is a diary of my battle to ski again and retain my blue leader's jacket. It also contains my deliberations on whether, after eight back-to-back seasons, I should end the Chalet Project. I have interleaved my usual bigoted and politically incorrect observations on people, life and Land Rover Defenders. And, just in case you hadn't had enough of it, I've added more chairlift philosophy. I hope you'll hop along with me and enjoy this, the very last *Skiing With Demons* book – I promise.

1. Right Place, Wrong Time

I've always hated the sight of blood - especially my own. It was therefore alarming to find myself lying in a pool of it on what was now a decidedly red piste. All I could hear were the words, '*je suis désolé,*' emanating repeatedly from Max, a young bare chested Swiss man, kneeling over my leg.

It was hard to be angry with someone who, so overwhelmed with remorse, had stripped naked to the waist in the freezing conditions. Max had taken his upper garments off to use his absorbent base layer as a compress but, despite his efforts, the blood (my blood!) was rapidly pooling around me.

He may not have been the cause of the collision, but it was his board which had sliced through my leg, so I guess he felt responsible and had taken charge of the situation. Both of us knew that this wasn't the time to be allocating blame. I wasn't in significant pain or in shock; I was just concerned about the loss of blood. I didn't think my leg or my life were in jeopardy - I didn't realise just how serious the situation was until I heard the sound of a helicopter.

I'd set off that January morning with the A-Team. Five of the best skiers I know: two former Ski Club leaders (Paul & Sarah), the Ski Nazis (Val & David) and Carol whose attitude towards skiing made the others look like skiing socialists. Even though they all knew the area well, I was leading this elite bunch because the Portes du Soleil (PdS) was my backyard and, after spending seven consecutive seasons in Morzine, I knew it better than most.

Season 8 had got off to a cracking start. Unburdened by chalet problems, Land Rover issues or hangovers, I'd been skiing well - although any skiing self-assessment is seldom an accurate one. I'd been training hard with other hopefuls, in a deluded attempt to improve my ski-instructor grading, by passing another course later that season. Despite a loathing of ski lessons, I'd recently invested a lot of time (and money) in them, and it seemed like some of the instruction had found its way to my legs.

That day, the off-piste had been uninviting, so we had opted for a piste tour of Switzerland. We had just crossed the border and were descending down the Swiss side of Mossettes, the highest peak in the PdS. We'd taken the steep, yet relatively easy, black run into Les Crosets and the Swiss canton of Valais. Any danger seemingly behind us, we schussed into the busy skiing crossroads at its centre.

Skiers and boarders were converging from several directions. I seemed to be on a collision course with a boarder. We both noticed that our trajectories intersected; we both changed to a new course but unfortunately they too intersected. Finally, at the last minute, we both turned sharply in opposite directions and the edge of the snowboard sliced across my right leg.

The impact didn't knock me over. It felt like I'd been kicked in the shin while playing football – so, instinctively, I went down for a penalty. As I lay there protesting, I noticed a large slash in my salopettes. This pissed me off because they were brand new that season. Then I noticed blood trickling out of the tear and the realisation that I hadn't been kicked with a football boot but with a sharp snowboard, sank in.

I hastily rolled my trouser leg up to reveal a close-up from a horror movie. The edge of the snowboard had sliced cleanly through the right side of my leg – the kick I'd felt had been the board hitting my shinbone.

'That's going to need more stitches to repair than my salopettes,' I thought.

Thankfully Max had changed from snowboarding assassin into a bare chested superhero and immediately set about stemming the flow of claret. At the time, I didn't realise they were the same person.

I had thought the boarder I'd collided with was female and I was pretty sure she had been wearing clothes.

Val had skied over just in time for the gory reveal. She gasped and the look of horror on her face confirmed to me that I needed urgent medical attention – 'Get me a pisteur,' I cried, pointing at the closest lift station assuming they could quickly call for a paramedic. 'A pastor?' she questioned, having misheard me. A *'pisteur,'* I repeated, thinking it was a little early for the clergy to get involved.

I wanted the lift-station attendant to call in a paramedic, as nobody else seemed to be bothering! There was actually a Poste de Secours (first aid post) only fifty metres behind me but I didn't realise this or that Sarah had been over already and requested assistance. There was a delay because all the paramedics were attending other incidents.

Sarah subsequently returned to the post and explained the urgency of my situation – I was losing a lot of blood. Most skiing injuries are broken bones and ripped tendons, none of which require especially urgent attention, but blood is finite and I knew time was critical. Max was doing a good job but his undergarment was already soaked and, unlike my female friends, I didn't want him to strip off any further.

Max was babbling on in French. Paul knelt by my head and acted as translator while trying to keep me calm. He suggested that I didn't look at my injury – a statement that is only ever going to further alarm a victim who isn't calm. I felt relatively calm and it seemed to me that those around me were not, which was alarming. Then Max, through Paul, asked me some seemingly unimportant question:

How old are you? – 'Too young to die,' I told him.

Can you feel your foot? – 'No, it's too far away for me to reach.'

The rest of the A-Team and some bystanders peered over my two attendants creating a tepee of concerned faces above me, some offering advice on whether it was a good idea to take my boot off. David, apparently more concerned for Max than me, took his jacket off and placed it around Max's bare shoulders. Someone was trying to make me eat a piece of Mars bar and drink water. 'Sod the water, where's the St Bernard with the brandy?' I thought. More importantly, 'where is the real paramedic with a sledge?'

Eventually one turned up – a paramedic, not a dog that is. More accustomed to the sight of blood than the rest of us, the medic casually placed an industrial sized compress over my wound and secured it tightly with what appeared to be gaffer tape. He had a greater grasp of English than Max:

'Where are you from?' he asked.

'England,' I proudly declared, wondering why my nationality was important and hoping it wasn't going to influence his decision making.

'No, where are you staying?' he added.

'Morzine,' I confirmed.

This was apparently quite important. He explained that he could simply take me to the nearest Swiss medical centre but the logistics of getting back to France after treatment would be worse for me than death – 'easy for him to say,' I thought. I then realised my passport was back in France. Knowing I was going to cross a border that day, I should really have been carrying it. I was an illegal immigrant and weirdly more scared of the resulting paperwork than of death.

So I agreed: a helicopter back to Morzine was the best option. Knowing that helicopter rides weren't cheap, I accepted that the incident was definitely going to cost me an arm if not a leg.

Pointing to Val, the paramedic asked if my 'wife' wanted to travel with me. Her face turned from horrified to mortified and she quickly informed him we were just friends. Paul and Val then had a delicate discussion about who would be best to accompany me – a free helicopter ride was the prize at stake.

I asked Paul if he would come along. Instinctively, I knew he would be good in a crisis. Not only was his French effective but he was also a relatively casual friend. In order to appear brave and stoic, I needed the audience of a relative stranger. Val and I were too close – she knew I was neither brave nor stoic and it would have been hard keeping up pretences.

Using humour to deal with a crisis is a very British thing. In fact the best humour is borne from crisis and perhaps that's why our humour is so renowned. To make light of a bad situation gives us perspective and helps us deal with turmoil; humour helps us emotionally disengage from a crisis and deal with it more effectively; humour is worn as armour to protect us from fear; humour in a crisis relies on the common understanding that life is mostly absurd - once you stop laughing at life you are sunk.

It turned out there wasn't enough room for a chaperone on the helicopter, so after helping me aboard, Paul stood back and waved me off - with a small trace of disappointment on his face. I was disappointed too; I'd lost my translator and my audience - my sense of humour would soon follow.

The noise of the engine and the whopping of the rotor blades increased and we took off. I waved back at Paul smearing blood from my glove onto the window - my day's skiing had turned into a war movie.

Once airborne I was distracted by the views and started to think more optimistically. They'd just sew me up at the medical centre in Morzine and I'd be joking in the bar with everyone that evening. I was unlikely to lose my leg and I was fairly confident I had renewed my travel insurance – so I'd be keeping both my arms too.

It was fascinating seeing the PdS from the air. We flew round Mossettes then swooped down the beautiful Abricotine valley. I could make out the pistes and the ant like figures skiing down them. I'd stood on those pistes many times and looked up at passing helicopters wondering who had been injured and how seriously – and this time it just happened to be me.

We banked hard left then passed over the Field of Dreams - a favourite off-piste skiing area of mine. We then flew down the Ardent valley and over Lake Montriond, which I had walked around two days earlier with friends. Through the chopper's window, my favourite ski resort resembled a model railway layout. Instead of miniature tracks and trains, tiny skiers moved around the pistes. I was one of those figurines - extracted for repair by a giant hand.

The on-board medic tried to get my attention. He handed me a form to fill in and sign. I didn't have my insurance details on me – who does? So I left all the boxes blank and simply signed the box next to a figure of €965 and waved my credit card at him. I'm not sure what the point of the form was. The price could have been €6,000 and I'd still have signed. Does anyone in that situation ever say, 'that's outrageous, drop me off here'? Anyway, if I was paying for the ride, I wanted to look out the window, not fill in a form.

We landed at Montriond, just outside Morzine, where an ambulance was waiting. Once I was loaded into the ambulance, the driver asked me how I was going to pay for the 1.5 km trip to Morzine's medical centre. I waved my credit card again and we set off. The ubiquitous form appeared but no pen could be found – so I offered to sign it in blood. I don't believe the French would actually leave someone to die if they couldn't pay – France isn't America after all - but they certainly give you the impression they will. I was delivered to the medical centre, transferred to a gurney and wheeled down a corridor into a windowless room.

The ambulance driver skilfully took my ski boots off, which was impressive; I find it a hard enough thing to do when both my legs are fully attached. He put the boots, along with the rest of my equipment (skis, helmet, jacket and gloves), into a cloakroom then busied himself cleaning up the trail of blood we'd left along the corridor. He then produced a credit-card machine. I got my pin code wrong a couple of times, which was alarming for us both, then the machine finally accepted I was the card's rightful owner and spat out a receipt. He wished me '*bonne chance*', then left - the good luck wish had only cost me €125.

I lay on the gurney for about twenty minutes listening to the sound of blood dripping onto the floor and wishing I'd extracted my phone before parting with my jacket. Then the infamous Dr Julian appeared and slowly started to gather suturing equipment. I asked him to retrieve my phone – he obliged.

Anyone who has been injured in Morzine in the last two decades will have met Dr Julian - not all encounters are reported favourably. He must be tired of treating Brits with what are essentially, self-inflicted injuries so his bedside manner should be excused. I had met him several times before, while accompanying injured guests, but this was my first encounter as a patient. His familiar grumpy face was reassuring.

Dr J called his assistant into the room. I watched her face gasp as he removed the final layer of the paramedic's compress. After poking around in my wound for a bit he put his tools down. 'This is too deep, you're going to need surgery in the hospital at Thonon', he declared (Thonon-les-Bains); to his credit, this was the right course of action.

My heart sank. I was going to enter the French medical system. I knew from personal experience how hard it was to escape from that institution. I'd pulled it off once before in Reims a few years back, but I'd had the use of both legs that time. Even though I've seen the Steve McQueen movie 'Papillion' several times, I still maintain that it's easier to escape a French penal colony than a French hospital.

By way of resignation, Dr J peeled off his gloves then left his assistant to apply a new dressing to my wound, which she secured with the now familiar, gaffer tape. She took her gloves off too then left me alone in the room with my thoughts. I reflected on the accident.

It wasn't really Max's fault. He may well have sharpened the edges of his board the night before, but we were both culpable for the collision. It could easily have been one of my edges that had sliced through one of his limbs. If his board had hit me four inches lower, the only damage would have been a badly scratched boot. If the impact had been four inches higher his blade would have sliced through my knee – the consequence of which I didn't want to contemplate. I concluded that I had actually been lucky.

Luck had also chosen a good place for my first serious skiing accident - the bottom of a piste near a first-aid station. Had I been deep off-piste, medical attention and evacuation wouldn't have been so swift. However, I had been unlucky that no paramedics were immediately available. I'd been injured in the right place - but at the wrong time.

Luck had also been kind with the weather. It had been a still day with good visibility. I've often skied in conditions where helicopters would have been grounded.

In a childish way, I had hoped that, should I be injured, it would be during some foolishly gnarly descent and hopefully caught on video. A survival story, that got more heroic every time I told it, might have emerged. But as luck would have it, I got felled at low speed on a flat area, in good conditions with lots of people around to help. I wanted a story of misadventure, not one of random bad luck – but those are the breaks you get.

I contemplated what I could have done differently to avoid the accident. Perhaps luck, or bad luck, had nothing to do with it? I could have chosen another route and taken the red instead of the black run to descend into Les Crosets; I could have headed to a different lift, there were two others nearby; that day, we could have decided not to ski over to Switzerland at all.

We had discussed having coffee only twenty minutes earlier, but the Ski Nazis were having none of it. I could have skied more slowly, put in more turns or paused to enjoy the view half way down the black run – but I was leading the charge. If we hadn't loitered for a second cup of tea before leaving the chalet, the whole time frame would have been different and the collision would not have occurred.

Had I made a different choice at each juncture I wouldn't have found myself in that place and at that time but my choices, however unknowingly, had led me to my destiny. Of course, in a parallel universe, Max might not have existed or I might have been a seagull – but that's enough fatalism for now.

Next I contemplated whether or not to call Debbie (Dr Debs), my soon-to-be wife. What could she do in England other than worry? Legs weren't really her medical speciality. She at least needed to know my intended location (Thonon) in case I passed out, so I reluctantly made the call.

2. Adventure Before Dementia

On the day of the accident, I had no logical reason to be in those foreign mountains. What would any human gain from going up into such a hostile environment? There was no treasure to be found, no bounty to plunder, no pursuing enemies to evade and no paradise to be discovered – there was no Shangri-La nestled between those snowy peaks. I'd gone up there simply to have fun.

Well, 'fun' isn't quite the right word – it's too small a word. Skiing is often more frustrating, painful and frightening than fun. Mountains are often places of purgatory not pleasure. Just getting to the top of one, suitably equipped, is a prolonged and expensive ball ache.

So why put life and limb at risk, to do something that is a load of hassle, has no reward, is dangerous and often isn't very much fun? Surely all skiers can't be masochists?

It might be the effortless speed that can be obtained that makes skiing so appealing. I don't think it's possible for any self-propelled human to go faster than they can on a pair of skis without jumping out of an aeroplane – but you don't have to be a speed freak to enjoy skiing.

It might be that skiers enjoy the challenge of learning how to dance with gravity. There are many complicated steps to learn, some requiring fitness and agility. But not all skiers are frustrated ballerinas nor indeed are all of them built for gymnastics.

Maybe it's the adrenaline rush you get when taking on a gnarly descent that many skiers find so addictive. Or is it just the endorphin-induced euphoria they feel after exercising all day in the fresh air? But not all who ski are junkies.

Skiing's biggest appeal could be that it provides total distraction. When skiing, you become so engaged with navigating the slope ahead that you forget everything else that is seemingly important –

including, in my case once, that it was my wife's birthday. However, skiing is more than just escapism, if often the cause of divorce.

Perhaps it's the mountains themselves. Some people have an inexplicable urge to stand on top of them. As Mallory said, 'because it's there' – we all want to climb our own Everest. For us lesser mortals, climbing the alpine peaks isn't feasible but we can ski down most of them – especially if someone has flattened the snow for us and fenced off all the really dangerous bits. However, not all skiers are obsessed with summits.

Is it the lure of the off-piste that rings so many skiing bells? The freedom of plotting your own line of descent on unprepared snow certainly tinkles mine. There is a self-expressive joy in bouncing down a fresh field of powder, leaving your own lines of poetry in the snow. However, most skiers don't go off-piste.

For some skiers, a journey into the backcountry has all the thrill of a polar expedition. It is to go where no man has been before – or at least not yet that morning. To enter a wilderness uninvited, to battle the elements and survive, is indeed an enriching experience. The Alps are one of the few remaining wild places that a modestly funded, relatively fit and reasonably sane fifty-year-old can explore. Perhaps older skiers, like me, are simply after a little more adventure before dementia sets in.

It could be the après scene that attracts the masses. Simply doing something energetic with friends then having a few well-earned drinks afterwards could be skiing's main craic. But skiing and drinking are not team sports, no matter how much some people try to make them so, and most après sessions run past any credit earned.

Maybe I'm looking too closely at the act itself to explain why so many Brits go skiing. 'Skiing' isn't just about the skiing but also about the environment in which it is done. Usually there is a breath-taking backdrop and a charming foreground, unless you're skiing in the Snow Dome at Tamworth, that is.

There is indeed a lot to enjoy in the Alps without donning the planks: the food, the drink and the fresh air. Eating local specialities and drinking mulled wine in a restaurant half way up a mountain is definitely a hoot – especially when people in funny leather trousers serve it. The Alps are a winter wonderland where every week feels like Christmas – even better, a Christmas without the irritating relatives.

There are many types of skiing and many types of skier, each with their own reasons for loving their discipline. Not all of us are speed freaks, adrenaline junkies, escapists, frustrated mountaineers or wannabe polar explorers, but all of us enjoy the physical and mental challenges skiing presents and love the environment it is done in – and most of us are probably masochists.

So what *was* I doing in those foreign mountains on the day of the accident, seemingly without purpose? I was there for all of the above reasons, but mostly I was simply having 'fun' (for want of a bigger word) before having a few drinks with my mates afterwards.

3. THE SEVEN YEAR ITCH

The Chalet Project's business plan had been incredibly simple: rent a chalet for the entire season, keep a room for myself and sublet the rest. Essentially, I would fund my own skiing by cooking, cleaning and driving. It was so simple that even I couldn't cock it up – or so I thought.

For five halcyon years, I managed to make the project work financially – or at least it broke even. I didn't intend to make any money, nor indeed did I. The mission was to live a winter dream, which was on the whole successful.

However, the problems began at the end of Season 5 when the Project's home (Chalet Neige) was sold from under my feet. While struggling to find a new winter home, I started to realise just how perfect Chalet Neige had been. It could sleep ten adults in en-suite luxury yet the rent was very reasonable. Critically, it was an easy stroll into town although not really feasible with ski gear, so I ran guests around in my battered Land Rover.

Driving around the Alps in a Land Rover Defender was part of the winter dream, but after five years, I had learnt the reality of owning an old Defender. The iconic vehicle is rugged and capable - but only when it wants to be. And yet, despite the reality, the Defender symbolises intrepid adventure, so I had to have one.

It's estimated that around 70% of all the Defenders ever made are still on the road. Officially, just over two million were made, so that means at least 1.4 million must still, however vaguely, be working. Defenders have distributed themselves evenly across the globe. Whether you're in the hostile deserts of North Africa or the mean streets of Chelsea, you'll usually see one. There is usually one parked on every road, in every town, in every county, in every corner of the world – or at least the corners I have been to. Where there are people there are Defenders, varying in age and states of decay. They may breakdown but they are cheap and easy to fix if you have the spare parts, which is where the other 30% come in handy. They are so ubiquitous it is almost impossible to watch the TV without one making a cameo appearance – or at least they do in the type of programmes I tend to watch.

Maybe I should have ended the Project after five years, declaring it a good innings. But life in the UK was still not going especially well and I found myself in the middle of an existential crisis. Thoughts of winter were still getting me through the summers. I still defined myself through skiing – if not a chalet host, who was I? So, on a friend's recommendation, without even viewing it first, I booked Chalet Framboise for Season 6.

A beautiful chalet in a stunning location, Framboise only slept eight, reducing my potential income. More significantly it was too far out of town. It wasn't accessible on foot especially if, due to intoxication, putting one foot in front of the other had become difficult. This was a big problem for my après-orientated regulars who now required a late-night taxi service and ideally not one operated by a grumpy driver in an unreliable vehicle.

Landie has only once ground to a halt and left me stranded on a hard shoulder. She malfunctions sometime and makes worrying noises - and gives me the impression she is going to die - but she usually limps home. Her main problem is that she is twenty-five years old and doesn't like the cold and prefers to sleep in a garage. Landie does go through periods of reliability – but anything that is periodically reliable can't actually be called 'reliable'.

During Season 6, I decided to skip most of February to avoid the busy school holidays even though large family groups had historically generated most of my income. I also outsourced the laundry and cleaning. I thought I was optimising the Project to reduce the hassle for me, but what I'd really done was optimise out my margin and Season 6 left me significantly out of pocket.

Despite all the out-sourcing, that season my stress levels went up. Framboise was at the top of a steep, narrow and usually icy lane. I started referring to it as the 'Cresta Run' because my heart was in my mouth every time I ascended or descended it. In January and most of February this required snow chains, which were a hindrance once in town. Landie and I were getting a little too old for running a twenty-four-hour shuttle service, especially in challenging road conditions.

To add to my financial problems, the snow never really turned up in Morzine that season and it was hard to fill my empty beds with late bookings. Landie had an equally bad year for breakdowns, and shortly after it began, I wanted Season 6 to end - I swore it would be my last.

If you count all the nuts and bolts, a Defender is made from 8,900 parts, and it seems like I have changed most of them. I've lost count, but it would be easier to list the parts I haven't changed than list the ones I have. Some parts I have replaced more than once – I'm currently on my fourth fuel pump. Landie's steering wheel is original along with the rear number plate, but that's about it. I have in fact got a very new Defender so my anxiety about her breaking down is probably now unwarranted. The only nut that is loose now, is the one behind the steering wheel.

The snow, Landie and I managed a bit of a rally toward the end of the Season 6. The drive became free of ice and I actually went skiing. Easter saw some late snow and some of my favourite guests returned – so I reassessed my plans to end the chalet project.

Season 6 had been sent to test my resolve, I decided. The prevailing forces of entropy would abate. Morzine was well overdue for a bumper snow season and it would be a shame to weather a storm and not enjoy the calm that usually follows it. What I needed was a more conveniently located chalet or a more reliable vehicle - and possibly both.

It is hard to explain to the unafflicted, why Defender owners get so attached to their vehicles. There is no real logic to justify this automotive love. Some owners claim they are still the ultimate off-road vehicle, but most never take their beloved off the tarmac. Perhaps, the crude engineering and lack of modern comfort appeals to those who crave a rugged outdoor life - even if they live in Sutton Coldfield. Maybe it's a common human desire to be somewhere that is wilder and muddier than one's current location. When Defender owners pass each other on urban roads, we wave while admiring each other's snorkels and winches. It's really a mutual nod, to a common gene that makes us ignore logic. We never wave at Discovery or Range Rover drivers – they are not similarly afflicted.

Unfortunately, I couldn't find a more suitable chalet, or at least not one I could afford, so I rebooked Chalet Framboise. Sentimentality prevailed and instead of replacing Landie, I'd spent that summer overhauling her, hoping she might live up to the Defender's movie-star image. I spent a fortune on new parts and equipped her with expensive winter tyres – effectively doubling her value. Landie and I rode south together again the following winter with high hopes.

However, Season 7 was an unmitigated disaster. Landie made it to Morzine but promptly died. The weather and snow were atrocious and instead of living the dream, I relived the nightmare or Season 6. I limped Landie home that April, double swearing that there wouldn't be a Season 8 – inevitably there was.

After much counselling and several honest discussions, Landie and I concluded that our relationship was going through a classic seven-year itch. Fundamentally, we still loved each other and it was worth giving that love one last chance. We would relocate to a better chalet for the ill-fated Season 8 – we just needed a new home and a fresh start.

We moved to the inaccurately named Chalet Benjamin. It was actually the top floor apartment of a large building. Four flights of stairs up, it was more of an Eagle's Nest than a chalet, but it didn't have a scary drive and was a practical walking distance from town – which would take all the pressure off Landie.

Season 8 got off to a great start. Early snow meant the skiing was good and Landie decided to behave herself - possibly because she feared redundancy. I felt that I'd finally got my winter life sorted. Then, on that day in Les Crosets, injury struck and my season lay bleeding next to me in tatters.

4. Escape From Thonon

'Hi Debbie, it's me. I've had a bit of an accident.' It was a phone call she'd hoped never to receive and one that I'd hoped never to make. She was at work and in the middle of a heart transplant! A cardiac anaesthetist, she plied her trade at Birmingham's Queen Elizabeth Hospital (the QE).

Luckily she had just popped out of theatre for a break and had turned her phone back on. I felt bad that I had interrupted her important work – even I could see a man between hearts trumped a man with a cut leg. However, anaesthetists are like airline pilots, all the clever bits are done at the beginning and the end of a job, so she had time to talk.

I described my injury and that Dr Julian was sending me to hospital in Thonon for surgery. No stranger to a medical crisis, she was calm and collected. She told me it was time to pause and assess.

How urgent was the surgery? Did I really want my leg reattached by an unknown surgeon and then have a lengthy stay in a foreign hospital? Was it possible to get patched up, fly home and have her colleagues, some of the best trauma surgeons in the country, sew my leg back together? I agreed a dash back to the QE was my best option. So, she would see if there was a flight to Birmingham that evening, and then call me back. Before we hung up she imparted one vital piece of medical advice, 'Get yourself a phone charger', because there would be many more phone conversations required.

Few skiers carry a phone charger in their rucksacks, but my accident has made me reassess what is and isn't vital skiing equipment. A fully charged phone is essential, preferably one with the local mountain rescue number already programmed into it. Carrying a small roll of gaffer tap is also a good idea too. You'll have to take all the kidnapper jokes on the chin, but it makes for the ultimate bandage, can be used to make a splint and repair torn clothing. A long piece of paracord also has a myriad of uses too: it's great for making a tourniquet, rescuing people from vertical predicaments and useful if a hostage does need to be taken. More seriously, if you carry a first aid kit, I suggest you empty it out and only put the items, the purpose of which you can identify, back in it.

Having spoken to Dr Debs, and agreed on a plan, I calmed down a bit and realised I need the loo. I'd actually needed a pee before the accident, but three hours had passed since then and urinating had returned to the top of my agenda. I called for help. 'Hello, hello, *excusez-moi*, anyone.' After a while, I decided to abandon my English politeness and started shouting, which did get the attention of a passing nurse. '*Le toilet, monsieur, très urgent*', I declared in my equally desperate French. He returned with a cardboard urinal device and left me to it. Thanks to childhood conditioning, peeing while lying down was physiologically very tricky, but I had viscous pressure on my side. Mid flow, Dr Julian's assistant appeared, which was a tad embarrassing. I handed her the now warm, receptacle, and expressed my desire to fly to the UK for surgery. '*Non, c'est impossible*', she replied, emphasising the ludicrous nature of my request with the Gallic facial expression French people reserved for imbeciles.

When you encounter the word '*non*' in France you know you're up against it, but often '*non*' can be turned into '*oui*', with a little persuasive charm. When a French woman in uniform utters the word, while holding a pot of your warm urine, you know you've more chance of extracting a hippo from a swamp than changing her mind – but I tried. I explained my 'wife' was a doctor and she could get me into surgery within hours of my landing in the UK. But '*non*' was still '*non*'.

I got Debbie on the phone so she could talk doctor language, but she failed too. The cut was too deep and too long to even consider getting on an aeroplane. I was Thonon bound and we had to lump it. Without sight of the injury, it was hard for Debbie to argue.

I called Paul and asked if he could ski back to the chalet grab some essentials and rush them to the medical centre, before I left for Thonon. Having come to terms with narrowly missing out on a helicopter ride, he agreed. Most importantly, he needed to reunite me with my phone charger.

Before long a fresh pair of ambulance vultures appeared and started wheeling me out of the room. I braced my arms against the doorframe in comical defiance. 'I'm not leaving until Paul arrives', I insisted. Not really understanding and presumably thinking I'd gone into some sort of shock they proceeded to forcefully wheel me down the corridor.

They told me *'votre ami'* was in reception. I didn't believe them, but there he was clutching a carrier bag. How he had managed to ski back from Switzerland, grab everything I'd requested from the chalet then driven to the medical centre in such a short space of time, still confounds me - it had taken me an hour using a helicopter.

He kindly offered to follow the ambulance to Thonon. At the time, this seemed unnecessary, but I accepted his offer and was extremely grateful I'd have a hand to hold.

Once underway, I phoned the Ski Club of Great Britain from the back of the ambulance. I was supposed to be leading a holiday for them the following week. Clearly, I wouldn't be able to honour that commitment and they needed to know ASAP. I don't recall whom I spoke to, but they sounded pissed off. So I apologised and told then I was literally hopping mad about missing the gig too.

On arrival at Thonon, I was wheeled into casualty and put on a gurney. My credit card was inspected again and I was parked alongside a couple of other patients in normal clothes – a frail old lady and an old man who was clearly a chain smoker. I felt a bit out of place in my ski gear. An attractive young nurse then approached me clutching a syringe. She was after a blood sample. I suggested that she didn't need to use the syringe because there was blood on tap coming out of my leg - sadly the joke was lost in translation.

Left alone, I went through the grab bag Paul had given me. He'd done a good job apart from packing a pair of Debbie's shoes, not mine and had forgotten the European adapter for my phone charger rendering it useless.

The nurse hooked me up to an antibiotic drip and wheeled me into a private treatment room and helped me change into a hospital gown. That morning I'd got dressed in haste and it was a relief to discover I was wearing a relatively respectable pair of underpants.

Paul turned up shortly afterward. I was impressed he had found me in such a large hospital, but he was turning into a bit of a bloodhound. I explained, 'Thanks for getting my stuff Paul, but I still can't charge my phone – no adaptor'. He slapped his forehead and departed for Thonon town centre to buy one.

Then my next bit of luck happened – I was allocated an Italian A&E consultant. His English was perfect and he could more eloquently explain my internal injuries. He supported my foot and asked me to try and move it. Alarmingly I couldn't make it move. I could wiggle my toes though, which was reassuring.

I swallowed my concern and mustered a joke, 'I guess my football career is over?' 'With the right surgeon, you might still be able to play for Hull City', he suggested, not knowing that was my team. It amused me that Hull City FC was a byword for footballing mediocrity in Italy. Having realised the extent of my injury, I did however start to wonder if my skiing career was over.

He poked various parts of my lower leg and foot with a pen, while asking if I felt anything. Alarmingly, I couldn't feel anything on the top of my foot or on the left side of my leg below the cut.

He brought in a younger, yet apparently more senior Spanish consultant for a second opinion. After playing with my foot, she concluded, a plastic surgeon was definitely needed and quickly. She explained that for the best outcome, I needed surgery within 48 hours. If nerves are reconnected within 48 hours they usually make a full recovery. However, I would need to go to a specialist centre – possibly in Geneva or maybe Annemasse? My heart sank. I was heading for another ambulance ride then a long stay in a foreign hospital.

Paul returned and was triumphantly holding a French USB charger. Hoping he wouldn't, I suggested that he headed back to the chalet and resume his holiday. He refused to go until my destiny was certain. This was lucky again, because he was still to play a pivotal part in my repatriation.

As we sat there together, he laughed at my crap jokes and generally kept my spirits up. He said, 'It could be worse, we could be waiting in an NHS corridor listening to people wailing and children crying.' At the moment the sound of a screaming child drifted into the room, shortly followed by the nurse, who wheeled me into the corridor to make way for another casualty.

This was almost the best piece of luck I'd had all day. While lying in the corridor the Spanish consultant walked passed and I arm tackled her. I was going to make one last plea for repatriation, she was Spanish not French - it might work.

My opening salvo was, even if I say so myself, brilliant. 'My wife is a consultant too and she has found a surgeon in the UK ready to operate on me tomorrow. How are you getting along finding one in France?'

Then, I grabbed her hand and pleaded. 'Please just sew me up and let me go'. She agreed, as long as I signed a disclaimer. I let go of her arm and she scurried off. I high-fived Paul then called Debbie to give her the good news and she busied herself booking me a special assistance flight home.

I don't know if it was relief, the blood loss or the fact I'd not eaten or drunk anything since breakfast (it was now 5pm) but I started to feel faint. 'Don't pass out now, they'll never let you go', I told myself. Paul dropped the backrest on the gurney, lowering my head, and I shook it off.

Shortly after that, the Italian doctor returned. He wheeled me into a treatment room and started the procedure of closing the wound. While he injected each side of the wound with local anaesthetic, I helped him learn some new English swear words.

After the procedure, I got dressed into the clothes Paul had brought and I wedged one of Debbie's shoes onto my good foot. He found a wheelchair and we waited for the paperwork; a release form, a prescription for painkillers and a 'whatever-happens-its-not-our-fault-form'. A couple of hours later the documents arrived. In France the paperwork always takes longer than the job it pertains to.

I signed the forms and we set off. Chicaning round various obstacles and people, Paul rolled me ever closer to the front door. The door slid open but three gendarmes and prisoner in handcuffs blocked our passage. We let them pass and I felt like wishing the prisoner, 'bonne chance' with his escape, but thought better of it.

Finally I was outside and heading for the car park. The sun had set since I'd last seen the sky, so I vacantly marvelled at the stars while Paul struggled to push me up the hill to his car. 'You're a heavy sod', he mutters. 'Yer, I know', I replied in my best Little Briton accent.

I lowered myself into the front seat of Paul's car and thanked my lucky stars I wasn't being driven back to Zine in Landie. This journey would be a comfortable, warm and dry one and significantly shorter in duration.

We sped towards Morzine and I realised the chemist would shut before we got back to town. Painkillers and crutches were essential for the next part of my repatriation. We took a photo of my prescription and emailed it to Val. Luckily, she managed to dive through the pharmacy door before they locked it. She managed to procure the crutches and surprisingly, without my presence, the prescribed horse tranquilisers too.

We arrived back at Chalet Benjamin with only two more hurdles to jump. First I had to get over the mound of ice debris the snowplough had conveniently piled up on the path to the building, then I had to ascend the four flights of stairs up to the chalet's door – I'd not given much thought to disabled access when booking the place. With Paul's help, I hopped over the ice then slowly dragged myself up the stairs on my arse – undignified but effective.

Exhausted, I finally summited the stairs and planted my flag on the nearest settee. I was greeted with presents: a pair of crutches, a bag of painkillers and an e-boarding card. Debbie had got me onto a 10am flight the following morning.

Chalet life continued around me, while I lay on the settee inanimate. I reflected on the day's events and just how lucky I was to be returning to England in the morning. I was grateful that, thanks to my friends, I was heading to Birmingham and the QE, where a team of top surgeons and a lovely anaesthetist would be waiting.

Val cooked dinner for the guests and later David cracked open a special bottle of whisky I'd been saving. It seemed appropriate so I didn't mind, although my drugs prevented me from tasting it. They then offered to run the chalet for the next few days in my absence, which was worth celebrating. Once again, I'd been very lucky that, at the time of my accident, they had been in residence.

5. Return to the Royal Town

The day after my accident, I woke up in the Alps with the clock ticking. The consultants in Thonon had emphasised that I needed my leg repairing within forty-eight hours if the outcome was to be favourable. I only had thirty-six hours of 'leg time' left. My mission for the day was to get my leg to the Queen Elizabeth Hospital in Birmingham (QE).

I hadn't really slept much. I'd been worried that I might inadvertently knock my leg and start it bleeding again but the temporary stitches had held. Paul and Sarah had kindly offered to drive me to Geneva Airport (GVA) to save me the rigours of catching a transfer bus. Debbie's father would collect me from Birmingham airport (BHX) and ferry me to the QE at the other end.

For some unknown reason, when booking my flight, Debbie had told the airline that I had a nut allergy – I don't. She had beaten a wheelchair retreat through GVA herself two years earlier and had briefed me on the process. I wondered if having a nut allergy granted some additional privilege too subtle for her to explain. Being deprived of nuts was the least of my problems. I wasn't allowed to have breakfast with surgery imminent, I was 'nil-by-mouth' and starving.

A beginner on crutches, I was presented with a sequence of challenges: going to the loo, putting my trousers on, descending the chalet staircase. Before I could reach Paul's car, I had to traverse through a new set of séracs left by the morning snowplough. If I fell and my leg started to bleed, I'd have to abort the whole mission – airlines don't accept leaky passengers.

I made it to the car without incident and before long we arrived at GVA. Sarah jumped out and retrieved a wheelchair from the special assistance desk. Being a major skiing hub, GVA is seriously geared up to handle wheelchair passengers – but only outbound passengers for some reason.

Sarah returned and wheeled me towards the departures hall then stopping abruptly at the pedestrian crossing outside. She had spotted a distracted transfer driver rolling towards the crossing; I'd spotted him too, but with my front wheels already on the crossing, I was completely at her mercy. He stopped and I recognised his face and gave him a smile, then made a mental note to chastise my friend when we next met. Most of my friends were trying to help me – not run me over.

This was my first experience of the crotch-level world. I was immediately stuck by my lack of control over my orientation. When parked I had to look in the direction I was pointed or at whatever derrière I was lined up behind – some were more pleasing then others.

When we got to the check-in desk, the girl behind it directed her questions to Sarah: 'Does he have any bags?' 'I'm down here', I announced. I wanted to leap up and do a one-legged dance to confirm I was a sentient being but I thought that might piss off everyone in the queue we'd just pushed in front of, so I didn't. Sarah handed me over to the special assistance porter and I gushed with thanks and bid her and Paul goodbye.

The porter was a jolly chap considering he had to deal with injured, and presumably miserable, people all day. He wheeled me toward security and picked up another wheelchair punter on route. Impressively he could push two wheelchairs at once. He told me that at peak times he often pushed three chairs simultaneously although he didn't explain how. It's always great to see a man who takes pride in his work.

I chatted to my fellow charioteer (Edgar) on our journey, side by side, through the airport. We swapped injury horror stories but agreed mine was the better one. He was still wearing his pyjama bottoms – at least I was going home in trousers.

Edgar had injured his leg in Verbier and was also heading to Birmingham for medical treatment. We bonded in our adversity – there seemed to be a fellowship between all wheelchair users.

They parked us in a special 'sick lounge' with about twelve other invalids. I was parked toe-to-toe with an old lady wearing a hijab. Once again, not being in charge of my orientation proved awkward. I smiled; she grudgingly smiled back then got her phone out to terminate the cultural encounter.

I wondered about the others in the room. Did the obese fellow in the corner become fat because he couldn't walk or did he just give up on walking after he reached a certain size? Did the old lady have a debilitating condition or was she just being lazy? Nobody had asked me for any medical proof that I couldn't walk.

Being in a wheelchair was proving to be a pleasant and more expedient way to traverse GVA than on foot. The last time I'd flown out of GVA, it had taken me two hours of shuffling to get through security. It had taken only fifteen minutes in a wheelchair. Passenger Assist was a free service and maybe some of the people in the 'sick lounge' were just taking advantage of it. It was something I'd certainly consider doing in the future.

Edgar and I were loaded onto the plane first, using something that looked like a Portakabin on scissors. 'This would have made a good siege tower in Medieval times', I thought. We were given a full row of seats to ourselves so we could put our legs up. The flight attendants were very sympathetic and I found their Essex accents strangely comforting.

I was aware that time was critical. I now only had thirty-two hours of 'leg time' left. The flight departed on time, which was unusual for GVA so, once again, luck smiled on me.

After we took off, the cabin manager announced over the tannoy that, due to a passenger having a severe allergy, they would not be serving nuts on the flight – 'That would be me,' I thought.

During the flight, having had no breakfast, I was worried about fainting - but I didn't. I was also worried that the cabin pressure changes would start my leg bleeding - but they didn't. I'm only really happy when I've got something to worry about.

We landed on time and another wheelchair was waiting at BHX. With no luggage to collect I was soon parked outside arrivals wondering where Debbie's father was. Surgeons were waiting for me at the QE - all they needed was a patient.

I don't think he had quite grasped the urgency of the situation. He was late then stopped for petrol en route to the QE. It was comforting to see the old fellow and I was extremely grateful for his help. 'At least this ambulance driver didn't ask me for my credit card before setting off,' I thought.

We finally arrived at the hospital and Dr Debs, dressed in theatre blues, was waiting by the A&E front door. She was in the middle of an operation but had left theatre to escort me through Casualty - obviously having left a colleague in charge during her absence.

Seeing her for the first time in four weeks warranted a tear of joy, but my eyes welled up with another emotion - a feeling of utter relief. I could now hand all responsibility for repairing my leg over to her. I secretly congratulated myself on my choice of fiancée. For some reason my first words to her where: 'So - why the nut allergy?'

It was apparently just a simple booking mistake. The conversation moved on to more pressing matters such as how long had it been since I'd had a shower? Clearly I wasn't at my most fragrant.

After a sequence of medics had poked about with my leg, tickling my feet and asking me to wiggle my toes, I got tired of describing the accident, especially to nurses and porters, each time reliving the horror. So I started telling casual enquirers I'd been bitten by a shark.

After being x-rayed I was relieved to be installed in a private room in the burns unit. It was the last bed available in the whole hospital and Debbie had pulled some strings to secure it – no one needs to doubt that the NHS is in crisis.

The nurses settled me in. My carers now had Brummie not French accents, which was more reassuring than alluring. One seemed a little concerned that I'd been in a 'dirty foreign hospital' and proceeded to swab me for MRSA bugs in some rather intimate places.

Without warning, a surgical team of four came marching into my room. Judging by their number, Debbie has applied a three-line whip. I talked them through the shark attack and they deliberated on the best way to proceed. I signed something that basically gave them permission to explore and fix whatever they found beneath the temporary stitches.

Debbie had explained, rather flatteringly, that 'I skied professionally' and, if it was possible for one person to need two working legs more than another, that person was me. I tried to clarify this for them before they started asking for further autographs. 'A Winter Olympics medal is not one of the things in jeopardy here, chaps', I told them.

Then I asked them the classic question, 'How long do you think the operation will take?' To which the answer is always, 'about three seconds': I'd go to sleep and then, hopefully, wake up. They couldn't accurately estimate the elapsed time until they opened the wound and inspected the damage.

They decided enough 'leg time' was left to leave the surgery until the next morning, so I was allowed to eat. Despite its reputation, hospital food is absolutely fine – you just have to be really hungry to eat it.

After dinner, I spend the night in my precious bed while mentally preparing myself for surgery. I'd never had a general anaesthetic before, which tells you how lucky my life has been. Although millions of people a year 'take the gas' and survive I was worried it might not work on me.

My mother always said I was a 'one in a million'; perhaps she meant I had a unique physiology that might cause problems. I decided this particular neurosis was the result of living with an anaesthetist. I'd heard too many horror stories from Debbie of complications she had encountered. Being married to the NHS has its downsides.

It was frustrating to be less than eight miles from my own bed and Debbie, who had returned home to feed the other needy males in her life: dog, children, father. Later that evening I called her and, amused by the role-reversal, I reiterated the words she had so often used when calling me, 'Hi honey, I won't be home tonight. I'm stuck at the hospital.' I'd often thought it would be interesting to shadow Dr Debs at work for a day – skipping the gory bits obviously. Now I'd finally got my opportunity to see her working environment, although I had envisaged me being more of a fly on the wall than the meat on the table.

Next morning, when I was finally rolled into the anaesthetic room, I made my peace with God (just in case he does exist) and nervously joked with the anaesthetic team, I think they had already given me a happy shot. Debbie wasn't there; it's not good practise for medics to work on a relative.

Unsurprisingly, the drugs worked on me and about three seconds later I found myself waking up – the surgery had actually taken four hours.

I was back in my room when Debbie appeared. She had spoken to the surgeons who had reported the extent of my internal leg injuries to her. The snowboard had severed everything on the right side of my leg (muscles, veins, nerves) and had even left its tag mark – a notch on my tibia. No wonder it had taken four hours to sew everything back together. The only thing the board had missed was my posterior tibial artery, located at the back of the calf. If that had been severed I might well have bled-out on the mountain. Once again, luck had smiled.

The surgeons had mummified my lower leg and foot with bandages and a plaster cast backboard that held my ankle in the optimum position for healing – foot pointed slightly downwards. I seldom wear high-heel shoes, but I imagine they are similarly uncomfortable.

All that was left now was for me to escape one more hospital, but it turned out that's no easier to do in the UK than in France. First, my blood pressure, pulse and respiration rates had to be within normal bounds and I had to prove I could urinate. The latter proved hardest to do on demand, especially for a man with a fifty-year-old prostate. Debbie offered to pee in the bottle for me – which was rather romantic.

All tests passed, I then had to wait for the physiotherapist to teach me how to use crutches. When she finally arrived, I explained that I'd managed to peg my way from the Alps to Birmingham, crossing a sérac field en route, and I could probably teach her a thing or two about off-piste crutch work. She explained that was all well and good, but I hadn't done so wearing a high-heeled shoe. She informed me that my leg would remain mummified for two weeks then I'd need to wear a plastic boot for four weeks. After that I'd probably need three months of physiotherapy to shake the repaired muscles out of stasis. The sensory nerves in my skin were too numerous and too small to be reattached; they would probably regrow but the process might take years.

All this assumed that the surgeons had got it right. If not, my foot might move up when I commanded it to go down or move left when I wanted it to move right. I'd experienced leg command and control failures before when I'd over done the sauce, but it had never taken three months to regain control. It dawned on me that I wouldn't find out if the surgery had been successful for several weeks.

Finally released, I triumphantly pegged out of the QE. I thanked the ward nurses before I left and warned then not to go swimming in shark-infested waters. I manoeuvred my way to Debbie's car and we set off for home.

We drove across the grey city or rather under it, utilising the A38 tunnels to the Aston Expressway then onto Spaghetti Junction. We passed through the motorway landmarks and into Erdington, an impoverished suburb. This was Dr Deb's daily commute and I wasn't envious of it. I'd forgotten that, like all UK cities, Birmingham is a depressing place in the winter.

Finally we passed the sign declaring us in 'The Royal Town of Sutton Coldfield'. You wouldn't notice that you had moved into the jurisdiction of another local authority if the sign wasn't there. Presumably it was erected out of civic pride, to underline that Sutton is a separate place to Birmingham.

Once home, Debbie unloaded me from the car onto my crutches. I paused at the open front door. I'd never noticed before just how high my doorstep was and I pondered on the best way to negotiate it. The last step of my journey home turned out to be a hop.

Oscar the Labrador was going crazy in the hall - dogs know how to give a welcome home - but on seeing my leg he laid flat on the floor. Somehow he knew I was injured and the traditional head-butt in the nuts wouldn't be appreciated. For once, I was delighted to have returned to the Royal Town; the place I'd spent so much time trying to escape was now a place of sanctuary.

6. A New Skiing Challenge

In 1993, after a late introduction and a disastrous first date, I finally fell in love with skiing. Well, not just the act of skiing but everything that went with a skiing holiday. But my love was initially unrequited. The object of my desire didn't fall into my arms easily - it took a lot of blood, sweat and beers.

In the beginning, I was absolutely hopeless at skiing. But, as Homer Simpson once pointed out, 'You cannot give up hope on something, just because it is hopeless', so I persisted.

Like any great challenge, learning to ski has to be broken into smaller sub-challenges. 'The only way to eat an elephant is one bite at a time,' as Bubbe, my Jewish grandma, was fond of saying. When she did, I'd glance at the slow cooker, which permanently gurgled in her kitchen, and wonder if elephant was kosher.

In essence skiing's sub-challenges are: standing still, moving, steering and stopping, using two planks. Then the same four challenges are repeated on increasingly steeper slopes in varying states of hangover. Then, if you want to become an off-piste skier, the same four fundamental challenges are taken in deeper and less well organised snow. Next you add obstacles to make the challenges more difficult: couloirs, rocks, trees, rivers, cliffs, crevasses and other terrain traps.[1] And, most importantly, the challenges have to be completed without getting buried alive.

Often, without choosing, the challenges are undertaken in less than optimum conditions. Sometimes they need to be performed in high winds, sometimes in poor visibility and often done while suffering from mild hypothermia. At all stages of the evolution, the

---

1 A 'terrain trap' is any place from where you cannot escape using gravity and skis. The only way to escape a terrain trap is to climb, walk or crawl out of it.

snow queen can make the challenges easier or harder, depending on what kind of mood she is in: fluffy, slushy, icy, crusty or just plain nasty.

With any big challenge you'll experience multiple failures before success. If you don't, it wasn't really a challenge. During these skiing failures you'll pick up your own eclectic group of Skiing Demons that will goad and undermine you at critical moments - to conquer them is the real challenge of skiing.

Only when you have completed all the above challenges can you declare yourself an all-mountain skier.

The term 'all-mountain ski' has only become part of the skiing lexicon recently. The term was invented by ski manufacturers to describe skis that worked well both on and off piste. Given that narrow stiff skis work best on-piste and wide flexible ones are better off-piste, an all-mountain ski is a jack–of-all-trades, yet master of none. So, if someone described you as a 'pretty good all-mountain skier', it's a bit of a backhanded compliment.

After seven full seasons there was pretty much nowhere on a snow-covered mountain a human might reasonably go and expect to survive, that I wasn't capable of skiing or at least surviving. I wasn't interested in anything more extreme. There were no more skiing challenges my aging body was capable of taking on.

I had gained some validation too. I was the owner of a Ski Club of Great Britain Leader's jacket and it had a British Association of Snowsport Instructors (BASI) Level-1 Alpine Instructor medal pinned to it – the ski instructor's equivalent of a Blue Peter Badge.

Maybe I was looking for a new challenge or further validation, but in a moment of summer bravado, despite the expense, I booked my place on a BASI Level-2 instructor course being held in Morzine the following March. I made passing it my skiing challenge for Season 8.

With one month left, before the course started, the enormity of this challenge was sinking in. The feedback I kept getting from my pre-course training instructors wasn't very positive. They kept telling me I was a 'pretty good all-mountain skier but…' - so it looked like I was heading towards failure.

Along with failure, I was worried about how I was going to attend the course for two weeks and run the chalet effectively: Could I expect guests to have breakfast at 6am? Who would pick them up from the lifts? How was I going to get enough sleep if they were party animals?

Just before the accident, I'd been concerned about a bunch of other logistical problems too. How to get to my upcoming Ski Club leading gig, where to leave Landie for my February recess and where everyone was going to sleep in March – I'd slightly over booked the chalet. We are often told to 'cross our bridges when we come to them' – but what if we arrive at the river and there's no bridge?

Then, on that January day in Les Crosets, all my perceived problems went away. I wouldn't be able to attend the course, let alone fail it. My leading gig would be cancelled, Landie would simply remain in the last place I parked her and the chalet would have one less occupant in March (me). It's annoying when you stress about things that ultimately never happen. Premeditation is a curse given to all intelligent life forms.

The accident not only wiped away all my problems; it provided me with a new skiing challenge - to ski again. It had kindly set me a deadline too. I needed to return to my previous skiing form by December, if I wanted to keep my blue jacket - the BASI badge I wasn't so worried about.

Every five years Ski Club Leaders have to take (and pass) a refresher course. Unfortunately my five years were up and I had to 'refresh' the following December. Luck had finally failed me - it was a very bad year to get injured.

Before undertaking this new challenge, I had some sub-challenges to face. First I had to learn how to function as a tripod (one leg, two crutches) then regain my status as a biped. I decided to slice these elephants into bite-size chunks and made a list of objectives:

Things to achieve as a tripod:

1. Move around the house without bashing my dangling leg. This included getting in and out of bed, performing ablutions and getting dressed without assistance.

2. Master staircases. Any Dalek will tell you, staircases can often foil plans for world domination. Anyone who has been on crutches will never take the ability to move between floors for granted.

3. Have sex. Obviously the presence of someone else would be required for this one – but I felt it was an important challenge to list.

4. Perform my other duties as a househusband. Vacuum, mop, dust, do laundry, iron, cook and wash up and - the most important 'man-task' of all – take the rubbish out.

5. Survive a day on my own. Get up and perform all tasks listed above. Feed and water myself. Make a hot drink and a snack and consume them in a location of my choosing.

Things to perform as a biped:

1. Wear proper clothes. The only trousers I could get over my mummified foot were the bottoms of my old tracksuit - often referred to as my 'skanky pants' by Debbie. Along with proper trousers, I needed to wear matching socks and shoes. The odd sock drawer would prove useful during my tripod era (so would Oscar who is capable of retrieving only one slipper) but I needed to restore symmetry.

2. Walk unaided. Sub-challenges included: walking with two crutches then with one and finally none. The ultimate goal was to walk without a comedy limp.

3. Drive a normal car. I had to convince others that I could do so safely and still be insured. Driving Landie would be an altogether more difficult task, especially as it was still in Morzine.

4. Take Oscar for a walk. This involved driving to the park and being able to restrain a 40-kilogram mammal with a mind, however small, of its own.

5. Walk up a mountain. None being available in Sutton Coldfield, I had my sight set on a Lakeland fell. Being able to fell walk was actually more important to me in the long term, than being able to ski. I had another dream, to live in the Lake District, after I'd done with all this skiing nonsense.

A few years back I had become a disciple of Alfred Wainwright (OBE) - the godfather of all Lakeland Fell walkers. Like many, his definitive guidebooks to walking the Lakes had become my scripture and I had set myself another challenge – to climb all of the 214 fells mentioned in his books. It was really just an excuse to get my mountain fix during the summer.

Things to perform as a skier:
1. Get a pair of ski boots on. Given that my own boots are almost impossible to get onto a fully functioning foot, I'd probably need to rent some badly fitted hire boots.

2. Mount a pair of skis. Clipping into my own bindings needs a significant amount of downward pressure. My own skis and bindings would need to be abandoned for some sloppy hired ones too. Ultimately, I would need to mount my own all-mountain skis before skiing off-piste again.

3. Ski a green run, then a blue, then a red, building up to a steep black run covered in moguls. I needed to regain confidence

that my right foot wouldn't let me down if I put it under full load.

4. Ski off-piste. Not just bounce down a fresh powder field, but also survive a variety of snow conditions in a variety of terrains. I needed to be capable of performing long traverses, in both directions, to jump-turn down a narrow couloir, to sideslip ice sheets and to remount my skis after a fall. I'd need to be able to do all the above - and look like I was enjoying it.

5. Drive a Defender across France. This would require a lot more leg strength than driving a normal car and a much higher level of endurance. I'd probably needed to enlist a co-pilot to help – an even harder task.

6. Run 5K (regularly). Technically a biped task, but I would need to run in order to gain aerobic fitness and leg strength. If refresher courses were anything like the Leaders' course itself, I'd need to be at my peak fitness by December – which admittedly isn't *that* fit. My first goal was to out-run Oscar. Given that he is old, fat and arthritic, this seemed achievable. Once he was vanquished, I'd try and run round the block (1K) in under 20 mins. I'd then needed to run 5K, in under 40 mins, three times a week. This was the training routine that got me through the Leaders course five years ago, so it would be a good benchmark.

7. And finally - Pass the Ski Club of GB refresher course. This required proving to the usual protagonists that I was still a 'pretty good all-mountain skier'.

Everything on the list needed to be completed within 10 months. Given that most of the latter tasks would require the presence of snow-covered mountains and most of the remaining months were summer ones, this looked a little unachievable.

After a few days back in Sutton Coldfield, stuck in an armchair with my foot up, I realised there was one task missing from my list and possibly the most difficult of them all. I had to survive the boredom of being housebound for two months. I'd have to endure the frustration of being in England during a ski season, a task not made easy by my Facebook friends who constantly posted pictures of their recently made fresh tracks.

I would at least have plenty of time to finish this book and, even better, I had a new and improved narrative for it. I hoped that writing would combat the boredom, but it was depressing to know I was going to spend the rest of Season 8 writing about skiing instead of doing it.

7. Marooned on Labrador Island

After the accident, I quickly discovered that losing the use of a leg meant losing the use of both hands too, or at least when moving around. When you become a perambulating tripod (one leg, two crutches) it is impossible to carry anything while moving – other than a crutch in each hand.

Carrying things while moving has become an essential requirement for modern humans. Ever since that first ape picked up a stick and thought, 'this might be useful,' we have been carrying stuff from one place to other. Being able to use tools may have allowed us to conquer the world, but the disadvantage of having opposable thumbs is that you accumulate possessions. You soon need something to help carry them all, like pockets. To have pockets you need clothes and then you accumulate those and a wardrobe is needed. This, in turn, will require a permanent dwelling to house it. All of a sudden, you are no longer a wandering free spirit. You now spend your life maintaining and protecting a house full of possessions. Perhaps having opposable thumbs and being able to carry stuff while moving, isn't such an advantage after all.

Being a tripod is not dissimilar to being a skier; our hands are fully occupied with poles all day. It's not entirely obvious why we need poles when actually skiing, but they are very useful when manoeuvring on the flat (ask any jealous snowboarder).

When you first don the planks and pick up the poles, you soon learn how to move on the flat while hobbled by skis. Initially beginners are bemused that they can't move their legs independently, but they soon work out how to use their poles to assist their compromised legs. Learning to use crutches is a similar experience.

If you are a veteran skier, or just an unlucky one, you will probably be a proficient crutch user too, leg injuries being so common in our sport. Our knees, in particular, were not designed to handle feet that are six foot long. The force those six-foot levers can apply to our leg joints often exceeds their design specification and they break.

Given that, sooner or later, a committed skier will have to spend time on crutches, being able to use them might be considered a skiing skill - perhaps BASI should run 'crutch instructor' courses? Being committed to skiing, it was inevitable that I would (sooner or later) need to acquire that skill myself.

Like my first week on skis, my first week on crutches was a frustrating and exhausting experience. Although much easier to master, there is no respite from crutches. You don't have to learn how to shower on skis or go to the toilet without taking them off. And, no one has ever had to ski up a staircase before they can go to bed either.

I spent most of my early tripod life stuck in the living room with another largely inert mammal who didn't have the use of opposable thumbs - Oscar. Like him, I spent most of my days waiting for Debbie to come home and feed me. With little else to do, I decided to document my experience of being marooned on Labrador Island and kept what I called a 'leg diary':

Day 1 (Friday)

Finally home, I'm sat in my armchair with my leg raised on a pouffe. I keep wiggling my toes. They stick out from the end of my bandage and it's very reassuring to see them move. I'm paranoid that Oscar or some other lumbering beast (a teenager for instance) will accidentally knock my leg, undoing all the surgeon's good work.

Oscar keeps sniffing my leg and it is freaking me out. Dogs can smell disease and even know when someone is about to die. I've heard anecdotes of dogs in care homes, sitting outside the doors of an inmate who was about to check out. Maybe I've picked up a super bug at the hospital and Oscar can smell it?

Debbie looks knackered. She hasn't slept much since my accident. In many ways, having taken on the responsibility of getting me home and sewn back together, her ordeal has been worse than mine. Before I can go to bed I need a shower, if only for her sake.

I will soon discover just how difficult it is to shower while standing on one leg and why 'soap on a rope' was invented. But first the stairs need to be mastered. I decide a backwards approach on my arse will work best. It's a time-consuming and undignified process. I attempted to seal my leg in a bin liner before showering, but it's a massive fail and my bandage gets damp.

Later, I lay awake in bed with my damp leg raised on a pillow, keeping Debbie at a distance in case she kicks my foot in her sleep. I desperately want to have a cuddle but it is too dangerous to attempt.

I feel a sense of relief that no further medical intervention should be needed and the healing process has begun. I also feel outfaced by the prospect of a lengthy rehabilitation. The physical pain is bearable, but the thought it might endure for months is not. It is not the pain that is keeping me awake but the dozens of logistical problems my incapacitation has caused. Who is going to run the chalet in March? How will I get Landie home? Will the insurance company pay up? 'At least I don't have to take that fucking BASI level-2 course,' I think.

Day 2 (Saturday)

Today I realised that my injured leg isn't my main problem – the foot attached to it is. My toes are swollen and I'm starting to lose feeling in them too. Dr Debs explains, 'Because you are not using the muscles inside the leg, waste fluids from your foot are not being pumped out'. She is very good at explaining things to a muggle like me.

That evening some friends come round with their new puppy which dashes around like a lunatic, putting my leg in jeopardy. We have a Chinese take-away, something that is not possible to do in

Morzine where I often miss such traditional British cuisine - I'm not allowed to drink so the drunks get boring.

Day 3 (Sunday)

Dr Debs has to go to work today and I feel rather anxious. I'm not looking forward to spending the day on my own, not because I will have to feed myself, but because I won't have medical backup. I'll only have Oscar to rely on and he can't dial 999 (no opposable thumbs) and he isn't much of a conversationalist.

I complete my one-legged ablutions then start my commute. My new place of work is the living-room armchair where I intend to spend the day writing. My commute involves throwing my crutches down the stairs then hopping down after them holding the banister. The first time I tried this technique I caused great alarm. Everyone thought I had fallen down the stairs – perhaps I should have warned them. But no one is home today and Oscar seems unalarmed by the clattering noise.

Finally, I sit down with my laptop to discover it needs charging and the charger is upstairs. I must plan my future forays more meticulously. Perhaps doing a risk-and-reward assessment first. Do I really need sugar in my tea? Can I read the paper without my glasses? Is the reward worth the jeopardy I would put my leg under? I also learn to:

1   Carry a rucksack at all times. Use it like a handbag. Fill it with things you may or may not need but lug them all around anyway in case you do.

2   Unless I want to drink my tea standing next to the kettle, I need to make it in a thermos flask then carry it to the armchair in my rucksack. Any food needs to be made in sealable containers. You have to treat every meal as if it were a picnic.

3   Master the one-man chain gang technique. If you need something that's at one end of the kitchen to be at the other end, you move it in steps around the work surfaces.

I reunited my laptop with its charger and powered it up; messages from friends, family and readers flooded in through social media. Instead of writing, I spent most of the day answering messages on Facebook. Unsurprisingly, many had stories of their own skiing injuries and long periods of being a tripod. Most were messages of encouragement. However, one warned me that, 'The sympathy would die out before the pain did'. I guessed he was having a bad day.

Luckily the dog walker comes in for a chat and relieves my solitude. She has recently read my books and seems to have enjoyed them. She proceeds to tell me her life story – she has read my life story (the skiing part at least) and it seems only fair I should hear hers. I'm a captive audience but I'm glad of the company. Meanwhile Oscar looks longingly at the front door.

Day 4 (Monday)

Debbie was rather grumpy last night, or maybe 'exhausted' is a better word, coming home from work then having to wait on me. Unlike Oscar, I'm not happy with a scoop of dog food served in the same bowl then a belly rub. Well, at least she doesn't have to let me out of the door every time I need a wee.

I have essentially become another teenager in her life complete with avoidance- of-movement strategies. It is particularly critical for me to avoid unnecessary trips up and down the stairs. So, shouting for her to throw things I need up or down the stair works well. If I want to communicate with her I don't really need to shout; I can use text messages to make requests from my bedroom, to find out what's happening about my last request, or when and what's for tea.

I'm also excused all household chores and if I'm asked to do a task that is within my abilities I've learnt to wince in pain to prevent the request reoccurring.

I can't drive and public transport involves too much pegging, so I use Mum's Taxi whenever I need to go somewhere. I'm also starting to feel comfortable watching others load and unload heavy items from the car.

It takes a herculean effort for a tripod to get showered and dressed. So, like a teen, I avoid the former and, if allowed, I would stay in my pyjamas all day. Worst of all, I've noticed that I'm becoming so used to having a servant that I've stopped saying please and thank you.

Debbie is not amused by my teenager analogy. I remind her that, 'It is not my fault. I didn't ask to be born - I mean, injured. I never wanted to be a teenager again and this time round, my legs actually *don't* work'.

I notice that Millennials seem to be burdened with metaphoric crutches. One hand is needed to message on a smartphone and the other is invariably holding a supersized calorific drink in a non-recyclable container. This means they can't carry anything while moving either. They can't take anything up or down the stairs. They can't use light switches when leaving a room and have to close doors by slamming them with a foot. Maybe I should have more sympathy for teenagers – they have permanently lost the use of their hands while moving.

I detect that Debbie's patience is running out; I had always assumed it was limitless. She had managed to cope on her own when a snapped anterior cruciate ligament left her on crutches. I had been in France during that period and was of no help to her whatsoever – so my needy behaviour must be annoying. At least that night we work out how to have a cuddle.

Day 5 (Tuesday)

I have watched too much TV today when I should really have been writing. Daytime TV is very depressing. The cheap advertising slots are filled with charity appeals designed to pull on the heartstrings of retired folk. Viewers are bombarded with images of suffering dogs, cats, bears, tigers, pandas, donkeys and humans. All except the pandas have my sympathy - if not my generosity. You can't help a species that is disinterested in sex.

More depressing are the adverts for 'over-50s' life insurance. I'm really not worried about who's going to pay for my funeral - I don't see it as *my* problem. The only reason the ads annoy me is that they remind me of my mortality.

This evening, a friend from the Lake District visits bearing traditional hospital presents: a bottle of Lucozade, a copy of the Beano and some jellybeans that he described as 'fruit'. Unfortunately I can't plan any fell walking expeditions until I know when I'll be back on both feet. His visit makes me very impatient for that to happen.

Day 6 (Wednesday)

This morning I feel like a tripod master – a 'BASI level 2 crutch instructor' at least. I'm the master of Labrador Island and can traverse it from shore to shore.

Debbie came home at lunchtime and decided to take Oscar and me for a walk in the park – or more accurately in my case, a roll. She retrieves a wheel chair from the garage (a family heirloom). Oscar is more excited at the sight of his lead than I am on seeing the wheel chair. I am apprehensive about leaving the house. It has only been six days and I've developed agoraphobia. My world seems to have shrunk from the expanse of the Alps to the confines of a suburban house.

Debbie drives us to Sutton Park, helps me into the chair then throws a blanket over my legs to complete my Chelsea Pensioner look. It is interesting to see the park from a different perspective (lower down). The wheelchair makes for an excellent observation platform. While I'm being gently wheeled I scan the trees for birds with my binoculars.

It's a freezing day and I can hear Debbie's rapid breathing behind my head when she pushes me up a hill. A puff of water vapour passes my ear each time she exhales. I joke, 'Is this a steam powered wheel chair?' She threatens to leave me in the park. I try to think light thoughts to ease her burden. It starts to snow, making the park look and feel like the Antarctic. I tie Oscar's lead to my chair but he makes for a very poor husky.

Day 7 (Thursday)

Another boring day stuck on Labrador Island. I had aspirations to earn a living writing but after a week of solitude and introspective reflection I've had enough of working from home.

At least the Winter Olympics starts tomorrow. I don't usually get to watch much of the games, usually being in the Alps skiing myself when they occur. This time I can watch them from start to finish. I might skip the curling – only the Scottish could make a sport out of sweeping up.

In the evening, the Ski Nazis come round with a suitcase of my clothes from the chalet they have kindly brought back from Morzine with them. I'm keen to hear how they dealt with the aftermath of my sudden departure. Turns out, they had collected my skis from the medical centre and stashed them in a locker along with my other stuff. David had even cleaned the blood out of my boots. They left Landie parked in the chalet's communal car park, which is worrying. How long will it be before someone reports it as abandoned and it gets towed away?

Day 8 (Friday)

I've become aware that Debbie has been coming home each evening to a slob sat in a chair surrounded by dirty Tupperware. He is invariably wearing his skanky pants and usually a stained tee shirt. When she gets home, all he does is moan about his ailments. Not wanting to put her off marriage by presenting a vision of me in the future - a revolting old man, I decide to do something about it.

I have a shave sitting down, put on a shirt and generally attend to my appearance. I even throw in another shower, which is a highly risky manoeuvre in an empty house. I make sure I'm sat in a different chair when she comes home. However my improved appearance and fragrance is completely masked by Oscar who has developed weapons-grade flatulence. God knows what he ate in the park the other day.

I seem to have put on an entire stone since my accident – I'm now almost as fat as Oscar! I put this down to lack of activity and snacking out of boredom. Unlike Oscar, I can open the fridge whenever I like and make a snack – damn those opposable thumbs.

Day 9 (Saturday)

Woke up with existential angst. If I didn't ski again, what was the point to my existence? If I wasn't a chalet host or a Ski Club leader who was I? If I gave up the chalet business then failed the refresher course in December, I'd be neither.

Would I regain enough control of my foot to ski at the required level to pass the course? I'd need time to gain the required fitness too. I probably wouldn't have passed the course before the accident, having let things slide over the last five years. Maybe I shouldn't even try? Everything needs an end.

My parents arrive to give Debbie some respite from care. They take me for another wheel in the park. The last time my mother pushed me round a park in a chair I was three years old. She leaves the actual donkeywork to my stepfather. I use hand signals to indicate my desired direction of travel and chastise him for being unfit, 'Debbie managed to get me up this hill without stopping', I told him. He retaliated with jokes about my newfound weight.

Day 10 – (Sunday)

I managed to distract myself with more practical problems today. I've cracked on with my insurance claim and submitted my expenses totalling €2,244! I don't have much hope of a full repayment but I hope, at least, they will cover the unpaid helicopter bill (€968) and the Les Crosets rescue people (€320). They both keep sending me threatening letters. I feel bad they have not been paid and hope I'm not blacklisted – I may need their services again.

I'm worried that, along with my right foot, the rest of my right leg is withering away. I've done nothing but dangle it for almost two weeks. On the upside, my upper body is getting a great workout along with my left leg, which is doing twice the work carrying all the extra weight I've put on.

Day 11 (Monday)

Today I tried to sort out the mess I'd left in Morzine. Luckily (again) I'd not taken the chalet for February so it was only those who had booked for March I had to contact and explain their holiday would now be a self-catering affair. Surprisingly, no one wanted their money back and everyone was very sympathetic.

I had a lot of random people offer to run the chalet for me but I don't think they had thought it through. It might sound fun being a chalet host but I assure you a lot of the time it is not. I also don't think they understood how difficult Landie was to operate. She has so many foibles that would flummox anyone but her long-term owner. Beside which if something failed (like the brakes) and people got hurt, I'd never forgive myself.

Day 12 (Tuesday)

I tentatively started putting some weight through my bad leg today to see how it felt. I even managed to stand on two legs while taking a pee - one small piddle for a man but one giant pee for mankind.

I agree to let a friend (Liz) in Morzine use Landie to pull her car from of a ditch. The driving conditions in Morzine are apparently appalling, so I'm a little worried Landie will end up in the ditch too. She has recruited an expert Defender driver to help her – there is one in every bar.

Defender drivers can be identified by a hole in the left side of their jumpers. Defender door latches have been designed to hook your jumper when you get out of the vehicle – it's possibly some sort of safety feature. Once you see the hole in their jumper, look down and you'll see that only their right shoe is wet. The water has come from the mandatory leak under the steering wheel above the accelerator pedal - in a Defender the foot 'wells' never dry up. When you get closer, you'll get a whiff of WD40 and notice oil under their fingernails. Beer bellies, beards and bald patches are fairly standard Defender-owner options too but not mandatory. However an 'Old Guys Rule' T-shirt worn under the holey jumper is definitely mandatory.

I'm disappointed to hear Landie failed to extract Liz's car from the ditch but even a Defender can't grip on icy roads (I forgot to mention that Landie had a set of snow chains in the back, which might have helped). I'm however, encouraged that Landie started first time and wonder if her clutch survived the ordeal.

Oscar's flatulence hasn't abated. I hope Debbie doesn't think it's me when she gets home.

Day 13 (Wednesday)

I'm trying to work out how to repatriate Landie - seems nobody is keen to drive her home for me and the cheapest transportation company wants £3K to tow her home - that's £1K more than she is worth. The insurance company have washed their hands of the problem and are even refusing to reimburse me for my flight home because, 'I didn't have a return flight already booked'. The logic of which defies me. I decided not to argue. I don't know what's worse – recovering from a skiing injury or dealing with the resulting insurance claim.

Day 14 (Thursday)

I'm having my cast removed and an air boot fitted tomorrow, so my life on Labrador Island is coming to an end. During my stay, I have come to admire Oscar's attitude to life. He has never had opposable thumbs and therefore has no possessions, unless you count squeaky toys, so he's never needed pockets, clothes or a house. Perhaps that's why he lives without angst. His only major worry is that that the humans may have forgotten it's approaching his dinnertime. He doesn't worry about being old – he doesn't even know he is going to die. He doesn't worry about the purpose of his life, let alone getting into heaven. He has no ambitions other than, maybe, to actually *catch* a rabbit one day. He is the ultimate existentialist, living from meal to meal – we can learn a lot from our pets.

Once the boot is fitted, I'll be able to put my bad leg on the ground. I'll still need two crutches until I've mastered walking on two feet again. I'm essentially being reconfigured into a quadruped – my metamorphosis into a Labrador will be complete.

8. Return to Framboise

On the 4th January 2017, a year before my accident, I found myself transporting another cargo of bacon to the Alps. Despite all my protestations, declarations and better judgment, I was driving Landie back to Morzine for a seventh time. Having been unable to find a willing or available co-pilot, Bacon Run 7 was turning out to be a solo affair.

Landie and I were heading to Chalet Framboise for a second year. Despite its problematic location and the financial loss I'd made there the previous season, my hopes were high. Advanced bookings where promising and I had full occupancy for my first week of residency. It looked like things would work out better in Framboise this time.

I suffer more anxiety on a bacon run, than on a wine run (my return journey). If I don't literally bring home the bacon on time, my first set of guests will have their holiday compromised. They would probably survive without bacon but find things logistically difficult without a vehicle and driver. On the other hand, wine, unlike bacon, isn't perishable and nobody in the UK is waiting for it to be delivered – apart from Debbie maybe. I could take a week getting back to the UK and it would be of no consequence. Time is critical on a bacon run because I need to arrive at the chalet before my guests do – if only to let them in.

That year, Landie and I made it down to Dover and across the channel in record time. New and improved Landie was firing on all cylinders. The summer refurbishment had seemingly given her a new lease of life. She was going like a steam train – and sounding not dissimilar.

Despite being on my own, I stopped at the Chateau De Cocove just south of Calais. It was a romantic location in which I'd spent several entertaining evenings with Dr Debs on our shared journeys to and from Morzine. The excitement of being back in France, or indeed returning to England, usually meant that spirits were high and indeed, consumed in quantity, along with the fine food on offer at the chateau. Although staying there on your own isn't as much fun, it is the perfect geographical location to rest the horses, before pushing on to the Alps.

Having reached the gates of this important way marker, I noticed something was amiss. The chateau's drive, a rough track that meanders through the chateau's wooded grounds, was unlit. I put Landie's headlights on full beam, clearing the drive of startled rabbits and proceeded into the woods. I turned into the empty car park and instead of being greeted by a magnificent flood-lit chateau, it too was plunged into darkness. It looked shut.

I'd booked a room online several weeks ago. 'Surely it isn't closed – perhaps it has gone bust,' I thought. I got my torch out and found my way to the front door. An owl was hooting somewhere behind me and I could hear the squeaking of bats in the damp air – I thought I'd walked into an episode of Scooby-Doo.

I pushed the door and it creaked open revealing a dark reception area. Once inside, I could make out the shape of a Christmas tree and the bands of tinsel draped around it twinkled in my torchlight. A ghoulish fairy, impaled on the tree, looked down at me, but the room was devoid of actual people.

'Hello, hello… I mean *bonjour, bonjour,*' I called out. No reply was forthcoming. Then, I heard footsteps and a ghostly apparition carrying a candle, appeared at the end of the corridor. The candlelight flickered across the features of the approaching entity but it wasn't until it was almost upon me that I realised it was an old lady in a dressing gown. Seemingly confused, she started babbling in French.

My French is appalling but I got the gist: there had been a power cut and she couldn't find her room. I tried to explain that I wasn't a member of staff and had just stumbled into the dark abyss myself. Mercifully the real receptionist appeared with torches and more candles and showed us both to our rooms.

The power remained off for most of the night but the staff adopted the spirit from the nearby town of Dunkirk and more and more candles were lit and the place slowly came back to life. I assumed dinner would be off and resigned myself to eating more Land Rover rations but no, the restaurant would open and the chef would offer a reduced menu of things he could grill on a gas barbeque.

After a shower, I took my usual table by the window in the dining room and ate a perfectly grilled steak by candle light while caressing a bottle of red wine. It was the most romantic meal I've ever had – on my own. I went to bed after reassuring myself that all was well with Landie and we would have a seminal season. Apart from being woken in the small hours by all the lights coming back on, I slept well.

Next morning I set off early. Landie started first time and powered her way south. Being a veteran of driving an old diesel car in the Alps, I knew it was important to arrive in Morzine with an empty fuel tank or a tank full of proper winter diesel. However, despite desperately wanting to tell you all about fuel gel points and the EU standards for winter diesel, I won't because this isn't a book about petrochemistry. If you have a modern diesel car, you probably live in a world where you choose your fuel simply on price and I won't wake you up from that happy place. But untreated diesel becomes waxy below -18c and clogs up the fuel-delivery system. Defenders are particular prone to this problem, especially when you leave them outside on a cold night on the top of a mountain.

On a bacon run, my refuelling strategy is closely linked to my bladder-emptying strategy. There was a time when man and machine were in perfect harmony, I could synchronise pee stops with fuel stops. Sadly, now I'm older, this is no longer the case. Whenever Dr Debs is called upon for her medical opinion, she invariably asks, 'What is the patient's urinary output?' Peeing is apparently a vital life sign. The more pee you produce the further from death you are. Descartes concluded that, 'I think therefore I am', was proof of his existence. Maybe mine should be, 'I *pee*, therefore I am', and I should celebrate every trip to the loo.

Desperate for a pee, I pulled into a service station near Dijon. Not wanting to stop again, I filled up with what I thought was winter diesel. But the brand of diesel was unknown to me.

I made it to Morzine late the following evening. It had started snowing somewhere around Bourg-en-Bresse and by the time I got to Morzine six or so inches of snow covered the Cresta Run (the access road to the chalet). 'Here we go again', I thought, the icy drive having turned Landie into a toboggan several times the previous season.

To my delight, Landie haul herself up to the chalet without any drama, despite her heavy load. My investment in winter tyres had paid off. I parked Landie then patted her on the bonnet by way of thanks. After I'd unloaded the precious cargo into the chalet's freezer, I opened a bottle of wine and made a toast to Bacon Run 7 – it had been an unmitigated success.

It was good to be back in my winter home. I opened the balcony window and called out for my old adversary, the Chat Noir. Then I remembered the feral cat that had plagued me the previous season now lived in England having been adopted by guests. Her reign of terror was over. 'Maybe this season,' I thought, 'I'll have less bad luck'. I finished the bottle and went to bed, thinking warm thoughts about Defenders, not realising the temperature outside was plummeting.

I woke the following morning with a list of errands to run in preparation for my first set of guests. Landie started first time but then I noticed she wouldn't rev. My heart sank. I knew this meant the diesel had waxed; I also knew the amount of hassle and time it would take to resolve the problem.

Having been plagued with waxing problems in the early years of the Project, I was livid with myself for letting it happen again. I was also livid with the service station in Dijon for misrepresenting their fuel and, most of all, I was livid with my bladder for not holding until I'd reached a more familiar vendor.

I called the AA to arrange for the local automotive vultures to collect Landie and take her to the world's most expense parking space (inside their warm garage). She would have to sit there until the fuel thawed out.

The AA's French call centre is in Lyon. I have spent many a reassuring hour talking to their fine operatives. Not a year goes past that I don't speak to my friends in Lyon. They have become my therapists. My European breakdown policy pays for a hire-car while Landie is off the road but, sadly, not the parts and repair bills from the garages. Each year I expect my premium to go up but it doesn't. (It is always around £100). How the actuary at the AA calculates the premium for a twenty-five-year-old Defender leads me to speculate: either, he is a Land Rover lover, or has statistics to prove that Defenders are actually quite reliable – the latter seems the least likely.

After a few days I got Landie back. They had changed the fuel pump for no apparent reason other than to inflate the bill, put some anti waxing additive in the fuel tank, and told me all would be fine. However, the following Saturday (the next change-over day) the problems resurfaced. It was ground hog day – guests arriving and no food or booze in the larder.

I was now livid with the garage. I explained to the mechanic that the anti-waxing additive he had used would only mix with the diesel if it was warm (+5°C) and their garage wasn't the warm place I'd been paying for. I insisted he drained the tank, filled it with proper winter diesel and replaced *only* the fuel filter. He tried to argue but he was never going to win against a man who was livid with everything in the world including one of his own organs.

Once my instructions had been followed, the problem never resurfaced; I should probably have drained the tank myself in the first instance. However, I'm reluctant to get my spanners out in Morzine. If I snap something, on a summer's day in Sutton Coldfield it's of little consequence, but if I undo the wrong nut in Morzine and something major falls off, my season is ruined. In any case, performing even the simplest of mechanical procedures in arctic conditions half way up a mountain is always difficult – your fingers freeze to the spanners.

The whole incident put me on the back foot with the Land Rover Demons. I lost sleep every night worrying about how cold it was outside and if Landie would run the next day. She usually did but my confidence in her was shattered.

Mentally exhausted, I simply forgot to go skiing that January. I'd forgotten how important it was to go skiing. I've previously criticised seasonaires who don't go skiing on their day off, but I too found skiing too much of an additional effort.

It didn't help that the skiing conditions were uninviting. Although it was cold at night, it was warm and rained during the day, creating icy pistes. High winds plagued the PdS too, closing many of the key lifts, often stranding people in the wrong valley.

Critically, I never got round to buying a season pass, which made deciding to go skiing psychologically difficult for a tight Yorkshireman. The thought of coughing up fifty euros for a day-pass to go 'girlfriend skiing' with guests wasn't very tempting. When the snow did turn up, my main off-piste buddy Morzine Mary broke her leg and was evacuated back to Liverpool - it felt like my skiing mojo had gone with her.

I did manage to go skiing with Sturmführer David, Carol and some associated Ski Nazis in mid-January. No matter what the conditions David always went skiing – it was part of his ideology. However, we found ourselves stranded in a mountain restaurant. During our lunch, a storm had rolled in, closing all the lifts and making it impossible for us to ski home. I wasn't too concerned - there are worse places to be marooned. It was a warm place and had ample food and drink. The afternoon rolled on, the wine flowed and we were just picking tables to sleep under when a piste patroller came in. He informed us that a piste basher was shuttling people back to Avoriaz from the bottom of a nearby green run. From there we could theoretically ski down le Crôt (a blue run) to Prodains, then catch a bus back to Morzine.

With thunder and lightning crashing all around us, we merrily mounted our skis and set off to rendezvous with the basher. It wasn't a difficult ski, but a simple matter of standing on the planks while they glided to their destination, leaving the passenger to ogle at the drama being played out in the sky. On arrival, we climbed into the mechanical behemoth giggling and joking, insulated from the maelstrom outside. Despite the gale-force winds buffeting it from side to side, the relentless monster crawled up the mountain and dumped us somewhere in Avoriaz - I wasn't exactly sure where.

The now-swirling snowstorm was obscuring most of the buildings and the wind was making communication difficult. Luckily, a local guided us to the top of le Crôt to make our way down to Prodains. Unfortunately it had been closed by a pisteur who tried to prevent us from using it. After insisting it was our only way off the mountain, he finally let us pass with the comforting words, *'I hop you ave zee good insurance?'*

We started our descent down to Prodains but, even though the run was quite steep for a blue, the wind kept blowing us back up it. We could only make downward progress between gusts. It was an epic battle between two great forces of nature: wind and gravity. Gravity finally won and we got down an hour later. By that time we were completely sober and exhausted from our adventure. No matter how unambitious your plans are, every time you head into them, you never know what the mountains may have in store.

I also avoided après skiing that January. Well, if you don't ski I guess it's just called drinking. My twenty-four-hour taxi service for guests really mandated that I stay sober in order to stay on the road. It was a bad idea to have a drink and then drive around town; it was an appalling idea to do so then ascend a mountain road covered in ice. With every foray from the chalet feeling like an expedition, I avoided any unnecessary journeys and became a bit of a hermit.

Worst of all, I stopped noticing the beauty around me. The views out of the chalet window were reason enough to live there, yet I stopped looking out at them. The danger with constantly being surrounded by beauty is that you stop noticing it – that's why it's good for my soul to return to Birmingham every summer.

January rolled on and the Agents of Entropy continued their Land Rover campaign. In a fiendish manoeuvre, they broke the bonnet-release cable, thus stopping me from accessing anything they might break under it – like the engine. I managed to open the bonnet with a bent wire coathanger and a 'coathanger' is now on my list of essential Land Rover maintenance tools.

Next the heat exchanger sprang a leak emptying the engine of coolant. This I knew how to deal with because it had happened a couple of times before - a simple matter of removing the unit from the coolant loop. I managed to complete the operation, without leaving too much frozen skin on my spanners. However, this meant

I had no cabin heating which made defrosting Landie impossible. A permafrost formed on all Landie's internal surfaces and left me driving round in an igloo for the rest of January.

Next, a drunken guest pulled the rear view mirror off the roof (don't ask how). This didn't matter much because I couldn't see through the back window anyway thanks to the permafrost. Then the rear indicator lights stopped working. That actually didn't matter too much either – nobody bothers signalling in France.

By the end of that January I was starting to hate my Defender and my love of Morzine was also waning. I kept asking myself two questions; 'Why on earth had I returned to Chalet Framboise? And why on earth had I returned to the Alps in Landie? The answer to both was obvious – 'stubborn stupidity'. Fortunately, I had a busman's holiday planned for my February recess.

9. Shaking a Fist at Age

The nightmare of January (Season 7) behind me, I headed to Arabba and the Dolomites. The Ski Nazis had organised a ski safari around the greater Sella Ronda. They would be skiing between a sequence of mountain refugio (refuges) and it sounded like an adventure I didn't want to miss. They had gathered a few of the usual suspects for the trip – old friends and new. But first I had to get myself to Lyon airport and catch a plane to Venice. Venice always seems a strange location to start a skiing holiday, but it is the nearest airport to Arabba.

One of the new friends was a septuagenarian called Helen. A Quaker, she lived in the Lakes but was resident in Les Gets during the winter - she was living my dream retirement scenario.

Skiing is not ageist. There are few sporting activities a grandparent can enjoy with their children and grandchildren, but skiing is one of them. Youth is no measure of ability either. Maybe at the highest levels athleticism counts, but the skiing skills learnt when young are never lost. Après skiing is often a family affair too. The age range in many après bars is unusually wide. Often teenagers 'hang' with their parents – admittedly this might be because their parents are buying their drinks.

The only thing that might prevent someone from skiing into old age is injury or worn-out joints. Skiing often takes its toll on knees and hips. However, I have skied with people who have had hip and knee replacements and once with a chap who'd had a complete set – although I thought that was cheating. On a recent Ski Club trip, I sat round a dinner table and discovered that I was the only diner who still had all his original parts!

I'd skied with Helen once before, with the SCGB in Avoriaz, but I didn't know her well. She had kindly offered me a lift to the airport, so all I had to do was drive Landie to her place and take her more civilised transport to Lyon. Having said goodbye to my last January guests the evening before, I departed Framboise for Les Gets at 4am.

It was freezing, and the previous day's rain had turned into sheet ice. Landie started, which seemed like a bonus, and we delicately drove through Morzine, passing a jack-knifed delivery lorry on the way. Once in *Les Gets* my satnav took me up a side road, which progressively got steeper and steeper.

I hadn't realised that Helen's place was almost 1500m above sea level and the drive to her building was even more impassable in ice than the Cresta Run. Even with her new tyres and diff lock engaged, Landie struggled to climb the icy road. We had several heart-stopping slides round vertiginous bends, none of which had barriers – but we made it.

I found Helen outside clearing ice from her front-wheel-drive town car. 'There's no way I'm going down that hill in that car', I thought. But not wanting to be impolite, I jumped in, said a silent prayer, and we set off.

I held my breath each time Helen drove round the icy hairpins, 'The ice seems particularly bad this morning,' she joked. 'If there's a God, I hope he's especially fond of Quakers,' I thought. He was and we made it to the main road. She proceeded to speed down the mountain like a transfer driver late for a pickup. Once on the motorway she upped the tempo further, overtaking everything that came into her sights - this was the fastest septuagenarian on wheels I'd ever seen.

En route, we chatted about the Lakes and the Ski Club and her ski-touring exploits and I couldn't believe she was still so active in her seventies. Perhaps the key to having a long and active life is not drinking – or maybe it would just seem longer? We chatted more at the airport then boarded our Air France flight.

About an hour into the flight, an alarmingly loud banging sound started emitting from the back of the plane. The captain announced something in French and repeated it in Italian (not English). Then the flight attendant started moving people from the back to the front of the plane. She was smiling, so it couldn't be too serious. I decided that I'd just watched too many episodes of Air Crash Investigations, on the Discovery channel - my TV guilty pleasure.

Then I thought, 'Maybe flight attendants are trained to smile in emergencies for just that reason.' I enquired into the problem but I didn't really understand her reply. It was something to do with one of the engines but it was *'D'accord'* because the plane had *'deux moteurs'*. She gave me a departing smile - which was worrying.

I looked over at Helen who was sat on the other side of the plane, hoping she might have a better understanding of what the pilot had said, but she looked fast asleep – heaven knows how she could sleep, given the mechanical racket the plane was making. 'Perhaps she's praying?' I thought, hoping that her god would save her and, because I was on the same plane, inadvertently save me too. Twenty nail-biting minutes later, the plane successfully touched down without any obvious intervention from heavenly bodies.

Once inside Venice Airport, we rendezvoused with the others then boarded the transfer coach. The driver proceeded to drive like an Italian (because he was) although he lacked Helen's cornering skills, he matched her speed on the straights. Spirits were high (apart from mine) and there was a lot of joking and laughter on board the coach while the driver wound his way up into the mountains. Through necessity he had to using both sides of the road to negotiate the more extreme hairpin bends and just trust to luck that there would be no oncoming traffic. Fortunately, *my* version of the Italian Job, ended with us getting *off* the coach in Arabba - not stuck *on* it, in a cliffhanger.

That night, still recovering from my horrendous journey, I slept like a log. Fortunately my roommate wasn't a snorer, although I'm not sure he was so lucky.

In the morning after hiring skis and procuring a ski pass, we set off with our guide who was called Mario (of course). We spent the rest of the day skiing to our first refugio. Still exhausted and on alien skis, I took up the rear. Helen bounced downs the runs taking every opportunity she could to go off-piste. It was a sunny day and, despite being UK school half-term, the pistes were empty. Once we'd gained some altitude I was struck by the beauty of the surrounding mountains. No stranger to Alpine vistas, the extra beauty of the Dolomites blew me away.

The Italian Alps are very different to the French Alps, both in shape and colour. Not especially high, the peaks form more dramatic spires, painted in shades of red. The colour has something to do with aragonite, although geology isn't one of my strong subjects.

During the course of the safari, Mario would explain the history of the region and the battles raged there between Italian and Austro-Hungarian forces in the First World War. I couldn't imagine being able to climb some of those mountains, never mind dragging artillery pieces to the top of them. It was hard to imagine the atrocities he described happening in such a beautiful place.

Our first refugio was surprisingly comfortable. A mountain restaurant by day, it had several en-suite rooms above the restaurant. The proprietor and his wife were old friends of Mario's. They did a lot of shouting in the kitchen then came out silently, smiling and bearing tasty offerings. Most were traditional dishes featuring a lot of polenta and pasta. A large plate of bloody pork chops formed the centrepiece but none of us would eat the seemingly undercooked pork – apart from me. Our host was perplexed and she returned the uneaten meat to the kitchen where an even louder discourse took place. We were too polite (or too scared) to explain that in the UK we don't eat under cooked pork.

We set off early the next day with the sun just poking its head over the red peaks. While other skiers were presumably parking and fighting their way to the lifts we were already carving down virgin pistes.

I found the off-piste skiing elements of our safari hard work. I blamed my rubbish hire skis and wished I had taken my trusty powder skis with me. The snow was a little wet and heavy but Helen seemed to carve through it with little effort. Not for the first time I was being out-skied by someone twenty years my senior.

We all assume that with age comes a reduction in flexibility, balance, strength and endurance, making us more prone to skiing injury. But skiing keeps us moving, aerobically fit and mentally dextrous, not to mention the therapeutic value of being in stunning Alpine scenery. The trick, according to Helen was to 'simply not fall over', which she never did. Skiing past seventy might be a risky business, but if Helen proved anything to me – it does keep you young.

We soon left the southern slopes of the Sella massif and skied past the impressive Marmolada (3342m) then checked into our next refugio on the Alpe di Lusia (2242m). This had another frightening matriarch in charge.

Foolishly my roommate decided to open the fire and put another log on it, but he jammed the glass door. He was desperately trying to close it when our host came and caught him in the act. Clearly unhappy she summoned her husband, who continued the interrogation until Mario smoothed over the waters. To me, all Italians sound irate even when they are happy. That night, feeling rather intimidated we all ate what was put in front of us without complaint.

After that I don't recall the names of the places we skied and stayed, other than that most of them ended with a double 'L' followed by an 'A' or an 'I'. I was enjoying being a follower not a leader. Like most of the folks who follow me, I had very little idea of where I was most of the time. I do recall that, on our return leg, we skied down the famous Hidden Valley near Lagazuoi - it was too beautiful to forget its name. There are few mountain valleys that, on first encounter, can still take my breath away but this one did.

We stopped at the refugio in the valley, but sadly only for lunch. The waiting staff wore lederhosen, making me wonder if we had accidentally skied into Austria. But the political complexity of the region, means allegiances to flags can change from valley to valley.

The only way out of the valley was to be towed by horse – which after a few shots of grappa was entertaining. Instead of moguls, our way was littered with piles of horse dung, which were equally hard to ski around given that they appeared spontaneously.

Most of the people I ski with are older than me. This, I guess, is because they are retired and can afford to ski all season. Sometimes I crave the company of folks younger than me, but this desire would probably not be reciprocated. I like to think that, while I'm skiing with the oldies, my peers will be sat in board meetings, trying to make their shareholders more money. I imagine my lawyer friends sat at their desks filling in time sheets and worrying that they haven't clocked up enough billable hours to secure a bonus. The thought of them makes me very happy to be skiing with retired people – it's a privilege I have obtained early.

From the Hidden Valley, we skied back to Arabba and cruised the relatively empty pistes there for our final day. The expedition was over and I felt like I'd conquered the Sella Ronda. Having skied only 298 of the 1,200 km of piste accessible with my lift pass, I'm not sure that feeling was entirely warranted.

After Arabba, I flew directly back to the UK for the rest of February to hide until the school holidays were over. On the flight home, which was mercifully uneventful, I reviewed my skiing options for the following winter. My Italian safari had opened my eyes to the many mountains I'd yet to see and the many ways I might ski around them.

Before the trip I had imagined a refugio would be more like a mountain hut, the sort of bunkhouse people on proper ski tours use when traversing the Alps, but mercifully they were not. You need a little more luxury when you are older, or at least an inside toilet. However the safari had the feel of an expedition that had a destination, even though we ultimately returned to the same place (Arabba). It felt like a journey with purpose even though it essentially was not. It was an adventure with a little luxury – and there is nothing wrong with that.

Sadly, Helen died the following November. She had a cardiac arrest while cycling in the Lakes – a fitting way for her to go, if a little prematurely. It was a pleasure to have skied with her and I'm glad our lives overlapped, if only briefly. I hope, like her, I will ski until my dying day. Its good to know that skiing has no fixed retirement age and like Landie, given enough replacement parts, I should be able to keep my own chassis going indefinitely. Skiing is one of the last fists we can shake at age and I intend to use it.

10. Square Meals on Round Plates

Some people are born to cook, some achieve culinary greatness and others, like me, have cooking thrust upon them. Fortunately, chalet chefs only need to master seven dishes of their own choosing – mercifully, few people stay longer than a week in a ski chalet.

I'd like to say that I enjoyed the challenge of learning to cook but that wouldn't be entirely accurate. I don't think challenges are meant to be enjoyable. If something is challenging it is, by definition, stressful - until it's no longer challenging; it's a bit like learning to ski in that respect. However, by the end of Season 5, I no longer found feeding ten drunken people challenging. Then, during Season 7, something changed.

I'm not sure if it was a change in my client base or the start of a national epidemic. Thanks to the success of my books, a more geographically and socially diverse range of British skiers were finding their way to my chalet door. Unfortunately, most of them seemed to have special dietary requirements. In my first missive, I'd ruthlessly mocked fussy eaters, vegetarians and others with eating disorders. But, seemingly to get their own back, they turned up en masse at Chalet Framboise.

I'd become used to dealing with vegetable phobic, salad-dodging children and the teenagers that result. I'd blamed the parents for letting their children dictate the family diet. My mother never asked me what I wanted for tea – unless it was my birthday; now most children seem to expect *a la carte* service. Then, during Season 7, grownups, armed with food intolerances, presented a new culinary challenge.

Joking aside, those who do have medically proven life-threatening allergies have my sympathy – as do vegetarians. It is those with self-diagnosed food intolerances I find hard to tolerate. Some I suspect don't know the difference between allergy and intolerance and, unless someone is carrying an epipen, I'm very sceptical of their claims. I try, but I find it hard to separate those with actual allergies and genuine intolerances from the 'I don't like' brigade of grown-up fussy eaters that now live amongst us.

The new culinary challenge is mostly a diplomatic one. You can't just laugh when someone claims to be allergic to turnips just because it's a comedy vegetable. In fact it's no laughing matter ensuring a specific vegetable isn't in bought stock or a sauce or just about anything that comes in a tin or a packet.

When a new guest walks through the door and announces their dietary requirements, first I've got to determine if it's a 'can not eat' or a 'will not eat' scenario. You can't just ask, 'Will it kill you or just make you grumpy?'

I have had a couple of notable walk-ins where my humour was tested. 'My brother and I are both intolerant to wheat and dairy products,' one chap announced. No milk, no cheese, no bread and no beer! They agreed, they were holidaying in the wrong country but had brought their own gluten-free bread and pasta to make amends.

'I'm allergic to nuts,' claimed another fella while he was scooping copious amounts of my complimentary peanuts into his mouth. He noticed my raised eyebrow and informed me peanuts were peas not nuts. He also needed a lie down if he had anything with wheat in it.

'I am allergic to fish,' one lady declared. 'Fish or shellfish?' I enquired. 'Both', was her answer. 'Luckily, we're a long way from the sea,' I informed her.

Given that fifty percent of all the things humans can eat live underwater, to rule out *all* fish seems akin to declaring an allergy to all land-based animals and should really be narrowed down. 'Is it all mammals that upset your constitution or can you eat reptiles? 'Are the number of legs important?' 'Are you okay with things that have wings?' 'How do you feel about amphibians?' There are many types of fish in the sea.

I suspect food intolerances are transmittable. When you hear how someone's life has been transformed by cutting out gluten or whatever, you're inclined to give it a go yourself, in case you have been similarly suffering. Then before you know it, you're interrogating a waiter in a restaurant and have become the very person you used to find so irritating.

Then there are the migraine suffers. I've had, 'peppers give me migraines', spicy foods, tomatoes, onions, chillies, citrus fruits and all things coloured red have been ruled out of bounds for a week. Actually, I think I might be allergic to red wine – it usually brings me out in a severe bout of idiocy. When one woman declared that egg white gave her a migraine, I thought she was yoking (boom, boom). I suffered many a migraine myself - mostly caused by reading and translating the small print on food packaging.

Then there are the 'won't eats'. Fish once again comes in for a battering along with vegetables, especially if they are green. The darker green the vegetable the more foreboding it seems to some. Having listened to one young girl list her dislikes, I tried to sum up her requirements in a single sentence: 'So, you won't eat anything found on land unless it has legs, or found underwater unless it has fingers?' She concurred, then added, 'I won't eat anything that grew below ground either, unless it's a potato?'

Morzine is a bit of an English ghetto and the supermarket in the centre of town has cashed in on this and now has an 'English Aisle'. There it stocks UK brands: Marmite, porridge, marmalade, golden syrup, Tuc biscuits, Colman's mustard, horseradish sauce, mango chutney and a surprising number of curry products. It's a snapshot of what the French think we eat; it's also a little sad that we still desire these products abroad. I guess it is mostly for the ex-pat community who often crave a little taste of home.

Then there are those who object to the shape of food. I'm not a pasta lover, but those who are seem to care about the shape it's been fashioned into. Even though the Italians have more names for pasta than the Eskimos do for snow, pasta tubes, strips, shells or sheets all taste the same to me. 'The surface area that a shape makes available to a specific sauce is critical', one lad informed me, while pulling a face at the length of his spaghetti - I'd foolishly chopped the strands in half to facilitate easy boiling.

I also used to cook a lot of stews in my slow cooker, mostly because I could load it in the morning then forget about it until dinnertime. But a stew is a fussy eater's nightmare. With all the chunks looking the same, eating stew is their equivalent of playing Russian roulette for a fussy eater, so stew was seldom chosen from my menu.

Breakfast has exposed a few funny fads too. You'd have thought a full English breakfast would go down well with a bunch of Brits but some people don't like baked beans, some dislike black pudding and one fellow didn't like bacon!! Existentialism aside, in my opinion, eating bacon and drinking beer are the two main reasons for living – that is why I could never become a Muslim.

Although I pride myself on being able to eat anything, and indeed on liking most French food oddities: snails, frogs, horses etc., I was defeated by my first encounter with Andouillette. Described as a 'local offal sausage' in a mountain restaurant in Les Arcs, I ordered it expecting something akin to black pudding. Despite the waiter and my French ski guide both raising their concerns, I insisted I wanted it. The horror of my mistake was realised when I sliced open the sausage and a load of tubes (pork intestines) spilled out reminiscent of a scene from an Aliens movie. The smell was so foul (I think it had been marinated in chicken excrement) my fellow diners started shuffling their chairs away from me. I got one fork of it in my mouth before I started gagging. Luckily, the guide took pity on me and swapped his plate for mine - he had ordered a chicken salad. Perhaps that's how a fussy eater feels when they first try broccoli?

Then there are the old ladies and their tea bags. In the chalet I'd only serve proper tea from the great plantations of Yorkshire. One week I counted six different zip-lock bags next to the kettle, each filled with a different type of tea bag: herbal, green, red, organic or some sort of lap sang sou shit – each morning I was greeted by a queue of winceyette nighties by the kettle.

Often it is not the food but the method of presentation that seems important. One lady objected strongly to having her scrambled eggs *on* the toasts, she wanted it by the *side* of the toast. Another pulled a painful face when I placed her smoked salmon and eggs in front of her - she only liked *cold* smoked salmon and I'd foolishly mixed it into the eggs.

Running a chalet full of fussy eaters is a bit like running a zoo. Each of the exhibited animals will only eat the food found in their natural habitat. The pandas will only eat bamboo shoots, the lions will only eat zebra meat and the penguins will only eat fish. Each morning I would feel like a zookeeper, creating special meals for a range of delicate species.

Before becoming a chalet chef I was oblivious to the intolerance epidemic - I even thought a coeliac was someone allergic to celery - but now I've had an education. I realise just how blessed I am to have inherited a sturdy immune system and an adventurous palate. I've recently led an over-fifties holiday for the Ski Club and to my surprise none of the sixteen members were fussy eaters. None of then had intolerances or allergies and no one grilled the waiter before every meal. They were all born when 'food' was 'food' and to have it put in front of you was a blessing.

Perhaps the most interesting guest I've catered for was one who didn't like ice cream or chocolate! Have you ever met anyone who doesn't like ice cream? Something clearly went wrong during her childhood. Her name was Debbie and she was a rather lovely doctor.

Even though my culinary skills are limited, I used to pride myself on providing square meals on round plates – but during Season 7 that no longer seemed possible.

11. Mad Dogs & Englishmen

Thanks to the Land Rover Demons, Season 7 had got off to a bad start. But I'd survived January, had a pleasant week in the Dolomite Mountains, then two weeks of R&R back in Sutton Coldfield. But March was looming and I had to return to the Morzine battlefields.

I'd unwittingly left Landie at the top of a mountain in Les Gets to survive the February weather alone. Had I realised Helen's pad was so remote I'd probably have made other travel arrangements and left Landie somewhere warmer. Going on January's form, I was pretty sure that after three weeks without any TLC, Landie wouldn't start. I'd been worrying about her ever since we parted.

When the transfer driver dropped me off at Helen's I was full of trepidation and my mind was full of contingency plans. Helen wasn't in residence so Landie was my only way off that mountain. It was all downhill from Les Gets to Morzine, and one plan was to freewheel all the way home. However, all that angst was unnecessary, she started first time without even using her auxiliary battery. 'Maybe the agents of entropy had forgotten about me,' I thought and hoped I'd have a trouble-free March.

Once back at Framboise, I awaited my first March guests, wondering what they would be like and what interesting food requirements they might have. They had a couple of intolerances (wheat, peanuts) but, what turned out to be worse, they were all health freaks. Amongst them was a dietician, who was held captive by the only subjects of conversation that seemed to be allowed – nutrition, health and fitness. For a middle-aged, overweight, borderline alcoholic who has never run more than 10K in his life, this soon grew tiresome - although I did quite enjoy the evening yoga sessions.

One of the things I love about skiing is that you don't have to be an athlete to enjoy it - nor indeed be good at skiing. You don't need a propensity to wear Lycra or, more importantly, look good in it. All body shapes and sizes work. You don't have to be 'good at sport' either. Even if you were the kid who got picked last for playground football (then put in goal), you can excel at skiing. Once you become a competent skier you don't have to be aerobically fit either– unless you fall over you seldom break sweat. Or at least that is true when skiing on the piste.

Luckily they chose to do most of their own healthy cooking and even fed me. I think the low-cholesterol, high-fibre, super-food diet put my body into shock.   A few days later the ensemble was supplemented by two 'geezanaires' (middle-aged ski bums) and their two Jack Russells who I had more in common with (the humans that is).

Despite having short legs (the dogs that is), their owners took them skiing which painted a rather lovely image of man and his best friend enjoying the mountains together. I was, however, slightly concerned that a golden eagle might mistake the dogs for marmots, swoop down and carry one off for lunch. Unfortunately, a thunderstorm blew in that week bringing monsoon rains and high winds to the PdS resulting in poor snow conditions and lift closures. But everyone still went skiing regardless.

Only mad dogs and Englishmen go skiing in the rain. It could be our stoic nature or our hatred of waste that forces us up a mountain when water is running down it. We don't want to waste the lift passes we have already procured or lose a precious day's skiing. My English guests set out optimistically hoping the precipitation might be snow higher up, but I knew they'd be down early looking like drowned rats and walking in that my-underpants-are-wet way.

I like chilling in the chalet when the rain is lashing against the windows. When it rains, it's time to enjoy living in the Alps rather than sliding down them. The rain always puts me in a reflective mood and I often have a productive day of writing. Even though I perversely enjoy rainy days, I do feel sorry for my guests who've been looking forward to their annual skiing trip only for it to turn into a snorkeling one.

Once the soggy-bottomed guests return, the chalet turns into a laundry with every available drying surface strung with damp garments. If there is a reward for going skiing in the rain, it's that it amplifies the feeling of being dry, warm and safe once you're finally back by the fire, wearing dry underwear. I've noticed that many of skiing's rewards come post-activity such as the exquisite feeling of relief when you finally take off your ski boots at the end of the day. Skiing is akin to banging your head against a wall – it's nice when you stop.

The following week, I exchanged my mad English guests for mad Dutch ones who had healthy living much lower on their agenda. I love the Dutch; I don't think I've met a Dutchman or woman I didn't like. I always know I'm in for a fun time when I have Dutch folk staying. They drink, they smoke, they eat anything and they understand British humour because it is identical to their own. To a man or woman, they all speak perfect English, which is a big help.

It was however, a tough week for my liver and for Landie. The temperatures plummeted and the Dutch partied all week. If they stayed in, I got paralytic with them and if they went into town, Landie and I would spend the wee hours responding to evacuation requests. On those evenings, the biggest problem was hunting them down. Like all inebriated people in a strange town, they were unable to describe their location accurately or to stay in one place together.

I had a second group (three English roses) stay with me towards the end of the week, who added to the bedlam. One night, I made five trips in and out of town before I got everyone home. Each trip I was deafened by stories of high jinks and flirtatious encounters. I wish I'd installed a webcam in the back of Landie – it would have made a great YouTube channel.

I think that week was all too much for Landie. She developed a rather worrying knocking noise whenever we went up the hill. I put it down to the Land Rover Demons tricking me into thinking something was wrong with Landie when in fact it was a normal-ish noise.

One of the joys of owning a Defender is listening to the new symphony they compose every time you drive them. But, this noise got worse with every trip into town and after another week, it became clear one of her percussion instruments was terribly out of tune.

I had three weeks left of my season and the middle week I was away, leading for the Ski Club in Switzerland, and didn't need Landie. I could probably live with the noise and its associated angst for the other two weeks but I didn't want to drive eight hundred miles back to England listening to it - so I finally took action.

Instead of calling the AA, who would send the French vultures round, I called a local English Land Rover mechanic, 'Landy Andy'. His existence was a recent discovery, one I wish I'd made earlier on in the Chalet Project's history. I suspect he might have been deliberately hiding from me.

Andy arrived and crawled around under Landie. 'Yer, your rear UJ is buggered mate,' he declared (a Universal Joint or 'UJ' attaches the prop shaft to the axle – but you knew that). Andy offered to replace it while I was away, if I got the new part delivered to his house. I gratefully accepted his offer and quickly ordered a new UJ online.

Unfortunately Andy gave me the wrong postcode and the new UJ was flown to France then sent back to the UK by the French courier. Why they couldn't have called someone in the UK and obtained the correct postcode I don't know. The supplier reposted the part, with the correct postcode, and it turned up at Andy's just before I departed for Switzerland. The part had crossed the channel three times in a week. Hopefully it would do it again attached to Landie in two weeks' time.

Meanwhile I had a fun bunch of lads from Tunbridge Wells (no food allergies). Amongst them was a budding ski instructor, Ukulele Dave. I was interested to hear that Tunbridge had a dry slope (Bowles) where he plied his skills. And (you guessed it) Dave never travelled without his ukulele. More skilled than me, at both skiing and plucking, he was planning to take a BASI Level-2 course in Morzine, in March the following season.

After one of Dave's postprandial concerts, he suggested I might go for my level-2 with him. I was tempted and seduced by his assumption I might be good enough to pass it. Having sown that seed, Dave and his merry band of jesters left. I donned my blue jacket, left my car keys with Landy Andy and departed Morzine myself. Andy would fix Landie while I was enjoying myself in the Swiss Alps. But life never works out as planned – well mine never does anyway.

12. Skiing With Dad's Army

Mercifully, Season 7 was almost over and I was delighted to be heading back to Laax. The Club had put me in charge of their popular Peak Experience (PE) holiday to that posh Swiss resort. Having learnt the leading ropes in Laax the previous season, I was very relaxed about the gig. The resort would have no hidden surprises and I would be able to ski every day for an entire week without having to cook breakfast first. I wouldn't have to deal with other people's dietary requirements or facilitate their inebriation and I wouldn't have to drive that bloody Land Rover.

I was always met with blank faces whenever I mention 'Laax'. Nobody had ever heard of the place. Then I discovered the reason why – I'd been pronouncing it with a Northern accent. Southern English folks, who predominantly go to the Swiss resort, pronounce it *'Larks'*, in the same way they inexplicably call a bath, a *'barth'*. Now, when I hear someone says, *'I did my gap-yer in Larks darling'*, I know they mean 'Laax'. They probably call a scone a *'scon'* too and have their dinner when I'm having *'mi tea'*. Anyway, now I've started calling it *'Larks Darling'*, it seems better known. Laax is more famous amongst the snowboarding community. It boasts an Olympic-sized half pipe and an enormous slope-style park, both of which are of absolutely no interest to me.

Despite being billed as a singles holiday, I knew from experience, it would be a sober affair. The word 'single' referred to the number of beds in a room rather than the marital status of their occupants. To go on a PE holiday you need to be over fifty-five so any nubile cavorting was unlikely. I take slight umbrage at the naming of the category. Being 54 myself, was I approaching the 'peak' of my skiing 'experience' - was it really all downhill from fifty-five?

Having led PE holidays before, I knew there would be no crazy suicide skiers and most folks would be in bed before 11pm, which suited me. On my previous visit to *'Larks'* there had been a more experienced leader in charge. However, this time I was to be the sheriff not his deputy. Indeed, I would have a deputy of my own, a newbie leader called Andy - his new blue jacket had yet to see action.

Having enjoyed the Swiss scenery on my train journey from Geneva to Zurich Airport, I waited at arrivals for the members' plane to land. I'd reviewed their rap sheets. The Club had sent me details of the participants: their age, skiing ability and any special dietary requirements – there were none!

One by one, my sixteen charges came through security. Most looked a little dishevelled after an early start and a delayed flight. Their ages varied, but all were over sixty, most approaching seventy and one chap was about to become an octogenarian. When the last of them came through, I asked everyone to line up so I could take a register, which proved difficult in a noisy airport. Some of the older fellas failed to respond to their names, reminiscent of a scene from Dad's Army.

I could see that a Private Walker, Godfrey, Frazer, Pike, Cheeseman and a Corporal Jones lookalike were all present. I realised this made me Captain Mainwaring and Andy, Sgt Wilson, but the similarities amused me. There were also three women in my home guard: Mavis, who looked like she could be Pike's mum, Mrs Fox who looked more of a 'flashy woman' and Dolly, who was actually Godfrey's younger sister. The Laax 1St Platoon B-company had a second section too, none of whom immediately warranted an alias.

The transfer from the airport to the hotel was uneventful and I spent the journey chatting to everyone and trying to learn their real names. On arrival at the hotel, I was pleased to find that the staff, and particularly the hotel's shuttle bus driver, Lenny, had not changed. He had been an entertaining part of my last visit to Laax. He would have made a good Bond villain and he even had a cat. I was pleased Interpol still hadn't found him. He remembered and greeted me, 'Ah, Mr Tomlinson, we have been expecting you'.

I apologised for being late.

During our first dinner together, despite the frugal amount of wine consumed, the platoon personalities started to come out. I sat next to Private Cheeseman, a retired public school headmaster. He spent the evening trying to convince me that global warming was actually an oil industry conspiracy. In subsequent dinners, he would explain that fracking was a great idea and that the Americans had faked the moon landings.

After dinner I issued my orders for the morning. Several people had booked their skis online from hire shops scattered around Flims. So I decided to take those who had their own skis directly up the mountain and Andy (a.k.a. Sgt Wilson) would oversee the business of collecting hire skis. We would regroup at a designated rendezvous point (RV) and then redeploy in two equal units.

'Do you think that's wise, sir?' asked Sgt Wilson, pointing out that I'd end up with too many skiers in my group (11). I admitted this was a sub-optimal number but we only had to ski together for an hour to reach the RV.

Several potentially better plans were simultaneously voiced. LCpl Jones wanted to get his edges sharpened before going into battle and Pike needed to buy some ski socks first – presumably his mother had forgotten to pack them.

Godfrey returning from the toilet overheard one of them and asked if the plan had changed – confusion reigned. So I had to shout 'Attention. Silence everyone, pay attention, Pike,' before I could reiterate the plan.

I marked the RV on Andy's piste map (a restaurant called Nagens) and went to bed with very little hope that anyone would be in the right place at the right time in the morning. Surprisingly, they were and I set off with eleven skiers of unknown ability in tow – a recipe for disaster.

Despite Godfrey having to make a toilet stop and Pike deciding to show off by overtaking me then skiing down the wrong piste ('stupid boy'), we arrived at the RV on time.

There was no sign of Sgt Wilson and his group so I phoned him. It turned out there had been a few issues at the various hire shops and he was going to be twenty minutes late, so I decided there was time for my group to do another run. Godfrey asked, 'Do you think I might be excused?' For unknown reasons, he and Mavis wanted to wait in the restaurant, so we set off without them. Halfway down the run, a thick fog floated in and we descended into chaos.

The Whiteout Demons seem to stalk me. My last visit to Laax had also been marred by poor visibility. Their *modus operandi* is to amplify your fear of skiing off a cliff or into some other type of terrain trap. They use sensory deprivation to fuel self-doubt. They make you wonder if you are actually lost and, if so, how badly. Navigational issues aside, when the line between the snow and the air becomes indistinct, the act of skiing becomes very tricky.

In thick fog, it's often hard to determine if you're moving or not. You think you've come to a halt then you lean on your downhill pole only to find you're still sliding. The pole jams under your ski and you fall over it. The solution is to stop near an object known to be stationary, like a rock or a chairlift pylon. Similarly, when you set off again, it's hard to determine which direction is actually downhill.

The Whiteout Demons can cause physical symptoms as well. Those susceptible to carsickness often feel a similar nausea when skiing in poor visibility. Well that's the usual excuse people give when they throw up in the fog.

Trying to bunch everyone up, I found a known stationary object, a piste marker pole, and stopped. Most of my troops spotted me and stopped too. Unfortunately Jones charged past with a determined look on his face. I told the others to follow the poles to the next lift station and wait for me there, while I retrieved Jones.

I finally caught up with him when he tried to ski up an adjoining piste. I escorted him to the lift station only to find that Private Frazer was now missing in action – he was 'doomed'. I sent the remaining troops up the lift and told them to wait in the restaurant at the top while I tried to call Frazer on the phone, but of course there was no answer. I don't know why old people have mobile phones - either they can't hear them or they are turned off.

Andy rang and was wondering why I wasn't at the RV. I explained I'd had a few issues of my own. Optimistically I asked, 'Is Private Frazer with you now?' forgetting to use his real name. He was baffled. I explained that I had a Dad's Army thing going on in my head. 'Does that mean I'm Sgt Wilson?' he asked indignantly. 'Yes, and I'm Captain Mainwaring. But that's not important right now,' I replied curtly, being rather stressed with the situation.

After cross-examination, he discovered that he did indeed have Frazer and I discovered he was in the wrong restaurant. I told him to stay put and I would meet him there.

After depositing what was left of my troop with Andy, I set off into the pea soup alone to retrieve Mavis and Godfrey, from the original RV – the Nagens restaurant.

The piste was now completely deserted. No sensible person would be skiing in such thick fog. Despite methodically following the left-hand marker poles, I didn't find the path to the Nagens restaurant. I called Godfrey and asked him to walk from the restaurant to the piste and stand next to a piste marker to distinguish it from the others but he refused. He wasn't leaving the building without a guide. So I caught the lift back up and re-descended, hoping I'd be more successful finding the path to the restaurant a second time.

I thought I'd found it, until it abruptly ended, leaving me 100m somewhere to the left of the piste. It was just a piste-basher track leading nowhere. 'Could this day get any worse?' I asked myself. I'd now managed to get myself lost and, worse still, lost off-piste.

It was then I heard a faint but unmistakable sound drifting toward me through the fog – the intro cords of Sweet Home Alabama.

The music could only be coming from one place - the restaurant. I skied toward the sound and like a Swiss version of Brigadoon, the lost restaurant and its outbuildings appeared in the mist. The music was emanating from a wooden deck outside the restaurant, where a DJ was doing a sound check.

I skied down towards the buildings, over the roof of a wood store and dropped onto the deck behind the DJ causing him to jump out of his skin. '*Guten morgen. Ist dies das Negans Restaurants?*' I enquired, in my perfect Denglisch. '*Ja,*' he replied pointing to the front door in case I had a general problem with determining normal points of entry. I took my skis off and triumphantly entered the building.

I found Mavis and Godfrey sat in the corner. They were a few glühweins into the start of a beautiful relationship and I was almost sorry to break up the party. I walked them back to the piste and thirty minutes later we re-joined the full platoon at the other restaurant.

Despite some mumblings of discontent about the limited amount of skiing that had been achieved that morning, I suggested we had an early lunch and waited for the fog to lift. If it didn't, I was prepared to face a complete mutiny and make everyone catch the lift down.

Sgt Wilson, or rather Andy, agreed that was the best course of action. His first morning as a Ski Club Leader had been a baptism of fog. At least I knew the resort and had a vague idea where the lifts and restaurants were supposed to be but he hadn't lost anyone or got lost himself – which was impressive.

Mercifully the fog did lift enough to ski safely. We split into two equal groups and headed off in different directions for an uneventful afternoon's skiing. The ability of the members in my group varied dramatically, frustrating the speedsters and exhausting the slow coaches. It's annoying when advanced skiers book a place on an intermediates holiday then complain everyone is going too slowly.

Having now seen everyone ski, Sgt Wilson and I reorganised the platoon into two ability groups (fast and slow) for the next morning. Those allocated to the slow group where not very happy and each night I would hear appeals for promotion to the fast group. People management is an important ski-leading skill and you sometimes need to be a politician.

The next morning I threw back the curtains to see a perfectly blue sky. 'The first day of any group skiing holiday is always carnage until everyone gets sorted out,' I thought. Today would be much less stressful. And indeed it was.

The week proceeded without event. Sgt Wilson and I alternated command of the groups each day, which gave me the opportunity to crack my limited repertoire of jokes twice.   Unfortunately, on the penultimate day injury struck.

My objective for the day was to ski to the furthest reaches of the resort, so we could ride the Lavadinas chairlift. Designed by Porsche, the chairlift is one of my favourites. Each of its chairs has six heated leather bucket seats. Once you embark, your chair accelerates to six m/s in only ten seconds – which isn't fast for a Porsche, but fast for a chairlift. The chair then rotates forty-five degrees, allowing you to admire the panoramic view, rather than stare at the chair in front. Just before it docks with the top station, the chair rotates square to the cable again – although it does leave it late enough to cause some anxiety. The chair's real surprise is that, despite costing millions, it goes from nowhere to nowhere, servicing two pistes that are often closed.

Just before arriving at the bottom of the Lavadinas Chair, LCpl Jones went absent without leave. Inexplicably, he swerved left and flew off the edge of the piste landing in a depression. He lay there, motionless for a worrying amount of time. Often, when people lay prostrate, by the time I've hiked back up to them, they have recovered - I'm sure some buggers lay motionless just to see me sweat. So I've learnt to delay the start of a medical emergency hike until it is clear there is no malingering going on.

Five minutes passed and Jones still lay motionless so I reluctantly kicked off my skis and started my hike. Before I'd got too far, he started shouting, 'Don't panic!, Don't panic!, I'm okay!' but I could see he was panicking so I continued climbing. By the time I'd got to him he'd remounted his skis and re-restarted his descent – typical. Unfortunately, every time he tried to make a left turn he fell over again. Clearly there was something wrong. So I relieved him of his skis and we walked down the last few hundred metres of the piste to the chairlift.

I knocked on the door of the lift station, wondering what the German for 'blood wagon' was. It is '*blutwagen*' the lift attendant kindly informed me in his perfect English. '*That'll cost him, a penny or two,*' piped up Private Walker, who was loitering behind me - but it didn't. The attendant offered to run Jones back to Flims on his skidoo - free of charge!

So, without any 'have you got insurance' questions or credit card debiting, Jones would be evacuated. The platoon lined up to salute their fallen comrade as he was whisked away by a true Swiss philanthropist. '*E could-a charge a fortune for that,*' Walker muttered disapprovingly.

On our return I found Jones propping up the hotel bar contemplating skiing again in the morning; mercifully he didn't. When he finally sought medical advice back in the UK he had actually snapped several things in his leg and had indeed been a real trooper.

On the last day of the holiday the dreaded fog returned. Not wanting to repeat the horrors of the first day, I headed for Lagens, a forested area above Laax. I knew that, forests being made from large numbers of stationary objects (trees), would make it hard for the Whiteout Demons to play their mind games.

We headed up on the Crap Sogn Gion chair that, despite its amusing name, is actually very pleasant. From there, it should have been a simple matter of following a blue run down into Lagens and the bosom of its trees but somehow I got lost. Then the mist thickened and the Whiteout Demons struck.

I knew I was still on a piste. The snow under foot had the fresh corduroy lines recently left by a piste basher. In an attempt to find a reassuring piste marker, I skied perpendicular to the corduroy, knowing that piste bashers go up and down pistes, but I was met with an increasingly steep gradient in both directions. I couldn't quite work out why both directions where uphill. So I went the only way gravity would let me, perpendicular to the corduroy lines, hoping to find a piste marker pole.

Finally I came across a strange pole with a red circle on it. I stopped, and scratched my head. Then I realised it marked the landing zone of a jump. I was stood somewhere in the middle of the slope-style park. I'd inadvertently skied my group down the giant half pipe, mistaking it for the blue, which explained the weird orientation of the corduroy tracks. Luckily no one was using the pipe or the jump in such poor visibility.

Location established, we skied on through the alien landscape of jibs, rails, berms, rollers and groms. With nobody about, the enormous man-made snow structures were imposing although easy to ski around. It was like moving through the abandoned remains of a once great civilisation. As each unnatural edifice loomed out of the fog, we speculated on its purpose.

Finally, we reached the safety of the trees. The fog persisted and I stayed within the forest for most of the day using the same runs over and over again. Eventually, I made everyone catch the bus back to Flims - a rather inauspicious end to my first week in charge of a ski club holiday.

There was a lot more banter across the dinner table that last evening. While anecdotes of previous ski trips were being told, I realised the wealth of skiing experience the platoon had collectively accumulated. By dismissing them as Dad's Army I had underestimated their fighting ability. I reflected on my week - I'd not had time to worry about Landie or any of my other Morzine troubles; I was physically tired, but mentally refreshed. It was a satisfying exhaustion.

I chuckled on the train back to Geneva. I must be the only leader ever to have taken a Peak Experience party down a giant half pipe and through a slope-style park. I wondered what the members might report back to the Club on their feedback forms.

Confirmation, that I'd not done too bad a job as Head Leader, came later the following summer. The Club allocated me the same leading slot for Season 8. I was pleased that I would be returning to *Larks Darling* for another episode of Dad's Army. Sadly, thanks to my injury, I never made it back.

13. Wine Run 7

I called Landie Andy on the transfer coach out of Laax. I was expecting an easy last week in Morzine - the only guest I had was Debbie. It had been a poor season for bookings but we could at least use the luxury chalet ourselves. Her intention was to drive home with me at the end of the week, assuming Landie had been fixed, but the phone call brought bad news.

Andy had taken off the rear prop-shaft and removed the broken UJ only to find the new one didn't fit. Despite the impressive number of air miles it had accumulated, it was the wrong size.

The problem with owning a car that has been in production for sixty-three years is that there are many subtle part variations depending on the vintage. I once incorrectly ordered a windshield wiper arm three times before I got the right one for my particular Defender.

I only had one week left to get Landie back on the road. Not wanting to take any chances, I ordered an entire new prop-shaft with UJs attached (even I could fit that) and paid a fortune for express delivery. With luck it would arrive on Friday, I'd fit it then I could set off for Blighty the following day.

Dr Debs couldn't trust luck, not mine anyway, and having important things to do the following week (saving people's lives etc.) she booked a flight home and I lost my co-pilot for Wine Run 7.

Getting parts delivered to France is tricky. They arrive in Morzine with impressive rapidity but the last mile to the chalet is always the hardest, relying as it does on the French postal system. Friday arrived and the tracking website said it was 'Out for delivery' – great news.

Knowing that French postmen simply cough outside your door and immediately conclude that nobody is home, I left the chalet door open all day. No delivery had been made by 3pm and I started to panic. I checked the tracking website and found to my horror the package status had changed to 'Failed delivery – returned to depot'. Livid, I sprinted down to the Post Office, to protest.

There was a queue. The official behind the desk did what all officials do when there is a queue – he proceeded slowly. I watched a young English couple in front of me hand over their failed delivery note. He asked them for identification. Unfortunately the parcel was addressed to their dad, and even though they had his passport '*le jobsworth*' wouldn't give them the parcel.

After their sheepish retreat and still with a little steam coming out of my ears, I stepped up to the desk and made a rookie mistake - I started the encounter in English. 'You failed to deliver a parcel to my chalet today, even though I was in all day. I believe it is back here now?' - 'Please don't send it back to England,' I added sarcastically. Sensing my sarcasm, his reply was, '*ne parle pas Anglais.*'

Realising my mistake, I apologised and tried again in Franglais. I gave him the tracking number and he typed it into his computer then gave me the French equivalent of 'the computer says no' – a Gallic shrug. I showed him the email proving '*Le carton, was dans la maison*'. 'Maybe tomorrow?' – he said, reverting to English.

I explained that I had to leave '*La house of raspberries de matin*' and pleaded with him to check again. He reluctantly turned back to his computer and, without typing anything, decided it was worth looking in the storeroom.

After a while, presumably spent drinking an espresso, he returned holding what could only be a prop-shaft. He placed it behind him and started the paperwork. 'This will take a while,' I thought but at least I could see the object of my desire.

But I couldn't prove I lived at the chalet made of raspberries; I didn't have a failed delivery card because a postman hadn't been anywhere near the place. Added to that, the first name on my passport

(James) didn't match that of the recipient on the package either – the official wasn't happy.

I thought about leaning over the counter, grabbing the prop-shaft and doing a runner with it but decided instead to state my intention not to leave the building without it. Which did the trick and, with reluctance, he handed it over.

For those who don't know me, and for those who think they do, my first name is in fact James, not Chris. My mother uses my second name 'Christian', which I abbreviate to Chris. It's a long story, rooted in parental disagreement. If parents can't agree, or one doesn't concede, in the naming of a child it is destined for a confusing childhood – or possibly a life of schizophrenia. There is an upside to this naming duality. If someone refers to me as 'James' I know they are from officialdom. Only the government calls me 'James'. And if someone (usually Mum or Debbie) uses my full name 'Christian', I know I've done something wrong.

I thought about leaning over the counter, grabbing the prop-shaft and doing a runner with it but decided instead to state my intention not to leave the building without it. Which did the trick and, with reluctance, he handed it over.

That evening I sat outside the chalet feeling very manly with my arms covered in grease and my fingernails impregnated with oil. I had successfully installed the new prop shaft – or so I hoped. After a thorough degreasing, I loaded my stash of cheap wine into the back of Landie along with my other belongings and went to bed.

The next morning I set off at 5:30am under a clear sky, the full moon illuminating my way, and the stars had turned out in numbers to bid me a celestial farewell. A deer and a fox were the only traffic I encountered while winding Landie down the mountain to Cluses where we joined the motorway.

Once on the motorway, I accelerated Landie up to 70mph apprehensively. This was always a key moment on any wine run because Landie hadn't been above 40mph for over three months and who knew what else might fail at such breakneck speed. 'Had I tightened the prop shaft bolts sufficiently?' I wondered. Mercifully, I couldn't hear any unusual noises above the familiar roar of her engine, the rattling of loose body panels and the clinking of wine bottles.

After an hour of uneventful motorway driving, my mind started to wander away from breakdown scenarios and the prospect of being imprisoned with only my thoughts for sixteen hours became daunting.

Having done the journey six times before, the navigation was easy: west past Geneva then turn north towards Dijon. I'm also very familiar with the psychological way markers. Dijon seemingly takes forever to reach. Once Dijon is captured the cities of Troyes, Reims and Saint-Quentin fall easily. Passing Reims is always poignant for me, having spent a night in its hospital. Finally, when the first sign to Calais appears, the smell of diesel fumes are diluted with the scent of victory.

I stopped for fuel just after Dijon and noticed something leaking out of my left rear hub. 'It wouldn't be a proper wine run without Landie leaving a trail of some kind of liquid,' I thought. I took no action, other than to drive faster in order to get to the ferry before whatever was leaking ran out.

During the journey, for distraction I tried to recall all the people who had visited me that year. Like the snow, my regulars had been a bit thin on the ground. A new type of guest, 'my readers' had filled the ranks. Many had come to visit the crime scene of *Skiing with Demons* and to meet the central protagonist. Some had made me feel like an attraction at a freak show. I wondered if they had been disappointed. I was no longer the party man of Morzine and was now a recluse, hiding in a remote chalet on its outskirts and seldom seen in its bars.

I reflected on the season in its entirety. Was Season 7 my worst season so far? Probably. The skiing conditions in Morzine had been mediocre at best but, even if they had been good, I'd still have spent most of my days fixing or worrying about Landie. I'd also made an unsustainable financial loss. On the plus side, I now knew how to fit a Defender prop shaft.

The ferry was full of the usual suspects: parties of annoying school kids, lorry drivers, bikers, European migrant workers and those too fat or too frightened to fly. I hid in the boat's posh restaurant and spent the voyage looking out of a window.

Above the muddy water, I noticed a couple of gannets gliding majestically above the waves. After a winter at sea they were returning to their breeding grounds in England. With no nest to build or eggs to lay, I didn't know what I was going to do with my summer. Hopefully, I would find some gainful employment because my coffers were running low.

When the white cliffs of Dover appeared in the window, I started to prepare mentally for the English part of the journey. The traffic on our motorways and their ubiquitous road works always made this section of the wine run the most painful. I have a habit of hitting the M25 in rush hour, and that wine run was no different.

Finally, Sutton Coldfield was in sight and the prospect of a canine welcome lifted my soul. It took me ten minutes to get past Oscar before I could embrace Debbie. She felt guilty that I'd had to drive home alone but alone had been better – the forced solitude had given me time to think. Landie had not only got me home one more time but also once again had been my decompression chamber as I transitioned from winter to summer life.

During my decompression, I reflected on the events of Season 7 and concluded that an aging vehicle had caused all my troubles. Landie was a millstone around my neck. Perhaps I could return to Zine without Landie? But she had become part of my persona and was often a source of misguided pride. I wouldn't be 'Chalet Chris' if I drove around in a more modern vehicle. 'You can take the man out of a Defender, but you can't take the Defender out of the man,' I thought.

I couldn't return to Chalet Framboise even if I'd wanted to. It wasn't available the following season – its owners were going to retire there. The prospect of finding yet another new home for the Project, filled me with apathy – the summer would be a whole lot easier if I didn't try.

Once again I'd concluded, the Chalet Project was over – there wouldn't be a Season 8. I'd focus on leading instead; I'd make myself available to the Ski Club all season. I'd offer to lead for them whenever or wherever they asked.

14. Cross Town Traffic

A few months after declaring Season 7 would be my last, I found myself sitting on a drum of electrical cable tucking into a Kurdish feast. The impromptu picnic was being held on the flat roof of a three-story building in the depths of an ugly conurbation. Traffic noise and the bustle of commerce, echoed from below.

My fellow diners - Farhad (a Kurd from Iran), Faridoon (a Kurd from Iraq) and Sayid (who was originally from Pakistan) - were similarly perched. A fifth diner 'James' (from Afghanistan) was munching on naan bread and shovelling bits of braised lamb into his mouth. No one could pronounce his Afghan name so he had chosen to be called 'James' to make life easier.

It was a humid day and we had been installing air-conditioning units for the restaurant below when Farhad decided to treat the most exotic of his employees (Chris from Yorkshire) to some of his national cuisine. English was supposedly our common language but Farsi and sign language worked best. Despite the communication problems and our ethnic differences, we all had one thing in common: a love of power tools - which was mostly what we talked about.

I couldn't have been further from the Alps or the white middle-class world of skiing but I was close to home. I was in Handsworth, a mere six miles from Sutton Coldfield. I'd joined this merry band of Brummie electricians as a rather old apprentice.

My co-workers, none of whom had been skiing, were mildly interested in my winter exploits. It was hard to explain the purpose of skiing or indeed its rewards. I was a novelty to them and they humoured me. They couldn't understand what this seemingly well-off middle-aged man was doing in their world. They were too busy earning a living to understand what an existential crisis was. I was on a quest to get a proper job.

One of the big questions posed by the Morzine Chalet Project was 'What do ski bums do in the summer?' and I still hadn't found a satisfactory answer. Telling people I was a writer wasn't cutting it and declaring I was a househusband raised eyebrows even further. The former seemed to suggest self-delusion and the latter an assumption that I was a kept man. So I decided a better answer was, 'I'm an electrician' and I'd set about making that true that summer.

Having a prehistoric degree in Electrical Engineering, I was technically more qualified than most of my new colleagues, but I lacked what really counted – practical experience. I had taken, and passed, a domestic wiring standards exam and was close to being able to call myself a 'sparky'.

I hadn't realised, when embarking on my new career, that I'd learn more than just how to wire a house. I'd lived for over twenty years in Birmingham's affluent centre and enjoyed its multiculturalism. However, I didn't really know the un-integrated nature of its suburbs where Farhad and his crew invariably worked. He had built a reputation amongst Birmingham's Asian communities for doing high quality work cost effectively.

The rundown areas of Brum still have their grand Victorian street names. Albert Road, King Edwards Drive and The Forge are echoes from a time when cloth capped Brummies lived there and actually made things. Now these places have been taken over by a different culture and infused with a different vibrancy. If my grandparents were alive and visited, the street names would be their only clue to their former inhabitants and their toil. It must be the same for the older French in Morzine – the place names are French but everything and everyone seems English.

I felt welcome, but coming from the middle class ghetto of Wylde Green, I stood out. So did Landie and her spare wheel cover –

emblazoned, as it was, with my logo (a devil holding skis, drinking beer). I was a little embarrassed to park her on the streets in largely Islamic communities. I'd often get some double takes when working in a school or a supermarket. However, because I wore a high visibility jacket with the word 'Electrician' written on my back, people soon realised I was with the contractors.

I call it my 'invisibility jacket' because once I've wandered around a building for a while in it, folk forget I'm there. I can listen into their daily conversations while I fiddle with something down by the skirting boards. Thanks to my invisibility jacket I can be a fly on the wall in places where I might otherwise be regarded with suspicion.

I soon replaced the wheel cover with a more appropriate one advertising my electrical services. I converted Landie into a builders van. I replaced two of the rear seats with tool storage lockers, added shelving and replaced my ski roof rack with ladder clamps. I made sure all the modifications were reversible so I could easily reconfigure her back into a troop carrier for skiers.

I developed 'van envy'. When driving to jobs, I found myself eyeing up other vans in the traffic. Admiring their livery and the ladder systems on their roof. I suspect lots of blokes secretly want to own a van – especially if, like me, they watched 'The A-Team' as a child.

Surfing the Screwfix website became my guilty evening pleasure. I spent more on tools than I earned each week, until I had an enviable set. My colleagues started to regard Landie as the ultimate toolbox. They also used her for shelter when it rained, filling the back of Landie with Persian banter.

Landie was even called into action once to drag a monster cable across a large building site. We weaved between JCBs and other large yellow mechanical dinosaurs that were flattening the buildings around us. We'd traversed some interesting landscape together before, but none quite so bizarre.

Despite the hard physical work and often appalling working conditions (under vermin ridden floorboards and in spider filled lofts) I mostly loved my new job. I'd spent most my working life sat in front of a computer. Although not so well paid, it was gratifying to be doing something practical with my hands while using my head. Once I became less conscious of being different, I enjoyed the banter of the building site and the inter-trade camaraderie.

I enjoyed not worrying about turning into a potato that summer. It was usually a battle each summer keeping fit. But knowing I'd be climbing ladders all day, I no longer needed to go running or take any ancillary exercise - my job kept me fit.

There was one big downside to my new career. I was back working in a crowded, noisy and dirty city. I was back in the rat race and now seemingly, further behind than the other runners. I spent a large part of my day driving between jobs scattered all over the conurbation. This involved sitting in horrendous traffic breathing diesel fumes – admittedly most of them coming from the back of Landie.

I'd forgotten that driving around town was hell, especially during rush hour. I'd forgotten the frustration, impatience and aggression that manifests on congested city roads. There was always a battle to find a parking space remotely near a job too and a constant worry about getting a parking ticket. Sitting in traffic gave me too much time to contemplate the quality of my existence.

One hot afternoon, covered in plaster dust from my last job and dripping in sweat, I hit the Aston Expressway during rush hour heading out of the city's commercial centre – seven lanes of traffic, four moving slowly. Landie wasn't built for traffic. A heavy clutch and lack of air conditioning meant my torture was more acute than those round me in their modern cars. I surveyed my fellow commuters in a cynical frame of mind.

I concluded that the occupants of the expensive German cars around me had spent their day playing monopoly. They had been in their shiny offices trying to make money out of property or help others with wealth make more money out of money, while keeping a slice for themselves.

Others had spent the day buying and selling things – essentially screwing suppliers and shafting customers. A few might have been administering the monopoly game, others keeping the score and a few making sure everyone stuck to the rules.

Nobody in that traffic jam looked like they had spent the day discovering, inventing, designing, creating, building or growing anything – other than investment portfolios.

They all looked well rewarded, but the fancy cars and the suburban houses, they were trying to reach, were likely as not, to be financed. They had to stay in the monopoly game to keep up the payments if they wanted to continue living the urban dream. That meant sitting in traffic jams twice daily until they'd paid everything off.

I suddenly felt less envious of their fancy air-conditioned cars. They were probably trapped, not just by the traffic, but by their car loans, their mortgages, their insurance policies, their children's school fees and whatever else was needed to live a dream mis-sold to them by capitalism. I was better off in my old Land Rover. They were self-indentured slaves to consumerism and I was not. I was free from all that – but yet, I seemed to be sat in the same traffic jam.

My self-validation session was interrupted by the sound of an ambulance siren and I tried to get Landie out of its way. Mounting a kerb and letting an ambulance past seems to be part of every journey through the city. There always seemed to be someone, somewhere, having a medical emergency.

The ambulance squeezed passed and I thought, 'Another player has had a heart attack and left the monopoly board.' Of course it could have been attending a pile up on the M6.

Landie was the oldest vehicle in the traffic jam. One of the central tenets of consumerism and indeed capitalism is to build obsolescence into everything. Once there are no more new markets to exploit, you need to sell the same things to the same people over and over again – technologically more advanced versions maybe. My fellow commuters and I were all sat in essentially the same product. Theirs' just had more buttons and dials and probably didn't leak. Their cars were allegedly more environmentally friendly but by keeping mine going, I was saving the earth the cost of building its replacement.

During one communal tea break Manjit, a master plumber and building site philosopher, explained consumerism to me – occasionally the conversation at work did move away from power tools.

'Capitalism only works in an expanding economy', he told me. 'Everyone needs to continually buy new stuff to keep the wheels of capitalism turning. Wages go up, profit margins fall and capitalists make up the difference by growing sales and increasing productivity. Cities have to expand too. Their populations need to increase to generate more consumer demand, not least for houses to live in. That in turn created more wages for tradesman, like you and me, to spend on consuming more products.' Then he started to admire my new impact driver.

The biggest problem with the grownup version of monopoly is the players don't all start with the same amount of capital. Some even start already owning properties they have inherited, with a full complement of hotels already installed.

I was pretty sure there were no farmers in my traffic jam. Thanks to modern intensive farming techniques, one agricultural worker can now feed approximately 150 people. Some help the farmer, some build tractors for him, some supply him electricity, some teach his children and some go to war for him – or at least in his name. But the rest are free to go and play monopoly in the cities and amass fortunes. Some don't have to bother going into a city they simply inherited great tracts of land and charge those who farm it rent.

The older I get, the more left wing my views have become. It might be because I'm not a millionaire and I resent those still trying to become one? Or it might just be the influence of my new comrades on the building site? Like all builders, I now also take two sugars in my tea.

However, given that our planet is over populated and running out of resources, a society based on expansion, avarice and greed cannot be sustainable. Hopefully I'll be dead before the world implodes but until then I'm going to keep driving my Defender.

The other big downside of my new career was the constant vista of ugliness. I'd often have to traverse across the city and work in the poorer, more rundown areas of the wider conurbation – I'd regularly visit suburbs I had previously only known by name and reputation.

With few trees or green spaces between them, one suburb merges into each other. The size and modernity of the houses might change slightly from place to place and the space between them fluctuates. But the conurbation seems to sprawl on in every direction like an unremitting desert. I felt suffocated, not just by the traffic but by the ugliness, surrounded by millions of other people with no easy escape from each other.

While driving around Birmingham, I felt many a pang for the Alps and I kept reviewing my decision to end the Chalet Project. I'd escaped the rat race once before, but now I seemed to be right back in it.

But it was good for my humility, if not my lungs, to spend time in the less salubrious parts of Birmingham. To appreciate your existence you need to compare it to that of others. Each night when I returned from work I felt grateful, no longer resentful, that I lived in Sutton Coldfield.

During Season 7 I'd started to take the spectacular vistas, the clean air and the abundance of space in the mountains for granted. Despite my whinging about being a chalet host, I was privileged to have spent so much time in the Alps – I was lucky that life had allowed me to try skiing at all, let alone live the ski bum dream, even if it was now over.

If it wasn't, I now had a proper job to see me through the summers and better still, one that seldom needed clarification. It involved working with my hands (and power tools) all day, not playing grownup monopoly. I could also now claim to be working-class and a socialist – all be it one with a bourgeois passion for skiing.

More importantly, I had a portable trade. If not the Alps, theoretically I could live anywhere and still find work. Communities will always need a sparky more than they need a writer - or for that matter a ski instructor.

15. The Lift Demons

If, like me, you are mildly, claustrophobic, agoraphobic and acrophobic or just a bit of a scaredy-cat, then Lift Demons can be hard to defeat. [2]I have an uneasy truce with them, rather than an outright victory.

I've never been very keen on using building elevators, always preferring to take the stairs. I hate being crammed in a small metal box and having to trust that the engineers who designed it did their maths correctly or that those responsible for servicing it were conscientious. So it was inevitable the Lift Demons would prey on me.

There are three main Lift Demons: the draglift demon, the chairlift demon and their big brother, the cable car demon – each has their own, subtly different, way of playing with my mind.

The Draglift Demon

The draglift demon fell without much of a fight. Learning how to get on and off a button lift was relatively easy. The journey in between proved more problematic to master. My legs would fight each other, desperate to form a snowplough and even on the shortest of drags, my thighs would start burning half way up. Once I could ski parallel, only T-bars remained a problem, until I became more discerning about whom I rode them with – preferably nobody. If I feel sociable, I will ride them with skiers of the same weight, height and ability.

Once on and moving, I'd worry about falling off somewhere too difficult for me to ski back down from – basically any draglift that wasn't next to a blue caused me anxiety. Once I became proficient enough to ski back down the drag path itself, without knocking anyone else off, draglifts held no fear.

---

2 Claustrophobia is an irrational fear of confined places, acrophobia is an irrational fear of heights and agoraphobia is a fear of entering open or crowded places, or places from which escape is difficult. A scaredy-cat is someone who is frightened of their own shadow.

These days I'm so chilled on a draglift I don't bother to hold onto the pole during the ride. Before I gave it up, I'd use my hands to light a fag and enjoy a smoke while surveying the scenery.

There are a couple of nasty old button lifts in the PdS. The springs have gone in the poles and they kick like mules, lifting you into the air, when you set off. Some of the really bad ones I call 'double kickers' because they do this twice before settling down. I usually warn guests before they get on a known 'double kickers' – unless I bear them malice.

The draglift demon seems to prey mostly on debutant snowboarders, who struggle to use a lift designed for skiers. If I had to use just one word to explain why I've never tried snowboarding it would be 'draglifts'.

The Chairlift Demon

The chairlift demon is more malevolent than his little brother. Even after we have mastered getting on and off a chairlift, he still likes to play mind games with us. Rather than using our fear of injury, he offers us the prospect of a long and chilly ordeal. He likes to randomly stop a chairlift, leaving his victims dangling over a precipice wondering how long it will be before it starts moving again.

Chairlifts stop for one of three reasons:

1. Someone has failed to get on or off it successfully. If a chairlift is accessible to beginners, bodies can often pile up at both terminuses. During half term, most chairlifts stop half a dozen times before getting you to the top thanks to embarkation and disembarkation carnage.
2. Wind. More specifically, a crosswind - they don't stop because of flatulent riders. On a gusty day modern chairlifts automatically slow down if they detect a side wind and even stop to let

strong gusts pass. If the wind persists, the lifties will have to shut the lift completely. If you got on one just before they do, you'll spend the next portion of your life inching forward in small bursts willing each pylon closer vowing never to get on chairlift again.

3. Malfunction. The chairlift has stopped working. If you're lucky, it might just be an intermittent fault. It might be a simple matter of resetting something or switching to a backup generator or engine. If the lift is broken-broken, you may need to be rescued from your vertical predicament – the nightmare scenario.

When a chairlift stops, leaving you swinging in the chilly air, you have no idea which of the three above reasons is at play and the chairlift demon strikes. The longer you wait the more he messes with your mind. You've seen the movie Frozen and heard other peoples' horror stories of being stuck for hours on chairlifts, and you think, 'Oh no. It is happening to me'.

After about ten minutes you can rule out reason one. No matter how many bodies are piled up at the bottom, it doesn't take more than ten minutes to untangle limbs and remount skis. If paramedics are needed, to extract a back injury, perhaps the delay will be longer. I know it's wrong to hope that someone has been seriously injured, but after twenty minutes of being stationary, I often do.

If it's a calm day, you can rule out reason two and after thirty minutes of being stationary you start to conclude that it is reason three and after forty minutes you know you're in the nightmare scenario.

I spend more time than most riding chairlifts and statistically I'm well overdue for a breakdown incident. Last season, the Chaux Fleurie Express in Avoriaz, a chairlift I use dozens of times each season, broke-broke. Mercifully I wasn't on it. It's not a chair I usually worry about because it's short, fast, seldom used by beginners, and relatively sheltered. Apart from one small section it never flies far above the ground. I don't know why that matters – there are very few chairlifts I'd consider jumping off.

This failure was un-rectifiable and rescue teams were sent to rope down the stranded riders. Three hours later everyone was off. Had I been one of the stranded, I would have had a good chapter for this book, but frankly I'm not that desperate for material. According to the chairlift demon, my good luck with injuries spectacularly ran out after seven seasons. So it is logical to assume my chairlift luck will soon run out too.

If it is a warm and sunny day, and you're sat with friends or interesting strangers, you can block out the chairlift demons by making conversation to pass the time. However on a cold and wet day, you start to wonder how long you have before hypothermia strikes. You're dressed for an active day skiing, which requires one less layer than sitting around being sandblasted with ice crystals, so you soon start shivering. In February, most people are borderline hypothermia when they get off a functioning chairlift, so survival time on a stationary chair is limited. In this scenario I, like many, start weighing up the possibly of a self-rescue.

Firstly you have to assess the location to determine if jumping is an option. Often the chair you're stuck on isn't that high above the snow. If it's less than three or four metres to the ground, a safe landing might be made. Whether you'd throw your skis and poles down first seems to be a matter of personal choice.

It is important you assess the whole landing zone before jumping. Is it reasonably easy to ski from the intended landing zone to a piste? Even with a broken ankle? You don't want to jump from the frying pan into the fire.

If you don't fancy jumping, creating a rope is your next best option. Belts, braces, and scarves might be used or daisy-chained ski poles together, using their wrist straps, will also get you closer to the ground before you drop. If you're stuck with a bunch of snowboarders you're buggered. If you're stuck with me, you'll always have access to a rope. But, even though I carry ten metres of paracord in my rucksack for such situations, I probably wouldn't admit to having it until well into the crisis.

If you don't have, or can't make a rope, there is always the zip wire escape. If you have a sturdy rucksack, you can sling it over the cable then, holding on to its straps, slide down to the pylon below. Assuming you survive the impact with the pylon, you can then climb down its maintenance ladder. The problem with this strategy is that if the chairlift starts moving mid slide, you'll look very stupid - just before you die.

If you don't have a rucksack, the same manoeuvre could be done utilising the Tyrolean traverse. This involves laying on the cable, using a dangling leg for balance and your arms for propulsion – it's probably best to go down feet first.

Then there is human ladder escape. One person dangles from the footrest. Then another person slides down him and dangles from his feet, then another performs the same manoeuvre making a human ladder. This of course means only the last person gets to the ground without a fall. However, acts of self-sacrifice aside, this will only really work if you're lucky enough to be stuck on a chair with members of the Cirque du Soleil.

I'm willing to admit that I may have overthought self-rescue and by dwelling on the subject, I'm simply feeding the chairlift demon ammunition. The only real practical advice I can give you is to always sit in the middle of a chair (its warmer there) and never get on a chair if you remotely require the loo.

Learning to get on and off a chairlift (conventionally at the top) might be relatively easy to master, but working out who to get on one with, is more complex. Here are my golden rules when it comes to choosing fellow riders:

1. Avoid getting on a chair with a beginner. If you do, make sure they are significantly smaller than you. They will throw a snowplough across your skis when you least expect it. If they fall when disembarking, they will instinctively grab hold of you and unless they are tiny, they will take you down with them. Small children are to be avoided too. If they do get into trouble, you'll feel obliged to try and save them.

2. Avoid getting on a chair with a snowboarder. Never sit to the left of one that is goofy or to the right of one who is regular.[3] If you sit the wrong side of a snowboarder, they will rest their board across your skis – but this is more annoying than problematic. The main danger is that an inexperienced goofy rider will fall to the right when disembarking and a regular rider will fall to the left. If you notice someone goofy sat to the left of a regular rider on your chair – prepare for carnage when getting off.

3. Avoid people with airbags. Actually, anyone wearing a large rucksack will have to sit precariously near the front of the chair making it difficult to get the safety bar up or down. Their airbag might also go off and suffocate you, not them.

4. Avoid nervous people. They will slam the safety bar down on your head before your bum has hit the seat. This is the main reason I wear a helmet. Conversely, people who lift the safety bar too early are equally dangerous – especially if you are the one wearing a large rucksack.

5. Never get on a chairlift with a Brexiteer. You might get stuck on a chair (or an island) with them for a very long time. The subject might crop up and you'll be tempted to push them off the chair.

---

3 'Goofy' riders have their right foot facing forward and keep it secured to their board when riding chairs. 'Regular' riders do the same with their left foot. Some boarders keep both feet bound to their board when using chairlifts, which is impressive, but makes them hard to categorise. 'Are they a dude or did they just forget to unclip a foot?'

6. Never get on a chairlift with someone known to carry paracord.
    If the lift stops, they might talk you into a self-rescue attempt,
    just before the lift starts moving again.

On a busy day, when etiquette dictates that every chair should go
up fully loaded, you may think you don't have a choice of chairlift
companions. You have to board the next chair with whoever gets to
the gates with you. But, with a bit of premeditation, that is under
your control. Someway back in the queue, you can assess those around
you for any of the above criteria. You can slide back in the queue
or even move forward if you want to avoid someone.

There is an art to ski lift queuing. By being assertive but not
rude, you can often get on a chair or two ahead of your friends who
haven't been paying attention. It's all about where you position your
skis. I know a few lift queue ninjas who, despite arriving at the back
of a queue with me, regularly board a chair several ahead of mine.
They have shared a few of their secret moves with me under the
strict instruction that I don't share them with you.

The Cable Car Demon

The Cable Car Demon is the most covert of all the lift demons. If
a cable car stops, you're not in any life threatening danger and self-
rescue is not an option unless you're packing an actual parachute
– not just parachute cord. There is usually an attendant on-board
in radio contact with the operators and if they don't look worried
there is no need for you to worry either. However, they almost never
stop mid transit. If they do something exceptional has happened, so
behind the operators calm face a serious problem might be hiding.

In September 2016, 33 passengers were stuck on the Panoramic Mont
Blanc cable car overnight. The lift running between Helbronner
in Italy, and the Aiguille du Midi (one of Mt Blanc's subordinate
peaks), jammed after its cables became entwined. Many people where
rescued by helicopter, before deteriorating weather and nightfall

forced the rescue operation to be suspended – knowing my luck, I'd have been one of the 33. They had to spend 17 hours in freezing conditions before finally being rescued. The cable car has since been replaced and cabins now contain emergency kits containing warm clothing, food and hopefully a Portaloo. Every time there is a cable car incident, I tend to read all about it. I really shouldn't, it simple empowers the Cable Car Demon.

Despite their many windows and the expanse around them, they are the most claustrophobic of lifts, especially if they are rammed. They span larger unsupported distances and fly over the deepest of chasms, so they are also the most acrophobic. There is also too much time to think, when waiting for a cable car to fill. I foolishly use this time to speculate on the car's maintenance regime. Depending on which country I'm in, I cast inaccurate aspersions on that nation's engineering prowess and attitude to health and safety - this is why I will never ski in Bulgaria.

If the cable car is rammed, I sometimes get agoraphobia – the fear of panicking and looking stupid. Strangely I'm not worried about the cable snapping and falling to my death - I just don't want to make a fool of myself first.

My fear of cable cars seems illogical, given I'm not the least bit nervous about flying. A cable car has a meaty steel cable holding it in the air. An aeroplane relies on Bernoulli's theory of laminar flow, to keep it from falling out of the sky. His theory explains why wings generate lift – but the fact it's still known as a 'theory', should be more worrying.

I'm relatively calm on a télécabine as long as my bubble isn't rammed. If it is my claustrophobia can kick in. I hate it when a gang of random folk cram in with me at the last minute when I'm expecting a spacious ride.

Unlike chairlifts, there is no effective way of choosing whom you ride them with. If you get in first you can scowl at anyone approaching the door and generally try and look like an unsavoury person to be in close confines with – but that seldom works.

I know I'm not the only one troubled by the lift demons. I see others twitching in cable cars and going quiet when chairlifts unexpectedly stop. Some text on phones, others make conversation with strangers and some suck on boiled sweets – I usually try and think about what I might have for dinner.

It might seem strange for someone who twitches in the smallest of elevators, to be so keen on skiing. But having to hang on to myself for a few minutes going up in a ski lift is small price to pay for the joy of coming down. If I ever completely lose my battle with the lift demons I'd have to take up ski touring, and I'm far too lazy for that.

16. One Man and His Van

Most people, at some stage in their life, have contemplated buggering off in a campervan. It is a common, if dimensionally constricted, dream. The idea of wandering with no fixed abode seems liberating. Being able to change the view from your windows on a whim is indeed a seductive proposition.

Even the most homely of home birds can sometimes feel they have been perched in one spot for too long. Once they have decorated the same house for the sixth time and worn out three mowers on the same lawn, the idea of a simple self-contained life on the road starts to appeal.

Many who live the campervan dream rent out their home to fund their travels, if only for a year or two. For others, a campervan is a cheap accommodation solution when travelling the world or living other dreams – to spend all summer surfing or all winter skiing. Campervans can also be a two-fingered salute to redundancy, divorce and other forms of financial disaster. It's a way of rejecting a rat race that has rejected you.

In my book (and this is my book), to qualify for a living-the-dream badge, you need to have burnt a few bridges before embarking on your new life - otherwise you're really just going on a long holiday. You need to pack in a job or sell your home to fund the dream. You have to opt heavily for more time and less money. If your home has wheels, because 'less money' has chosen you, it's important that you keep those wheels rolling. If you don't, you're not really living a dream but living in an oxymoron – a 'static caravan'.

Low on funds and wanting to establish an escape route from the metropolis, I thought about swapping Landie for a campervan. But even though the Chalet Project was over, I didn't want to sell her – a man never sells his Defender. Besides which, I didn't want to just go camper vanning, I wanted to go 'wild camper vanning', if indeed there was such a thing - if not, I was going to invent it.

I wanted to stay in places not accessible by road somewhere in the mountains and preferably within walking distance of a pub. I needed an all-terrain vehicle I could sleep in, so pimping my current ride (Landie) seemed the obvious solution.

Either by design or accident, there is just enough room in a Defender 110 (the long wheel base version) for an average sized man (me) to lie flat in the back. I'd discovered this accidentally on one of the early bacon runs, when a hotel bed couldn't be found.

In the dark days, when worst-case scenarios dominated my nocturnal thoughts, I'd contemplated how I could make Landie into a rudimentary home. Now, temporarily living in Landie was an exciting proposition. It was time to actualise the dream.

Well-off campervan dreamers might be tempted to buy a motor home or, God forbid, a caravan. But these boxes on wheels renege on their promise of nomadic freedom. It's true, the bigger your mobile home the more modern conveniences it will have - not to mention an actual convenience. But a campervan is easier to drive and park. If your charabanc is too large you are simply going to a poorer neighbourhood for your holidays – a trailer park.

I wanted the changes I made to Landie to be reversible. She had to be capable of continuing her new role, an electrician's van, and her old one, a troop carrier for skiers. With hindsight, keeping that last option open was the first indication that I wasn't truly done with the chalet business.

The modifications involved bolting equipment to the rear bench seat frames. I fashioned a rudimentary kitchen out of an old ammunition box and added a fridge – a plug in cool box. I installed curtains for privacy and for warmth I insulated the roof and carpeted the floor with rubber playground tiles.

I installed a bed that rolled out from under the cockpit bulkhead. The last time I'd slept in Landie, catering packs of bacon had been my mattress, but this time I wanted something that would attract fewer carnivores.

Despite their size, Defenders don't have any storage places: no glove box, door trays and no boot. So, I tried to create storage wherever possible. Finally, I installed cabin lights and a USB socket in the back. Like most modern humans, I can't sleep without a USB socket next to my bed. Essentially, I didn't want to be just a man with a bed in the back of a van.

Modifications made, I took the Landie-van for a field test. Not sure how things would work out, or the legality of wild camper vanning, I headed to a campsite I'd heard about on the banks of Ullswater.

The far corner of the site, next to a pebble beach, was only accessible by a 4x4. I managed to drive almost onto the beach and parked up for the night. I was slightly concerned that an AA van wouldn't be able to reach me, if Landie malfunctioned. I reminded myself that Landie was now reliable, and unlikely to let me down. In any case, I had no phone signal to summon rescue, so I set up camp. This involved pulling the hand brake on, setting up a deck chair on the beach and opening a can of beer.

Essentially, I was camping but my tent had windows, electricity and didn't need erecting. It was unlikely to be blown away too. I still had to put my trousers on while lying down and perform most tasks on my knees. The main advantage a campervan has over a tent, is that you don't have to constantly retrieve things you've forgotten from your car.

I sat on the beach and watched the sunset behind the mountains to the west (Helvellyn and its subordinate peaks) with a solitary merganser for company. I watched the duck floating around fishing and felt a kinship. We were both solitary travellers enjoying the tranquillity of our location. I contemplated why I felt so content - sunsets are usually more enjoyable when shared with humans than with waterfowl. I concluded it was because I was enjoying being on my own. With no internet or phone signal, I was isolated, but self-sufficient. I had everything I really needed to exist in my Landie-van. To celebrate my newfound liking for isolation, I decided to hike to the nearby pub and chat to some fellow walkers.

I have never lived in a house on my own. The Landie-van was essentially the first home I'd exclusively owned. It was a minimalist home, but I had chosen all the items in it. Each had a utilitarian purpose and was, quite literally, to hand. Everything was organised the way I wanted it to be. I had even chosen the cushions and the curtain material myself. Nobody else's detritus littered this home. There were no cast off clothes or other people's dirty dishes to navigate around. Nobody was going to put things back in the wrong place or not put them back at all. Everything was the way I liked it, because that's the way I left it. Unlike chalet or family life, the amount of chaos I lived with in the Landie-van was under my own control. I must be further along the obsessive-compulsive spectrum than I thought. Essentially, life boils down to two choices – you can spend it being irritated or being lonely.

That first night in my Landie-van I sat in my sleeping bag planning the following day's walk feeling cosy and content, surrounded by maps while reading my Wainwright guidebooks. A moth flapped around the cabin light causing shadows to dance across the pages as I turned them. Then the heavens opened up – I was in the Lake

District after all. The rain drummed down on Landie's aluminium roof adding to the ambience. The percussive noise went from therapeutic to downright annoying when I finally turned the lights out and tried to get some slumber. I lay there in the dark listening to the rain unable to sleep.

Along with the sound of rain, Landie echoed with memories created in the Alps. I replayed some of the amusing conversations I'd had while ferrying guests around Morzine. I could hear the raucous laughter and drunken singing that had taken place in my metal box. The echoes had French, Dutch and Irish accents along with those from almost every corner of the UK. There was even an echo of Farsi spoken by my new Kurdish colleagues. I was on my own, but I didn't feel alone.

I recalled the intense and frivolous conversations I'd had with co-pilots on the bacon and wine runs and the profound sadness I'd felt when I'd undertaken my winter migration solo, post marital separation. Landie and I had been through a lot together and now she was protecting me from the rain.

I remembered the hitchhikers I'd taken pity on and the inappropriately dressed youths Landie had saved from freezing to death in Morzine. I thought of my regular guests, most of whom I'd probably never see again, now the Chalet Project was officially over. I would miss them, the ex-pat community and the few French locals I had interacted with for so many years.

I would miss the Alps. I would visit them on holiday, of course, but that would compare badly to being part of Morzine's winter community. Surprisingly low on the list of things I'd miss, was skiing. The rain abated and the echoes stopped and I finally fell asleep.

I was woken early the following morning by two oystercatchers having an argument on the beach. I got a brew on, and I watched the sunrise through Landie's rear windows while still in my sleeping bag. I noticed I now had a neighbour. A white Ford transit van was parked above me in the field. A burley middle-aged man sporting a white mane and unkempt beard, climbed out of the van where he had obviously spent the night.

While I was having breakfast on the beach, my new neighbour wandered down for a chat. He was a Defender fan, having owned several of his own. I tried not to show my ignorance of Land Rover anthology when he described them and their relative merits.

When you own any type of classic vehicle, enthusiasts often accost you. When I rode a Harley Davison, this used to happen to me a lot. It's a nice thing: the enthusiast compliments your ride then starts babbling in petrol-head speak. I'd try to pretend I was equally discerning about motorbikes but, really, I'd just bought mine because it was black, had lots of chrome and made a wicked noise. I'm slightly more informed when it comes to Defenders – I think?

The beach conversation moved on to camper vanning. He'd sold his last Defender to buy his transit. 'More room for my stuff', he told me. 'You've got to be ruthless, when you're living in a van. There's no room for sentimental clutter'. He told me. 'I've got my mother's wedding album in my glove box and that's it', he admitted, paused and added, 'Along with my own'. An alarm bell went off in my head. 'Here comes the life story', I thought.

A retired fireman, he had been living in his transit for over two years. Mountaineering was his passion, although age had forced him to retire and give lectures on climbing instead of doing it – his climbing gear had become props. He invited me over to look at his collection of ropes, carabiners and belaying devices – some of which he had made himself. So, we walked up to his van. He had done practically nothing to the inside of his, other than install a bed and hooks for his climbing gear. A cargo net bellied down from the roof laden with clothes. He'd obviously chosen to live with a high level of chaos.

I listened to his climbing stories but was more fascinated with his current adventure. He had weathered out 'the beast from the east' in his van, a freezing snowstorm that had hit England a few months earlier. Which was impressive because his van wasn't insulated and had no obvious heating devices other than the engine.

I couldn't decide if he had chosen to live in a van or thanks to hard times, had ended up living in one. The reference to his wedding photos and the mention of a son, hinted at a marriage. Maybe he was divorced or maybe he was widowed? I didn't want to probe. I was enjoying the encounter, but didn't want it to turn into a therapy session. He was retired, so presumably had a pension. He'd been on many expeditions and maybe post-marriage, he had turned the rest of his life into one.

Transit van man seemed happy enough. By the look of him, he ate well and enjoyed a pint or two. Presumably, when he felt the need for company, he went down to the nearest pub too – not just accost strangers on campsites.

Although his life had appeal, it seemed like a tragic one. He might have been living his dream, but I was living out a fantasy. I had a real home, a real job and a viable future wife. I had access to all the trappings of a conventional life to fall back on.

I was pleased that I now had a mobile man cave and in the summer, when I felt trapped in Sutton Coldfield, I could bugger off in it. I could temporarily live in a van through choice not necessity and I was profoundly grateful for that.

The temporary solitude was refreshing although I wouldn't want to live alone permanently – and not in a van. If loneliness is the price of freedom, I'm not prepared to pay it.

17. The Hurt Locker

If you are my age, you will have been through the purchasing of shoes hundreds of times - or at least a dozen if you're a man. However, if you've never skied, you won't have faced the ultimate challenge in footwear procurement – the buying of ski boots.

A friend once asked, what type of shoes she should bring on her first skiing holiday. I thought it odd she was asking me, of all people, for fashion advice. I suggested walking boots would be sensible and thought no more of it. When she turned up at the chalet she proudly showed me her new walking boots and asked if they would work? They were a reasonable match with her handbag and went well with her jeans – so I said 'yes'. It wasn't until we went to the ski hire shop that I realise she thought that skis attached to regular footwear. I then watched her travel from a happy place, where ski boots didn't exist, to the 'hurt locker' a place filled with devices of torture.

Some skiers can spend a whole evening discussing their boots; their boot history and the purgatory they went through on their journey to ski boot nirvana. Others know to keep their own boot anthology brief, lest they become a boot bore. Having said that, I'm now going to fill an entire chapter with a discourse on ski boots. First, here is a quick anatomical review of a ski boot.

A ski boot is made up of two major components: the clog and the collar. The collar is the bit that wraps around your shin. The collar will flex forward slightly and spring back. The amount it flexes, is unsurprisingly known as 'the flex'. Theoretically, the higher the flex the more power your boot can produce in a turn. But really, the higher the flex the more uncomfortable the boot will be to walk in. The collar often has a 'canting' adjustment. Which means, if you have bandy legs (like me) the collar can be tilted outwards, or if you're knock-kneed it can be tilted inwards.

The clog is the part of the boot that isn't the collar (the actual shoe). The less room your foot has to move in the clog the more accurately you can press on the ski. Inside the clog is a foot bed that can be moulded to the shape of your sole. However the rest of the clog is shaped to fit a normal foot but nobody has normal feet – abnormal is normal when it comes to feet. The trick is to choose a brand of ski boot that thinks your foot shape is normal.

Without knowing any of the above, I borrowed a friend's boots for my first skiing holiday They were a pair of rear-entry boots, the type you occasionally see grandpas still wearing on the pistes today. I might as well have borrowed her false teeth; they couldn't have fitted any worse than the boots. They made the almost impossible task of learning to ski, actually impossible. Everyone kept telling me *all* ski boots hurt, but they weren't trying to eat a rare steak with somebody else's teeth.

Since then I've always owned my own properly fitted boots. I take them as hand luggage on aeroplanes for fear the airlines might lose them and ruin my ski trip. I change them every couple of seasons, but it's a painful task, both financially and emotionally. Your new boots are never as comfortable as your old ones.

I had my latest pair fitted at the Footlocker in Chamonix. Jules, the proprietor was, 'the world's best boot fitter', according to my instructor and Morzine Mary. By her own admission, she had 'funny feet' although they didn't seem to amuse her.

People who have oddly shaped feet, either from birth or after injury, suffer most when trying to find ski-boot tranquillity. I couldn't tell you exactly why Mary's feet were so problematic. I'd endured many a lengthy anatomical explanation on the subject, but had never come away with a summary.

I'd seen Mary's ski-boot graveyard back in Liverpool, which could have filled its own field in Normandy. She must have tried just about every make and model of boot that had ever come onto the market. Some were custom-made and some had been specially adapted. Yet, she still hadn't found the perfect ski boots. So, she wanted the Svengali of ski boots (Jules) to fit them. I decided to join her pilgrimage to Chamonix. I took my old boots to see if he could adjust them, although I knew I'd probably walk out with a new pair.

When I first met Jules I was surprised to find out he was an Englishman. We English always seem to be the best at everything in the skiing world - except the actual skiing that is.

He had just come back from fitting President Putin's boots, which I hoped for his sake, he'd got right. After examining and measuring my feet, he quickly decided on the make, model and size of my ideal boot – I didn't have much input into this decision. I made the mistake of telling him I was going through the BASI system and had aspirations to be an instructor. So he assumed I needed something hardcore.

To my horror, the boots he selected were a whole size smaller than my current pair and very uncomfortable - which seemed to please him. 'You can't ski in slippers,' he commented.

Boot fitters have ways of talking you into uncomfortable boots. 'They won't hurt when you are actually skiing,' 'they will slacken up', 'they just need breaking in', are some of their favourite phrases. Jules was a master of these platitudes. He had just talked a Russian president into a pair of boots, so I stood no chance.

I walked out of the shop using the same sized feet I'd walking in with, yet carrying a pair of boots a size smaller than the ones I'd taken in. But Jules had convinced me the smaller boots would ultimately be more comfortable.

You don't really 'break in' ski boots; they break you in. Your feet get moulded to their shape, not the other way round. The truth is that when your ski boots become comfortable, it's usually time to start a war with a new pair because they have lost the stiffness and flex needed for accurate ski control. This is known as the ski-boot paradox. Comfy boots are bad boots, or at least bad for skiing performance. A common theme in skiing is compromising comfort for effectiveness – we skiers have to suffer for our art. But, nothing illustrates the masochistic nature of skiing more than the footwear we are forced to wear.

Needless to say, the first time I tried to ski in my new boots my feet were in agony. I ended up stopping halfway down the first piste and frantically trying to rip the left boot off, like some wounded animal clawing at an injury. When I finally got it off, a small Allen key fell out! It had been used to adjust the cant but must have fallen into the boot – 'thanks Jules'.

Without any foreign bodies in my boots they became more comfortable – but only slightly. The torture went on for weeks and put me off going skiing. At one stage, I even started wearing my old boots again, especially if I was going Girlfriend Skiing, but I could tell their sloppy fit was adversely affecting my skiing. I started to refer to my new pair as my 'BASI boots' and only wore them when having lessons.

Nobody has two identically sized feet. Everyone has one foot slightly larger than the other, yet ski boots, like all shoes, come in matching pairs. So one ski boot is always going to hurt more than the other. If you buy a pair that fits your bigger foot, your smaller foot will have space to move, causing rubbing and blistering. If you buy boots for your smaller foot, your larger foot will suffer crush injuries. Deciding which way to go makes for a delicious choice if you're a masochist. My solution is to wear odd socks with a slightly thicker one on the smaller foot.

After a full season of being at war with my BASI boots I was enjoying a truce that lasted right up to my accident two years later. Even so it was battle to get them on each morning. If I didn't keep them in a warm place over night, they would be too stiff to get on. They had to be bone dry too, along with my socks, to prevent any friction during foot insertion.

There was a brief period when they were almost comfortable. I noticed that I'd stopped undoing the buckles when I sat down for lunch. Every skier goes through a 'happy time' with their boots. All relationships have a magical time: you fall in love, you struggle to co-exist, then you work things out, you're briefly happy together, then something changes, it all falls apart and you have to go your separate ways – ski boots are no different.

In my case, I think all the skiing we had done together had taken its toll on our relationship. I had started to take my boots for granted and they had become less supportive of my skiing goals - they had become all take and no give. They had become physically abusive too, giving me black toenails each season. It was probably time to end the relationship.

I'm often jealous of other people's relationships with their ski boots. You see them happily walking around town together long after skiing has finished. Some people even go dancing with theirs! Of course it could just be alcohol that keeps their footwear relationship alive.

If I passed the Refresher course, I promised myself a pair of sloppy touring boots and that I'd wear them for the rest of my skiing life. But until then, there would be many more visits to the hurt locker before I could divorce my BASI boots.

18. SHALL I COMPARE SKIING TO A SUMMER'S DAY?

You may not be the slightest bit interested in fell walking,[4] the Lake District or mountains that aren't covered in snow – you bought a book called 'Skiing with Demons' after all. However, a fell walker and a skier are kindred spirits and are often the same person. So, to analyse the appeal of one activity can help to understand that of the other.

I have walked in most of England's National Parks, but it is in the Lake District where I most feel like I'm on a skiing holiday. Arguably, it is England's most beautiful landscape – it's certainly our most mountainous. Its craggy peaks and plunging valleys are equal in drama to those of the Alps, even if the theatrical production is on a smaller scale. But it's not just the scenery that leads me to compare the two ways to enjoy mountains.

The obvious thing that skiing and fell walking have in common is they both involve pointlessly going up a mountain in order to almost immediately come back down it. Both methods of doing so involve taking on a physical and often mental, challenge for its own sake.

Most of the ski demons have fell walking cousins. Although the mental challenges are similar, once you've dropped into a skiing pitch it cannot be aborted no matter what the demons whisper in your ear. A descent on skis, once started, has to be completed – unlike a fell walk, there is no turning back. When walking, self-doubt stays with you until you reach a mountain's summit; when skiing, most of the self-doubt happens when you're stood on the top of it, staring down not up.

---

4 I struggled to find the right term for walking in mountainous regions. 'Hiking' suggest carrying a large backpack with camping gear and 'walking' alone could mean a stroll with the dog in the park. No rope is needed, so 'climbing' doesn't fit, even though a scramble up a rocky face is often needed. So, I settled on 'fell walking'. 'Fell' (fjall) being the Old Norse word for a high barren landscape.

But it is not just the nebulous reward of meeting a pointless challenge that drives us upwards or downwards. Both activities release endorphins to make us feel happy. Fell walking relies more on aerobic exercise to produce them and skiing more often relies on an adrenaline rush.

When skiing, satisfaction is felt at the bottom of a mountain; when walking it's usually felt at its top. Whether ascending or descending, the common reward is just being in a place that transcends endeavour – the mountains.

Unlike walking, skiing seems to have its own purpose. The act of walking isn't that exhilarating. You'd never spend a day walking up and down an artificial grass slope inside a large shed in Tamworth for instance. Remove the scenery, and walking is perfunctory yet skiing would still be therapeutic.

Skiing carries the greater risk of injury, partly because it's done at higher speed but mainly because most humans are very competent perambulators. Most of us obtained a Level-4 grade before leaving the care of our parents. Unlike skiing, walkers rarely walk into immovable objects or off cliffs. Collisions are also rare too - you're unlikely to be 'felled on a fell' by an out of control beginner or a French kamikaze walker.

Mountain biking, the fell walking equivalent of snowboarding, creates the only real danger of a collision on the fells. Fortunately you can hear mountain bikers coming. You learn to recognise the noise of spraying stones, like you do the scraping noise of a board and you usually have time to leap off the path into the adjacent heather.

Unlike the Alps, there are no bears, wolves or hostile natives in the Lakes. The only predators you need to worry about are midges and mosquitos. Assuming you're walking in the summer, the avalanche risk is low so the fells can't spontaneously decide to kill you. And, being able to move in the opposite direction to gravity, the only terrain traps you need to worry about when fell walking are bogs.

Some of the summit routes can turn into rock climbs and some paths often skirt precipitous cliffs that become treacherous in bad weather. But, keep an eye on the weather and your life is mostly in your own hands on the fells. In the Alps your life is often in the hands of the people above you.

Some of the more popular Lakeland fell paths can feel like pistes and during the school holidays can be equally crowded, although, overtaking on a fell path is much less hazardous. Some sort of salutation is traditionally offered, not a spray of snow. Pleasantries are often exchanged with strangers (fell-banter) and often a conversation can develop. Admittedly this sometimes happens on chairlifts too.

Unlike skiing, there is no great distinction between on and off-piste. There are no marker poles stopping you from wandering off the paths. When walking, you can easily find yourself using dead reckoning and geographical features to navigate - not dissimilar to picking an off-piste route. In skiing terms, fell walking is mostly done in the backcountry. Although, if you can read an OS map and know how to use a compass, no local guide is needed.

Along with skiing off-piste, carrying the right equipment when fell walking is essential. Minus a probe, a shovel, and a transceiver, my walking rucksack is similarly loaded to my skiing one (gaffer tape, paracord etc.) I'm always prepared to survive a night on the fells in case I get stranded. For completeness I should really carry a bottle of wine too, but even I'm not prepared to carry that much extra weight.

The most important piece of equipment for both activities is a fully charged mobile phone with the local mountain rescue number preprogramed into it. Unlike skiing, a fell rescue team will not debit your credit card or demand proof of insurance before coming to your assistance. The highest price you'll pay for a fell rescue is a chastisement from the helicopter crew for setting off in flip-flops armed with nothing more than a jumper.

Fell walking is far more accessible to beginners than skiing. There is no expensive equipment to rent and you don't need to procure a lift pass. You don't need to spend a week in walking school first either. Walking is free but skiing is limited by budget. All you need is time, not money, to wander on the fells.

When choosing whom to fell walk with, similar rules to skiing apply. They must be of a similar fitness and ability if you don't want to be, or spend all day waiting for, a Tail-End Charlie. Unlike skiing, fell walking companions need to be good conversationalists or mute. Ski lift journeys and lunch aside, you don't have to make conversation when actually skiing.

Unlike off-piste skiing, solo fell walking is relatively safe, especially on the popular fells in summer when there are plenty of people around. If you injure yourself on an empty piste, before too long someone will descend the same run and hopefully not ski past. In any case, all the pistes are swept every night by piste patrollers who *will* stop and help. Failing that the piste basher will come up the slope at some stage and hopefully you can get the driver's attention before he runs you over. If you're walking alone on an unpopular fell and injure yourself you might not be so lucky. For those fells, I always try and take a companion.

Assuming you're good at not getting lost, you can lose yourself on the fells, if you're after some quiet contemplation. When piste skiing alone you're constantly assessing the rapidly approaching terrain for hazards. There is no wandering lonely as a cloud in the Alps – you have to concentrate on skiing, when skiing. Your mind is free to roam when roaming the fells – assuming you're not walking with an incessant talker.

Leading a bunch of fell walkers is not dissimilar to leading on skis. Your concern is for the slowest, least able follower and managing their angst, while hiding your own. You must decide on what is an appropriate route for their ability and often feel responsible for their distress if you get the itinerary wrong. In both cases it means putting up with a lot of whinging and moaning from those who feel they could do a better job or doubt your ability to make good navigational decisions.

Their distrust undermines your self-confidence and you feel like saying, 'I'm not getting paid to do this job. I might have got it slightly wrong the last time we were out on the mountains together, but I'm not in control of the weather, the snow or the mud. If they didn't enjoy the day, you often have to face recriminations in the bar later.

When leading a group of skiers these burdens are amplified, because a poor off-piste route choice can have more dire consequences. Even if nobody dies, you often feel guilty for being the architect of their ordeal. Occasionally you'll be secretly thanked for taking them out of their comfort zone and giving them a story to exaggerate over dinner. You'll be cast as the crazy guide, then you'll point out they are all still alive, but secretly know it was more through luck than better judgment.

You meet a similar type of people on walking and skiing holidays, ones who don't enjoy lying by a swimming pool or drinking, without first taking exercise. The walking après scene is less wild, but the pleasure of drinking a pint you have earned, is similar. Unlike après ski, you don't have to chase it with a shot of Jägermeister and nobody intentionally gets wasted. Hedonism isn't rife in the Lakes and nobody ever dances, let alone on the tables.

Keswick is the central hub for serious fell walkers in the Lakes. People walk around in cagoules and muddy trousers, not expensive ski jackets and salopettes – but similarly everyone wears beanies. When entering a bar, you notice that lager has been replaced with proper beer and the mandatory item on the menu is Cumberland sausage not tartiflette. You also notice that young people have been replaced with silent middle-aged couples at every table. Most are tourists who outnumber the locals at the height of the season. It's even harder to find a Cumbrian in Keswick than a Frenchman in Morzine. If you do, they will probably resent the invasion of the 'off-comers', who now own most of the properties – in Morzine it's no different.

Then there are the mountains themselves. You might scoff at me calling the Lakeland fells 'mountains'; by Munro's definition, only four of them qualify.[5] But what they lack in stature they make up for in beauty – there is a reason why they have inspired so much literature and poetry. The Alps are a more brutal place than the Lakeland fells, although on a cold, wet and windy day, the Lakeland crags, cols and arêtes can seem equally hostile.

Skiing and fell walking may have a similar appeal, to those who like mountain challenges. Skiing challenges may take more skill to complete and are done on bigger mountains but walking presents the unequivocal victory of standing on top of one – however small. Few of us can climb an Alpine peak, but most of us can summit a Lakeland fell, take a summit selfie, plant a metaphoric flag and claim we have conquered a mountain.

Towards the end of a ski season I grow tired of looking at the monochrome landscape that is the Alps in winter. The mountains all seem to dress in grey and wear the same dark green skirt of pine forest. By April I look forward to seeing some summer colour. I miss the deciduous trees: mountain ash, copper beech and oak. I miss

---

5 A 'Munro' is any mountain over 3,000ft (914.4m) high. Named after Sir Hugh Munro (1856–1919), who produced the first list of such hills in Scotland, in 1891. His list is considered to be the epoch of the modern pastime of 'peak bagging' where walkers try to stand on every summit of an arbitrary list. Munro is therefore ultimately responsible for the photographic art form known as the 'summit selfie' where people take a picture of themselves stood next to a pile of stones (usually the summit cairn).

having a variety of stone to look at, not just lichen-covered granite. I miss the purple heather, the meadow flowers and the complex pallet of green moss, grass and bracken. I miss the wildlife – especially the birds. I miss wearing comfortable boots, light clothes and not having to look at everything through steamed-up goggles. I know the summer Alps are equal in beauty to the Lakes, and a great place to go hiking; they have a similarly rich mix of flora, fauna and wildlife – although some of it *can* kill you; I know it's foolish to compare anything to a summer's day in England; but I do, and fell walking always seems to win over skiing.

I'm contemplating living another dream and moving to the Lakes but I worry that after a few years living in another holiday destination I'd stop noticing the scenery and grow tired of the tourists. It might be akin to living in Morzine, only the half-term hell would last all summer. Fortunately, a surprisingly small percentage of Lakeland visitors actually go up onto the fells, so once you leave the ice-cream-eating hordes in the valleys behind, you can soon escape from humanity - this is not so easy to do when skiing.

Then, by the end of the summer I start missing the Alps in their winter wardrobe and start looking forward to the ski season. I seem to spend a lot of my time in the Alps wishing I were in the Lakes and vice versa.[6]

---

6 While wandering around my new summer love, the Lakes, I can't help but feel I'm being un-faithful to my first love, the Yorkshire Dales. There is no question the Lakes hold all the trump cards. The mountains are bigger, the crags are craggier and the sheep are more attractive – and of course, the Lakes has lakes.
Lakeland villages are too well groomed for my liking and full of spa hotels and gastro pubs. In the Dales it's still possible to find a real rural pub, with a bar adorned with a surly barmaid and a village idiot. Scampi still comes in a basket and halloumi cheese is never on the menu. Un-fortunately North Yorkshire, being more of a rolling landscape, has few discernible summits, so artificial purpose cannot be given to wandering its fells, by ticking them off an arbitrary list - it's not peak bagging country. At least, I'll always consider the Pennines to be my home mountains

19. Chalet Benjamin

It didn't take many months of working on building sites and sitting in Birmingham traffic to convince me that Season 8 had to happen. So I reversed my decision to end the Chalet Project and frantically started looking for a suitable chalet for Winter 2017/18.

I couldn't find one. I was far too late to the game. And it was the usual game: the available chalets were either in need of refurbishment or too far out of town. Essentially, any conveniently located chalets with en suite rooms had already taken bookings for the forthcoming winter. Places actually in town were either permanently leased by tour operators or dilapidated. French owners seem reluctant to renovate old places in town - I guess if your chalet gets fully booked every season, why spend money on it? In the end I booked one I'd rejected the previous year, Chalet Benjamin. It had known shortcomings, but it was better than having no chalet at all.

People often ask me, what is the best way to find somewhere for their own Chalet Project? My first book seems to have been turned into a blueprint by some who want to fund a season in Morzine themselves. Firstly, there are slim pickings, unless you get on the case the season before. Secondly, since the loss of Chalet Neige, I've struggled to find the ideal chalet myself. Anyway, if I did have a magic source of chalets, I'd probably keep it secret. However, I do offer them a few tips and pointers - along with several words of warning. If my books have inspired you to embark on your own chalet project, I suggest you read them again more carefully.

Although Benjamin was essentially the top-floor flat in a multi-occupancy building, it had a luxury chalet feel. A spacious living area and open-plan kitchen covered by a vaulted wooden ceiling made it look like a log cabin. A log fire and a massive dining table completed the illusion. It also had the usual chalet trimmings: stuffed marmots on the shelves and old wooden skis mounted on the wall, along with lots of other alpine chintz.

Benjamin did tick several of my other boxes. The living areas were drunk-proof. A tiled floor, leather settees and a pine table, meant everything could be scrubbed clean of red wine and the other substances commonly secreted by skiers. It had a large gas hob capable of cooking a meal for eight. Most importantly, it had a small, yet habitable, utility room just behind the kitchen for the staff (me). I'd spent five winters sleeping in a garage, then two in a laundry, so a room with a window, seemed like an upgrade.

The biggest problem with Chalet Benjamin was its lack of guest rooms. It allegedly slept eight, but four of the beds were on a mezzanine floor that was only separated from the living area by a blind and had just enough headroom for a hobbit. Whoever slept there would need to be a small party animal. If they weren't the last to bed, they'd be kept awake by those still up and if they were tall, they would probably bang their heads the next morning. The other two rooms were allegedly en suite - but one didn't have a toilet!

Old French chalets often don't have toilets in their bathrooms. I'm pretty sure the French don't 'powder their noses' less than the rest of us, so I assume they are simply less prudish about sharing Johns with other Jeans and don't mind bumping into scantily clad strangers in hallways late at night. Even when a chalet has been renovated, en suite toilets can still be missing – presumably to retrofit the plumbing was too difficult. However, because 'en suite' is a French term, I suppose they can define what collection of porcelain items it comprises.

Historically, the French have had a unique approach to sanitation. They still seem reluctant to fully embrace the water closet (WC) –

possibly because it was invented by an Englishman (John Crapper). Their stand up toilets, we English hate so much, still proliferate. Arguably, they are more hygienic and good for your core muscle strength - although often lethal if used while wearing ski boots. Nowadays, WCs are found in French public toilets, but often the seat has been removed by way of compromise. Seemingly keen to prevent people outstaying their welcome, the toilet light is often on a short timer - leaving the patrons fumbling for toilet paper in the dark with their trousers around their ankles.

In an attempt to lose their reputation for having the worst toilets in Europe, the French seem to have modernized many of the toilets in their mountain restaurants - if the sample set (no pun intended), that I regularly use in Morzine is indicative. I'm willing to admit that I'm a little obsessed with toilets and plumbing in general.

The rest of the plumbing in Chalet Benjamin was also very French. The showers didn't work or at least not simultaneously. The wiring was equally Gallic: the mains electricity switch tripped if the oven was on and someone tried to use a hairdryer. I only discovered these additional shortcomings once I'd moved in. Who asks if they can take a shower when viewing a potential property to rent?

Chalet Benjamin might have ticked most of my boxes, but it fell short of many people's idea of what makes the perfect skiing holiday accommodation. Skiers, usually the ones not tasked with finding a chalet, have the following on their wish list:

1. It must be ski-in/ski-out (SISO). There are few such chalets in Morzine. Like most rural alpine towns, Morzine was not designed for ski tourism. Its neighbour (Avoriaz) was, so most of its accommodation is SISO. If you mandate SISO you'll end up staying in a purpose built ski resort – which might be your preference. There is also a big danger when staying in a fully catered SISO chalet that you'll never see the rest of town. If you ski to your

accommodation, then intend to walk to the après bars - you won't. You'll be tempted to get showered and changed first and decide you can't be bothered and will stay in. You'll end up socializing with the chalet's other guests all week – which is always a gamble, even if you brought them with you. In any case après is only après if it's done immediately after skiing while still in ski boots.

2. It must be drink-in/drink-out (DIDO). Being able to get back to your accommodation under your own steam, especially while steamed, is important to most of my regulars. However, if you're staying bang in the centre of town or next to a bar, you're going to be kept awake by drunken revellers until the small hours. If you are one of those revellers, then it's not a problem. It is nice to be able to nip back to your accommodation mid-session, or indeed independently decide when your personal session is over. However DIDO accommodation can be detrimental to those wanting a more skiing-orientated ski holiday.

3. It must have en suite rooms (with toilets). This is more important for older skiers like me, whose idea of pulling an all-nighter is not getting up in the middle of one for a pee. If everyone in the chalet is a relative or a friend you don't mind them pilfering your toiletries, or seeing you wrapped in a towel. However, anyone who has shared student accommodation will know just how badly some children are brought up, and many have taken their appalling domestic habits into adulthood. You really don't want to share facilities with them.

4. It must have a bath. This is often important to oldies who like to soak their bones after skiing. Unfortunately, in France, any receptacle can be declared a 'bath' if it has taps attached to it and a plughole. Some are entertainingly shaped and some are designed to minimize the use of hot water. Unless your

accommodation is very expensive, it's unlikely your bath will be large enough to soak all your bones simultaneously.

5. It must have single beds. You can forget single rooms, unless you're staying in a hotel and can afford to pay a hefty supplement. In a chalet, any cupboard that can accommodate a single bed will have staff sleeping in it. Your average twin room will have the beds crammed together, so the only advantage is that you don't have to share a duvet. Back in the day when I was a male ski escort, I had to share a twin room with my sponsor – a female friend. On arrival, she rearranged the furniture putting the beds against the walls and the bedside tables between them. A task we had to perform every night, because the staff kept putting everything back each day. I had a job convincing her it wasn't me.

6. It must have a boot dryer. This seems more essential for the English who like to go skiing in the rain. Some people are reluctant to risk leaving their precious boots on dryers in case they melt their custom foot beds; others (like me) can't get their boots on if they are not preheated.

7. It must have a hot tub. I'll admit, there is something immensely decadent about sitting outside in hot bubbly water when the snow is falling on your head. However, unless you're sharing the chalet with underwear models, hot tubs don't always deliver on their promise. Once you're in, you have no control over whom you are effectively sharing bath water with. They can also cause arguments over whose turn it is to get the drinks in. I do recall one week when the hot tub on the balcony of the chalet opposite was permanently inhabited by a Russian grandpa who liked to wave at everyone who passed, often not with his hands.

I had an interesting conversation with an entrepreneurial fellow in Morzine who had set up a hot-tub maintenance company. He was the alpine equivalent of a 'pool boy'. Rather than describing a glamorous lifestyle, surrounded by women in bikinis, he relayed horror stories of the things he'd found in the aftermath of hot-tub parties. He once attended an emergency when a chalet girl spotted a 'brown thing' floating in her hot tub. He donned his rubber gloves and fished out the floaters – which turned out to be slices of chocolate cake. This and his other stories have permanently put me off using hot tubs.

Benjamin had a proper bath, if not a hot tub. It had one-and-a-half en suite rooms but no boot dryer. It wasn't SISO, but was just about DIDO and it had single beds with a respectable amount of separation. Most importantly, it was on a regular bus route and thus removed Landie as the critical point of failure for the Chalet Project's operation.

I later discovered that one toilet had an amazing view. It faced a roof window, which looked outwards to the mountain and upwards to the sky, a perfect place to loiter and star gaze at night, assuming there wasn't a queue. I called it my 'loo with a view'. 'We all sit on the toilet, but some of us are looking at the stars', I told prospective guests, paraphrasing Oscar Wilde.

However, none of my regulars were overly impressed with Benjamin. It was the usual game. Had I found their ideal chalet with all the items above (if indeed such a chalet exists), it would have been too expensive. They would have balked when I tried to pass the costs onto them and would no doubt have then found somewhere cheaper to stay.

If I were a wealthy man, I'd simply buy a chalet and not bother filling it with random holidaymakers. But, like most businesses, the Chalet Project suffered from the inconvenience of needing customers. I do sometimes regret not getting a mortgage and buying somewhere when the project began. Instead of paying an eye-watering amount of rent over the last eight years, I'd have paid off a significant amount of that mortgage by now. But, at the time, I didn't expect the project to last so long. My only consolation is that nobody would have lent me the money back then – or indeed now. It's the usual capitalist story - only those with money make money, the rest of us have to earn it.

Pleased that there was going to be a Season 8, I spent the rest of the summer convincing my regulars that Chalet Benjamin was the perfect skiing accommodation (using most of the arguments above), having never stayed there myself.

20. Never trust a Frenchman with a Belt Grinder

There is one set of skiing demons that can be bribed – or so the ski manufacturers would like us to believe. Their modus operandi is to undermine our confidence in the planks strapped to our feet. They can often talk even the poorest of skiers into buying the most expensive pair of skis.

For want of a better name, I call them the Ski Tech Demons. Unfortunately the acronym 'STD' has medical connotations, so I'll refrain from using it. Although, they have a similarity – you usually pick up a skiing STD through contact (if only conversational) with another infected person.

The Ski Tech Demons never used to bother me in the early part of my skiing 'career' as I'm now calling it.[7] Before I got infected, I used to believe in the adage that, 'a bad workman always blames his tools'. However, since my foray into the world of the electrician, I now know that it's essential to have the right tools to do a proper job. Now my head often swirls in the winter with a veritable host of Ski Tech Demons constantly asking me:

'Are these skis helping or hindering my skiing?'

'Are they the right skis for the conditions?'

'Do they need servicing?'

'Have they been serviced correctly?'

'Why isn't everyone else struggling with the conditions?'

'Have they got better skis than me?'

Before I got infected, I used to mock those who looked down at their skis and blamed their 'rubbish hire skis', or concluded their own skis needed a service. In my opinion, it was always the way they were standing on their skis that was the problem.

---

7 Even though I've never been directly paid to stand on a pair of skis, skiing is the vocation I'm currently pursuing. So I have a skiing career - it's just not a career that's going especially well.

I had a theory that skis were like horses – largely because neither had an effective braking system. Over the millennia, horses have evolved into faultless performers in all conditions. They almost never fall over when they are not being ridden. Put a rider on a horse, who tries to control the horse, and both frequently come a cropper. Skis are highly evolved beasts too. Most modern skis will cope with any conditions. You just have to stand on them in a way that leaves them in control - which is essentially known as carving. Nowadays the Ski Tech Demons often convince me that my steed is an old nag.

Once you've got an STD (whoops), hiring a pair of skis becomes problematic. Rather than accept the pair the dude in the hire shop selects for you, you question his assumptions about the conditions and your ability. What is actually more important than the make, model or even shape of the skis, is how well they have been serviced.

For the average holiday skier, owning a pair of skis makes no financial sense now that most airlines charge for ski carriage. The cost of ski ownership is now greater than the hire-cost savings, if you factor in the price of having skis serviced. Hauling your own skis to and from the Alps is a burdensome task too. However, those infected with an STD feel it is worth the cost and hassle to be assured they have the right tools for the job. I'll admit, owning your own skis will save you the time, and angst (if you have an STD) of hiring skis when you arrive.

The first skis I owned, a pair of Salomon X-Screams (circa 2001), were cast offs from the Ski Nazis. They were considered to be a 'game changing' ski at the time. They featured an aluminium strut in front of the bindings. I had absolutely no idea what purpose the struts served and neither did their former owner Val – but they made the skis look hi-tech.

A lot of skiers seem to be on a constant quest for the wonder skis of the future. They regurgitate the manufacturer's gobbledygook about honeycomb tips, reverse camber or the advantages of a double rocker. But I believe few truly game-changing skis have emerged on the market since carving skis were invented. Fortunately I have an arrangement with a hire shop in Morzine (Gravier Ski) and the owner (Michele) lets me borrow his skis, swapping and changing them without question. I always take my hiring guests to his shop in return. However, he mostly rents out Rossignol skis so the Ski Tech Demons have recently started to suggest that a more exotic brand might give me a better metaphorical edge.

My X-Screams were half a metre too long for Val and about 40cm too long for me. However, in those days, size really mattered. You were nobody if your skis didn't poke significantly above your head in a cable car. A common trick was to rest your skis on the toe of your ski boot to add a few extra inches.

Unsurprisingly, I struggled to make them turn unless I had a football field of space in which to persuade them. With hindsight, those skis severely hampered my skiing progression – but I loved them. I enjoyed the novelty of carrying them through airports. They were a proud declaration that I wasn't going on a mere skiing holiday but on a skiing expedition. After a couple of years and input from more informed skiers, I realised my Salomons had to go. So I went to Snow & Rock in Birmingham to buy some replacements.

The trick, when buying new skis, is not to sound too knowledgeable. If you engage in a science battle with the ski dude serving you, you'll lose and walk out with some weird skis, not really understanding what made them so expensive or why they were going to improve your skiing.

I walked into the shop and started furtively looking at the skis. Then one of the ski dudes pounced on me. 'Is there anything in particular you're looking for sir?' he asked. I told him, 'Skis - I'm after a red pair' - I had a red ski jacket at the time. He laughed, but I was serious. 'What kind of skiing do you do?' he enquired.

People always buy skis for the conditions they desire (usually deep power) rather than the conditions they mostly encounter (icy pistes). If you own skis, you'll probably be spending most of your time on the wrong planks for the conditions. Ideally, I'd like to have a quiver of skis in a bag and employ a ski caddy to drag it around the mountains behind me.

I was honest with the dude in Snow & Rock. I spent 99% of my time skiing down blue runs and 1% skiing off piste - and 0% skiing backwards off jumps. So I ended up being sold out-and-out piste skis (Rossignol Zeniths) – which fortuitously were red.

The problem with buying a pair of skis in England is you can't try them out first. If you procure them in resort, you might be able to try before you buy but you might randomly fall over on one pair but not on another, or you might just be skiing well during one test and not another.

Even if you're more scientific and ski the same runs with every pair you test, the snow conditions will vary. You might try to read some ski reviews but those who test skis, really don't ski like you and me. They might love a pair, but you might hate them. It really is a lottery buying skis – you might as well just choose them on colour.

My *red* Zeniths served me well until I started my campaign to conquer the off-piste. Being thin and stiff, they didn't give me much assistance in powder. The Tech Demons soon pointed out that the campaign wasn't going very well, because of my 'rubbish piste skis'. So I started looking for some game-changing skis of my own.

I settled on a pair of Rossignol S3-B98's. The best all-mountain ski Michele had in his shop. They were a rocker-camber-rocker revolution, as the Rossignol marketing men described them. I'll resist trying to explain what that means because, basically, I don't really know myself. I just know they felt good in most conditions. They were very light, which appealed to my laziness; they had twin tips (front and back) for doing tricks, which meant I'd look like a ski dude carrying them through town - assuming I kept my helmet and goggles on. The rear tips and rocker also accommodated my habit of leaning back when skiing steeps (look away now, if you're a ski instructor) and allowed me to turn using the backs of the skis.

The Service Demon

Perhaps the most pernicious of the STD's is the Service Demon. He constantly reminds you that just one careless pass through a poorly maintained grinding machine will utterly ruin your precious planks. He makes me worry about where to get my skis serviced and which technicians to trust. Most ski-hire shops offer ski servicing, but the type of machinery they own and the knowledge of how to use it correctly, varies.

I caught this STD from my skiing mentor, Andy Jerram. According to Andy, nobody in the whole of France knows how to service skis correctly. His motto is:

'Never trust a Frenchman with a belt grinder'.

He also jokes that he knows his students will always ski better towards the end of a course, even if they don't learn anything from him, because the terribly applied wax will have rubbed off their skis. He might have a point. I always seem to get on better with my skis before a service than after one. Despite most people worrying their edges are blunt, it is harder to ski on edges that are too sharp or have been filed at the wrong angle.

With my refresher course looming, I had to make a big decision – which skis to take? My S3's were battered and coming to the end of their life but they were tried and tested so maybe I should stick with them. I also had to decide if it was worth the risk of getting them serviced one last time. My first attempt to pass the actual leaders' course had been hampered by poorly serviced skis and I certainly didn't want to risk the same thing happening again.

21. Ski Resort Top Trumps

Season 8 started unexpectedly in Les Arcs. It started early too, just before Christmas. The Ski Club needed someone to fill in for an injured leader so I volunteered for the slot.

Sod's Law seems to dictates that injury is most likely to occur just before a skiing holiday. Case in point: I was felled just three days before my leading slot in Laax (darling). Every season, numerous other Ski Club Leaders have accidents just before their leading gigs. This could be because we are highly tuned athletes and therefore injury prone - or just that we roll the dice on the slopes too many times each season.

I don't know how many people get married with their arm in a sling or go down with food poisoning just before they have to fly, but the number of pre-skiing injuries seems disproportionate. Each season, more guests leave the chalet on crutches than arrive with them, but a surprising number turn up with limbs already in plaster. Broken wrists obtained practicing at indoor slopes seem popular with snowboarders. It's probably best to avoid any pre-skiing training, and save your injuries for the slopes.

The injured leader's bad luck was my good fortune. Before booking Chalet Benjamin, I had intended to sit in England on standby for the Club all winter – waiting, like a vulture, for others leaders to get injured. However, I didn't need to be in Morzine till January, so I could fit in this early season gig.

I'd been to Les Arcs a few decades ago but couldn't remember much about it. I generally dismiss purpose-built ski resorts for being too much like holiday camps, referring to them as 'Butlins in the Snow'. However, it was a red/silver on-piste holiday (for intermediate skiers) so theoretically the skiing would be the perfect warm-up for my season.

I picked up my charges (sixteen SKGB members) at Heathrow and headed to Les Arcs with high hopes for the season. Snow had been piling up in the Alps since mid-December and Chalet Benjamin was booked. Everywhere looked set for a bumper season and once I'd got pesky Christmas out the way, I'd be back in Morzine living the rekindled dream.

We arrived at our destination (Arc1800) in the dark and I hunted around the complex for our hotel. If the air hadn't been breathable and the ground covered in snow, instead of dust, I might have thought we were checking into a base on the moon. Those who designed Arc1800, back in in the 1970s, must have taken inspiration from what was then contemporary science fiction – and why not? After all, they were creating a habitat for humans to survive in a hostile environment.

Arc1800 is a labyrinth of connected blocks, atriums and covered walkways that follow the Bauhaus architectural principle that form should follow function. However, many of these structures are clad with wood, softening the concrete brutality that other purpose-built French ski resorts often suffer from. It has been cleverly laid out, so that buildings don't overlook each other, and most rooms have an exterior mountain view. Essentially, if you're building a holiday camp for the masses, you're going to need some large ugly buildings. But then, who really cares what a building looks like when they look out of its windows?

I eventually found the hotel entrance. We checked in then ate in a cosmopolitan self-service restaurant with few regional delicacies. The rooms were furnished in a style that might have once have been considered contemporary but they were warm, dry and everything worked including the plumbing. It wasn't until the next morning, when I threw back the curtains to reveal a magnificent view of the Aiguille Rouge peak (3226m), that I felt like I was back in the Alps.

As the week progressed my prejudice against purpose-built ski resorts eroded. My accommodation might have been Bauhaus but it was single occupancy, had an en suite (with a toilet and a bath), and it was both SISO and DIDO. The only footwear I needed for the week was my ski boots and a pair of slippers.

Although Les Arcs was bereft of Alpine charm, I was forced to reassess my preference for chalet-based ski holidays. Hotel-based skiing in a purpose-built resort is extremely low hassle. The snow was fantastic and, it being pre-Christmas, the pistes were empty – apart from a family of sumo wrestlers! Fancy dress skiing is normally the preserve of stag and hen parties. But, on Dad's insistence, Mum and their two teenagers always wore inflatable sumo suits when skiing. Despite their long faces, it was a family tradition that apparently needed upholding. It's important that, if you dress like a clown, you act like one and be jovial. Which was a point I made to the utterly miserable sumo teenagers in the hotel boot room. But then, teenagers always look pissed off when they are with their parents.

There is no better example of mountains being turned into theme parks than Les Arcs. Being a so-called 'third generation ski resort', Les Arcs was conceived and implemented solely for recreational purposes. Tourism there hasn't grown round an indigenous community and a traditional way of life. The pistes have not evolved from a network of mountain passes or droving routes, but have been carved across virgin mountains.

Les Arcs belongs to one giant corporation. The Compagnie des Alpes owns many other ski resorts and amusement parks. Its property portfolio expands beyond France and the Alps. Piste skiing may make us feel like intrepid mountain explorers, but we are all slightly deluded. There is some danger and risk – but we are essentially visiting an Alpine theme park.

The level of skiing required for the holiday might not have been challenging for me, but the lift system proved demanding – specifically the Vanoise Express. This double-decker cable car (linking Les Arcs to La Plagne) was once the biggest, longest and fastest in the world. On my first visit to Les Arcs, many years ago, it was being constructed and when I heard about its intended statistics, I vowed never to ride it. Then, a few years later, due to operator error, it crashed into the base station, proving my apprehension was warranted. If ever the Lift Demons were to get me, it would be on this cable car.

Unfortunately, the first time I was forced to use the lift, I'd woken up knowing that was the plan. We intended skiing over to La Plagne, which would involve using the cable car in both directions. Premeditation is always at the root of all phobic anxiety. An over-active imagination usually causes more suffering than the eventual reality. With hindsight, I really shouldn't have spent the night before reading about the accident.

After skiing over to the lift's bottom station, we stopped for coffee. This didn't help my anxiety, because the café had a great view of the cable car and the Ponthurin valley, 380 metres beneath it. When it was time to board, I headed for the upstairs cabin, keen to avoid standing next to the floor window in the lower deck.

Presumably worried that the cable car wouldn't be vertiginous enough, a Perspex panel was installed in the cabin's floor, so riders could admire the drop below their feet. In 2014, thirty 'lucky' thrill seekers, were served a gourmet meal around the window, while the cabins were stopped mid span – I get indigestion just thinking about that.

I boarded with trepidation, planning to find a corner and start a random conversation with whoever was unfortunate enough to stand

next to me. On entering, I spotted a passenger with a huge coil of
rope attached to his rucksack and I hoped that, for this journey, he
wouldn't need it. But it made my 10 metres of paracord seemed
wholly inadequate.

The Vanoise Express is in fact, two cable cars with independent cables
and engines. Theoretically, if one car gets stuck the other could pull
alongside and evacuate stranded passengers – presumably being asked
to 'mind the gap' while disembarking. To celebrate its 10th year of
operation, a French stuntman proved this was indeed possible, by
completing a slack wire walk between the two cabins mid span. I
suspect more than a single rope would be needed for most of us to
make the transfer successfully.

Once underway, I focused on the approaching top station. Normally
I count pylons, but the Vanoise Express is a single humungous 1.8
km span. One of my co-riders started talking about the accident,
which wasn't helpful, and I could feel panic building in my chest.
Then, the worst of all things happened - the cable car stopped!

Well, obviously that wasn't the 'worst thing' that could have
happened – we were still attached to the cable. But if the car had been
in free fall, there would have been nothing more for me to worry
about. An eternity of about fifteen seconds passed then, without any
explanation for the delay, we set off again. During that vast expanse
of time, my imagination ran riot:

Was I going to spend seventeen hours waiting for a helicopter
rescue?

Would the car slide back and crash into the base station - again?

Would I have to perform a Tyrolean traverse over to the other
cable car?

I vowed, 'If I ever get off this bloody cable car, I'll never get on
another one again' - forgetting the only practical way back to Les

Arcs was to retrace my route. I also vowed to spend the rest of my life in Holland or somewhere equally flat.

First by the doors when they opened at the top, I stepped back onto terra firma feeling strangely triumphant. The Lift Demons had done their worst and I hadn't died, or worse - made a fool of myself.

Three hours later, despite my vow, I found myself re-boarding the Vanoise Express for the return journey. It looked like I wouldn't be moving to Holland either because the journey back was surprisingly un-stressful. I put this down to 'flooding'.[8]

Having defeated the cable-car demon, I enjoyed the rest of the week. It was refreshing to see a different set of mountains and eat slightly different local cheeses. I was forced to reassess my allegiance to the PdS. However, I always try to avoid getting into what I call, a game of 'Ski Resort Top Trumps', where the vital statistics of ski resorts are compared.

When I did play the game, Morzine would usually win on 'size of ski area' and 'shortness of transfer', but it would frequently lose on 'highest altitude' and SISO accommodation. Now I realise that what makes a favourite skiing location is far more subjective than objective.

With ski resorts, first impressions count. If you are unlucky with the snow or the weather, or you made a poor accommodation choice, you're likely to have a lasting downer on a resort. If you went at the wrong time of year, or with the wrong people, your assessment will be blurred. If you left finding the best skiing, eating and drinking to mere luck, you'll probably make an inaccurate assessment.

I profess to dislike Tignes for instance. I might say this is because it has no tree skiing, its purpose-built architecture has no Alpine charm and the altitude seems to affects my performance (or so I've

---

8 'Flooding' is a therapy used by cruel psychologists. In order to demonstrate the irrationality of a patient's fear, psychologists often put them in a situation where they face their phobia at its worst. For many it's a room full of spiders, but for me it turned out to be just one ride on the Vanoise Express.

convinced myself), also it seems to attract a certain type of skier that I'm struggling to define – without using the words 'dick' and 'head'. However none of that is true. My prejudice against Tignes is purely down to a gritty first experience there and the gung-ho skiers I encountered on the piste – and having to share a room with three snorers.

Those who do like a game of Top Trumps will soon start talking about snow records and declaring their favourite place to be more 'snow sure' than yours. They will brag about altitude and the presence of a glacier. They will babble on about foehn winds and gulfstream heating then conclude, quod erat demonstrandum, Tignes is better. It certainly wins the 'early and late season snow' top trump. All I know is that the meteorological matrix is too complex for me to understand and soon, thanks to global warming, nowhere will have a glacier.

Like many, I also make gross generalisations about entire countries and mountain ranges based on very small sample sets. I dismissed the whole of the Rockies based on one visit made twenty years ago, because of America's approach to mountain food and their nannying off-piste culture.

I won't go to Bulgaria because the lifts are unsafe and Japan is mobbed with Australians – even though I like Australians. I have Canada down as 'too cold', Switzerland as 'boring and expensive' and the food as 'too salty' in Austria. I turn my nose up at Andorra, even though I've never been there. I glibly say, 'I'd rather spend a week on a child-friendly cruise ship than one in Andorra'.

Despite the French seemingly doing everything they can to put me off, I still prefer skiing in France. France used to get top trumps for 'quality of food', but I'm not so sure anymore, now they seem to be giving us what they think we want – crêpes, pizza and burgers.

I agree that the après ski in Austria is unbeatable having had many a memorable time there when I was younger and more alcoholically robust. But I have managed the odd wild night out in France too and I've since discovered that hangovers conform to a single international standard.

Italian lovers often say the Dolomites are the most beautiful mountains in the world and after my safari there, I'm inclined to agree with them; unfortunately, I'm just not that keen on pasta. For me the Cumbrian Mountains are hard to beat, although I'll admit the skiing there isn't exactly extensive.

Even within France, I have my prejudices. Courchevel is full of Russian oligarchs and Méribel is full of English chalet girls called Pippa; Megève is full of fur coats worn by folk who never go skiing; Chamonix holds all the trumps for extreme terrain but has all the charm of a capital city; Flaine suffers from lift queues and too much Stalinist architecture.

Morzine is not big on glitz. It's more hipster than *haute couture*. It's a place for drinking beer not sipping cocktails. You're more likely to meet a rugby team from Liverpool there than a pack of Sloane Rangers from Surrey. What I like most about my beloved Morzine is that it was a place before skiing. It has an indigenous population and it still feels French, despite being overrun by Brits in the winter. Best of all, the hands Morzine loses at Ski Resort Top Trumps are usually won by its neighbour Avoriaz (which is one lift away).

The truth is, having spent so much time there, I know how Morzine works. I know how to avoid the lift queues, where the best restaurants are and, on any given day, where to find the best skiing – and, on any given night, the best après. Even if (like me) you enjoy visiting other resorts, it's worth investing time learning one place really well because nothing can trump that knowledge.

Fortunately, my week in Les Arcs went without injury or major cable-car incidents. There were the usual people-management issues and there was the delicate matter of allocation of new skiing grades for the members at the end of the week. Betterment seems to be a common skiing purpose and everyone had their sights set on improving their grades.

Most skiers are keen to improve and seem to need recognition of that improvement. I, for instance, wanted to pass my BASI level-2 that season for no logical purpose. Unfortunately this quest for improvement means skiers are constantly analysing and getting frustrated with their technique. Sometimes I think it would be nice if everyone could just enjoy a day of skiing (however badly).

In the perfect conditions everyone skied well in Les Arcs that week - including me. No matter where or when you go skiing, truly perfect skiing conditions are seldom encountered. If you do, you tend to fall in love with the location of that encounter. Theme park or not, I ended up loving Les Arcs – but please don't tell the folks back in Morzine.

22. BACON RUN 8

After my perfect warm up in Les Arcs, I ate turkey with relatives then started preparing for my journey to Morzine for Season 8. I was about to do the thing I'd sworn I'd never do again – drive a Defender to the Alps.

I converted Landie back into skiing mode and doubled my efforts to make her reliable. I replaced parts that had yet to fail if there was the slightest suspicion that they might. I even addressed minor problems that I'd previously just lived with. By the time I'd finished, all the doors would open and shut without slamming, and could even be successfully locked. The air vents would stay open above 50mph and the hand brake could be used on a hill, not just on the flat.

Not stopping there, I tried to improve the comfort levels for Landie's occupants. I sound-insulated the engine bay and lagged the inside of the cockpit. With a rubber washer here and a new screw there, I eliminated most of the louder rattles. Although, I wasn't entirely successful, I tried to make Landie watertight.

While surfing the Defender forums online, I discovered a document that would change my life. When I opened a PDF called 'The Defender Water Ingress Manual', I knew I'd hit gold. It was a comprehensive guide (with diagrams) that explained how to fix the ten most common Defender leaks. Once I'd finished reading the scripture in this automotive bible, I knew I would never have to drive in wet socks again. It did make me wonder who, other than Land Rover, could sell you a vehicle then produce a manual telling you how to fix it. It really is a good job they never made submarines.

Inside Landie was now a relatively dry, warm and quite place - or so I told Dr Debs and she agreed to accompany me on, what would be, Bacon Run 8. Her usual reward was a night in the Chateau du

Cocove followed by a week of not having to ski. She professes to enjoy everything about a skiing holiday apart from the actual skiing bit.

As tradition dictated, it rained all the way to the Channel but we kept warm and dry in our Land Rover submarine. Despite the heavy cargo, Landie galloped her way to France and seemed keen to get back into winter action.

When we arrived at the chateau, I was slightly disappointingly to see that its floodlights were working. I'd wanted to relive my candle-lit dinner – this time with Dr Debs not just a bottle of wine for company. This time, instead of being met by a ghostly apparition, there was a posh Englishwoman frantically ringing the bell at the bar while loudly berating the lack of service.

'Honestly, that's the problem with the French, they're always in the kitchen,' she insightfully informed Stephanie, her young daughter. A barman appeared.

'Oh there you are. We've been waiting ages,' she declared then requested, 'a Negroni for me and a ginger beer for Stephanie please.' The barman looked confused. 'What do you mean you don't know what a Negroni is!?' she exclaimed. Then her husband, a doppelganger for Richard E Grant, stumbled into the adjacent reception. He was laden with leather suitcases and looked like he needed a drink even more than his wife. 'Where's the bloody porter?' he cursed.

'Darling, he doesn't know what a Negroni is!' she told him, ignoring his plight. 'Can you tell them?' Clearly she only drank cocktails but never made them. 'They don't have ginger beer either for Stephanie – can you believe this place?' The dutiful husband explained to the barman, in his suave upper-class accent, how to make a Negroni and I started to wonder if he was actually Mr Grant[9].

After the barman had made his first ever Negroni, he moved to the reception desk and checked us in. I felt like apologizing for my

---

9 The Negroni is a popular Italian cocktail, made of one part gin, one part vermouth rosso, and one part Campari, garnished with orange peel. A properly made Negroni is stirred, not shaken, and built over ice in an old-fashioned or 'rocks' glass. It is considered to be an apéritif – so don't have too many.

countrymen. We were fairly desperate for a drink too but Debbie always travels with a bottle of wine in her suitcase – 'room wine' as she calls it.

Mr Grant and his family entertained us more that evening at dinner. They made us look like alcoholic lightweights and took shifts at smoking outside and ordering more wine. Stephanie seemed to take it all in her stride - Mummy and Daddy were just getting 'squiffy' again I suppose. Until that evening I didn't realise such bluebloods still existed – but then, until that evening, I didn't know what a Negroni was either.

The Chateau De Cocove is used by lots of random Brits who have just rolled off the ferry. It's a transitory place, a watering hole, where a variety of social species come to rest and drink before continuing their journeys. Skiing can be like that too - where the impala drinks next to the hyena.

The rest of that bacon run was uneventful. Landie didn't miss a beat and my confidence in her was increasing. We did have one heart-stopping moment on the Nantua viaducts when a powerful side wind pushed us towards the guardrails but Landie, ballasted with bacon, stayed on the road.

Determined not to arrive in Morzine with even the smallest trace of summer diesel left in my tank, I almost ran out of fuel before I could reach a known supplier of proper winter diesel. Debbie thought this was ridiculous given the temperature was well above freezing but I use so little fuel (one tank lasts a season) that whatever fuel I turn up with will loiter through February when it gets much colder.

We pulled up at Chalet Benjamin in time to greet my first guests – friends from Sutton Coldfield. They had taken the easy way to Morzine, using an aeroplane. The chalet revealed its shortcomings as we settled in but I was mostly happy with my new winter home. I was with people I loved, a fully functioning Land Rover was parked outside (full of the correct diesel) and a season's supply of bacon was in the freezer – Bacon Run 8 had been a success.

23. THE CRÊPE HUT TIME MACHINE

My first week in Chalet Benjamin was a voyage of discovery. The first week in any foreign residence always presents a sequence of intelligence tests. Before you can use any device, you need to figure out what the symbols or words on its buttons and dials mean. In an old building, it's also hard to determine if the thing you're failing to comprehend is simply broken or never actually worked properly in the first case.

Learning how to perform even the simplest of tasks that week, like opening a window or switching a light on, required a process of experimentation. Well- designed products should be intuitive to use. Maybe those in Chalet Benjamin were - I just wasn't thinking like a Frenchman.

Luckily, my first guests were friends from home (with low expectations) and they were happy to help me decode the chalet. Debbie proved particularly adept at deciphering the controls on the over-complicated kitchen appliances including a toaster that, along with a timing dial, had four perplexing buttons.

What on earth did those buttons do? Toast is either bread or toast. There is only one way to make it, you expose bread to a heating element and you get toast. You may want to control the duration of the exposure, depending on how toasty you want your toast but, in my world, time is the only parameter that needs adjusting when making toast. Life is complicated enough without unnecessary buttons - perhaps that is why I like driving a Defender?

When you rent a French-owned chalet, there are always things you need to acquire to make it habitable for English people. A teapot is always missing and often the oven grill pan too. There is always an elaborate coffee maker but sometimes no kettle. There will be a lettuce-drying device but no sieve.

You can tell you're in a French kitchen by the selection of utensils on offer. There will always be a garlic crusher, and an olive-stone remover but not a bread knife or cooking tongs. The cups will be impractically large or small and there won't be any tumblers suitable for a gin and tonic, but always a set of champagne flutes – it is interesting to see what is important to one nation that isn't to another.

Whenever or wherever you stay in someone's holiday cottage you often end up using items they have rejected from their primary residence. For example, owners often decide their knife set needs replacing, so they buy a new set and relegate the old blunt knives to their cottage. I often sit in self-catering holiday accommodation looking at the furniture, crockery, ornaments and especially the paintings the owners have hung on the walls, and I think – 'they really should have thrown that out'.

By the end of the week, we had broken the chalet in, although we gave up trying to influence the heating system.   Debbie and my Sutton homeboys left and were replaced with my first proper guests along with the Sturmführer, David. He arrived bearing his traditional gift – an uncooked chicken. Having once been outraged by their local cost, he now always brings an uncooked chicken to Morzine in his suitcase.

With life now established at Chalet Benjamin, it was time for me to focus on my objective for Season 8 – to pass my BASI Level-2 instructors course in March. With hindsight, it might have been a good idea if I'd asked my skiing mentor and the course examiner (Andy Jerram) if I stood an earthly chance of passing it before I'd paid the course deposit – but I didn't.

There were a dozen or so other BASI-2 hopefuls training in Morzine that season, all booked onto the same course. Most were on a pre-course training programme run by The British Alpine Ski School (BASS), who kindly allowed me to dip in and out of their training sessions, whenever I wanted. They also informed me that BASI required me to clock up another thirty-five hours of 'shadowing' before I could even take the course. This involves watching and helping a real instructor give lessons.

So, with any spare time I had, I tried to either clock up some shadowing hours or train with BASS. Along with time, my funds were also limited. Unlike some of my fellow hopefuls, at £70 a day I couldn't really afford too many training sessions. You really do have to be rich to become a ski instructor - or sickeningly talented. A keen skier and proud father once told me that his talented son wanted to be a ski instructor. He estimated that getting his lad all the way to his BASI-4 would cost more than putting him through university. He agreed to fund his son's endeavour but with a warning, 'If you're going to live *my* dream, you better not cock it up'. Maybe the reason some people procreate, is to live a second life vicariously through their kids.

The feedback from the few training sessions I did attend, wasn't good. My skiing stance was 'all wrong' and my dodgy snowplough came under scrutiny. They kept saying I was a pretty good 'all-mountain skier' – which was worrying. It was frustrating for the BASS instructors (and me) that I couldn't implement their suggestions. My limbs and muscles simply didn't seem to work like theirs. The instructors implored me to attend more training sessions but I felt I would be throwing good money after bad.

When I had some free skiing time I faced a dilemma. Should I sign up for another expensive and frustrating training session or clock up some more shadowing hours? The shadowing was the easier option, although very boring, it usually involved standing around watching kids learn to snowplough – although admittedly I could have learnt a thing or two from some of them.

One week I shadowed an Irish family, who were trying to learn to ski together. Mum, Dad and daughter did make some progress, however their five-year-old son was hopeless. He fundamentally didn't understand how gravity works. He would just fall over, I'd pick him up and he'd fall over again. He had the attention span of a goldfish and didn't follow or even watch any of the instructor's demonstrations. The instructor had the patience of a saint and kept trying different teaching approaches, but nothing was getting through to this young chap. He seemed to be living in a snowy world of his own – one where gravity worked differently. My BASS instructors probably thought I lived in that world too.

One day, instead of opting for either form of BASI purgatory, I decided it would be more fun to ski with my ex-wife! She was holidaying with mutual friends in nearby St Jean d'Aulps, so I drove over to see them all.

Seven years after our gritty separation, my ex-wife and I were on good terms. We had even managed to orchestrate a very civilised divorce. There were many good times to reflect on but perhaps our greatest combined achievement was to get divorced without the use of solicitors. This was due to our mutual contempt for lawyers being greater than that for each other.

With no kids involved or other maintenance considerations, we split everything equally – she got the inside of the house, I got the outside. At the time, a friend suggested it would have been easier if, instead of getting married, I'd found a woman who already hated me and bought her a house - but it wasn't that simple.

The inaccurate jokes having now been made, the 'outside' included other properties and any arbitrary divide was better than a four way split with lawyers.

Despite living very separate lives, we occasionally met up in Birmingham's city centre. Many things have changed in the city's business district since I left my old stomping ground. New bars and restaurants have emerged, but the city vibe remains the same. It's a little nostalgic and slightly eerie to walk down those familiar streets – every corner seems to hold a memory of some, now regrettable, incident. Where once I would expect to bump into at least one business contact or drinking crony, I now wander unrecognised. Wearing a high visibility jacket and hoodie probably doesn't help – I wouldn't recognise myself.

When we meet, my new work attire perplexes my ex. She worries that someone important might spot us together and think she has taken pity on a tramp. She still wears the same clothes that she did before. Not actually the *same* clothes, but the same formal work attire. It was once a weekly chore but I'm very pleased I now never have to go to the dry cleaners. You know your life is good, when you don't have to wear anything you can't wash yourself. Since our separation, along with her clothes, everything else in her life has remained the same: same city, same job, same walk to work, same friends, and same home. Problematic husband aside, she liked her life – it was me who had the midlife crisis.

It was good to ski with my old marital crew again and catch up with their lives. We had been on many formative skiing trips together. Memories of your first few skiing holidays always stick with you. They are wonderful, if often gritty, experiences that leave indelible marks on your mind (and sometimes your body). You are still learning to ski and so every blue run seems like Everest and every après session seems outrageous. You're exploring an exciting new world of masochistic pleasure, euphoria and hedonism all set in a breath-taking location. Having said all that, I wouldn't want to be a beginner again.

My ski trip down memory lane came to a sudden halt when the Lift Demon struck. Three of us, including my ex, were half way up a draglift when it happened. After about twenty minutes, we decide to ski back to the bottom and find out why and discovered

159

that there was a mountain-wide power cut. I thanked my lucky stars, we hadn't been on a chairlift when the power had failed, not least because I'd forgotten my paracord. Although with hindsight, 'Stuck on a Chairlift with my Ex-Wife' would have made for a great chapter – if not an entire book.

The draglift was the only way out of the small valley we were now stuck in and there was very little information to be gained from the lift operator. He had no idea when, or if, the power would be restored.

With few other options, we decided to ski back to a small crêpe hut further down the valley and wait. The hut was crammed with other stranded skiers. It had no power but the proprietor was managing to cook omelettes on his gas-powered stove. We shared an omelette and drank beer in the damp gloom, reminiscing about our early skiing adventures together. Looking at my friend's familiar face, and indeed that of my ex-wife, I started to wonder if the hut was actually a time machine which had transported me back ten years.

Midlife divorce creates a fault line through your memories. Any nostalgic thoughts that cross that line are especially upsetting because divorce can turn sweet memories sour. After a separation, you can't revisit a place, a time or repeat an experience without feeling guilty that you're now doing it again with someone else. If you do return to somewhere, there will be a ghost that follows you around. My ex and I travelled extensively, so half the world now seems out of bounds. You can divorce your spouse but unfortunately not your memories. I think I have become the very person I used to hate – a sentimental old bastard.

Two hours later, the crêpe-hut time machine returned me back to 2018. There was a communal whoop of joy when the lights came back on and the whole mountain started working again. We left the hut, rode the draglift out of the valley then reunited our friend with her husband in a local bar. I'm guessing the whole experience had been a bit awkward for her too.

I had a couple of drinks with them all but had to get back to Morzine to what I now called, 'work'. I was slightly sad I couldn't remain with them for the rest of their holiday. However, my exclusion was self-inflicted. Like divorce, it was an unforeseen consequence of the choices I had made. I know that to enjoy the future, you need to stop wishing for a better past – and it's best to avoid time travel.

The next morning, I woke up free of nostalgia. After I'd served breakfast, I prepared a room for my next incoming guests - Paul and Sarah. I was looking forward to skiing with my new friends who would put me through my paces on the slopes – 'ex-wife skiing', isn't that demanding. Little did I know that disaster would strike the following day and instead of skiing with Paul, he would be wheeling me through a hospital in Thonon.

Up to that point, it seemed like my season was going to be seminal. Chalet Benjamin was working out well and Landie was behaving herself – as were most of my guests. After a couple of bad winters, the snow was good and I'd already had some exceptional skiing in Les Arcs. I was looking forward to my week in Laax (Darling). Apart from my self-inflicted BASI misery, I was once again enjoying 'living the dream' when, along with my leg, the rug was pulled from under Season 8. Even if I'd put my mind to it, I don't think I could have chosen a worse time to get injured. But then, disasters are never very convenient.

24. RETURN OF THE BIPED

Two weeks after my accident, I was back at Birmingham's Queen Elizabeth Hospital laying on another gurney. For once, I was pleased about this. My leg was about to be exhumed from its mummification and I was about to become a biped once again. A chatty nurse carefully unwrapped the bandages. I was both nervous and excited at the big reveal.

She seemed pleased that the wound had healed up nicely. A thin pink line wrapped around the right side of my calf. I was disappointed. I'd hoped for a more impressive scar – something I could show off down the pub. The thin line was testament to the sharpness of the snowboard that had caused the cut. It was also testament to the skill of the surgeon who had diligently weaved in a continuous subcuticular suture to close it. He was probably very good at hemming trousers too. 'Maybe I could tattoo a more gnarly scar over the top', I thought.

But there were more important issues to resolve. Could I move my foot up and down? While the nurse supported it, I gently tried. 'Did it move?' I asked. 'Yes I felt something,' she replied. I tried again and could see my foot nodding at me; in delight I nodded back. Dorsiflexion had been restored. Next I tried pronation (side to side). My foot waved at me and I waved back. Pronation had been restored too.

I forgave the surgeon for the girly scar and felt gratitude not disappointment. Through all that blood and gore, he had managed to reconnect all the right bits back together.

She scratched my leg below the scar, then the top of my foot. I still couldn't feel anything but I'd already been warned the sensory nerves would take longer to re-establish themselves – possibly the rest of my life. But who, other than a footballer, needs feeling on the top of their foot? The lack of feeling might even be an advantage when wearing ski boots.

It was important I didn't over extend my foot in any direction. The tendons and the muscles needed more time to strengthen, so I was fitted with an air boot to restrict foot movement. The large blue foam boot had a stiff back and footplate. It wouldn't have looked out of place in a ski shop had the word 'Lange' or 'Nordica' been printed on its side. It had a flex of about eighty, no canting adjustment or walk-mode switch (sorry - ski-boot anorak joke).

I was told to 'walk properly' but still use my crutches and slowly increase the amount of weight I put through the boot. After a quick demonstration, I soon found myself pegging out of the hospital wearing my new big blue boot - it was a vast improvement on the high heel shoe I'd gone in with.

The next four weeks as a remedial biped presented more challenges and needed even more mental endurance. I already had cabin fever having been stuck on Labrador Island for two weeks - but I was only a third of the way through my prison sentence, so I continued with my Leg Diary:

Week 1

After dangling it all the way to and from, the hospital my foot was very swollen. The first thing I did when I got home was to take a bath. I'm not a fan of baths, preferring showers, but I had one just because I could. Getting in was a bit of a palaver. I lay there admiring my right foot – continually waving at it then making it wave back.

Later, Debbie kindly gave it a massage, while I was laying on the settee. But, no matter how hard she rubbed, I couldn't feel her fingers. Then she touched an area just above my big toe and an electric shock surged into my brain causing me to leap into the air. 'What the hell was that?' she asked. 'I don't know. Maybe the surgeon wired something up incorrectly?' I suggested.

After that I was a little frightened of anything or anyone touching my foot. If anything did touch the magic spot, the electric shock sensation would recur. You could have stuck a pin in any other part of my foot and I wouldn't have felt it, yet hit the bull's eye and fireworks would go off in my head.

That first night, I slept with my foam boot on. Debbie informed me that it wasn't a very sexy look but I didn't trust my unconscious self (or hers) not to bash my foot or press the electric-shock button.

The week progressed, and I pretty much did the same things I did as a tripod – bugger all. I ate, drank, slept and watched TV - with the addition of an evening foot massage. I also bashed my frustration into a diary (this is a truncated version, you'll be pleased to know).

I felt sorry for Dr Debs. She spent her day dealing with sick people at work then came home to another patient. My foot was really getting in the way of life. Debbie, joked, 'there are now three of us in this relationship: me, you and your bloody right foot'. I too had started to refer to my foot in the third person.

The massages were a big help and slowly my foot and toes shrank back to their normal size. Initially, I was scared of using my right leg but, by the end of the week, I did manage to cast off a crutch and walk using the other one as a stick. I had returned to being a biped.

Week 2

I got my second week of biped life off to a good start by delivering a cup of tea to Debbie in bed (via the flask technique). It was her first lie-in for over four weeks, due to under staffing at the hospital, a lame boyfriend and various parenting demands from real teenagers.

The tea seemed to go down well until she declared, 'So you'll be able to do the housework now too, if you can bring me tea in bed?' My act of kindness had backfired.

That Wednesday, I had my first appointment with the physiotherapist. He couldn't believe how well I was walking having read the report from the surgeon. 'I'm definitely back on the hoovering now,' I thought. He complimented my leg muscles, 'Not bad for a fifty year old,' he said. 'That is what seven straight seasons of skiing does for you, I told him.' I rubbed my beer belly and added, 'It also does this.'

Using layman's terms, he explained the orthopaedic issues I was having. I understood his words more clearly than those the surgeon had used. All professions seem to develop their own language to confuse muggles. Skiers do it too - especially BASI. He gave me some exercises to improve the strength of my dorsiflexion and pronation (in their language).

Debbie was almost permanently at the hospital that week, so I decided to venture up North to my parents' house where there was less danger of being asked to do any housework. Driving wasn't an option yet, so I caught the train to East Yorkshire.

I took a crutch with me. Folks kept helping me on and off platforms etc. One old lady even tried to give me her seat. I felt a bit of a fraud. The crutch was a useful signpost to everyone saying, 'keep the hell away from my leg', but I didn't really need it to walk with. On the train I enjoyed telling some children about my encounter with the shark - that was until they requested a look at my scar - knowing the game would be up, I refused.

I arrived at my childhood home and waiter service was re-established. I enjoyed being a teenager again and doing absolutely nothing around the house except helping to empty the fridge. I went bird-watching with my stepfather and he relayed my mother's concern about me dying in an avalanche. My injury had reconfirmed to her that I was partaking in a very dangerous sport. I joked, 'If the avalanches don't get you the snowboarders will.' On a serious note, I explained that the mountains themselves pose less of a threat than the people you share them with.

I always enjoy returning to Yorkshire. I usually visit my parents mid-season during half term when it's best to be a very long way from the ski slopes. They live in South Cave. I wasn't brought up in a cave - it's a village to the west of Hull. It sits on the edge of the Humber Estuary's alluvial plain. It's a weird unremittingly flat landscape but rich in wildlife, and the banks of the Humber are a bird watcher's paradise. I often sit in a bird hide, staring out at the vast reed-covered marshes without a single mountain in sight and think, there is great beauty in the horizontal not just the vertical. Although North Yorkshire is mountainous, East Yorkshire is largely flat. It amuses me that a mountain lover, like me, should have been born in such a flat place. Perhaps if you're brought up in the mountains you don't hold them in such high regard?

Week 3

I returned to Sutton for my next physiotherapy session. Not being a skier, my physiotherapist asked what foot movement I needed for skiing, which was an interesting question that I bet most skiers wouldn't be able to answer. Most of us just ski, without really being aware of what limb movements we are making.

Being held tightly in a ski boot, you might assume your ankles and feet don't need to move. However, we do flex our ankles forward and backwards at various stages of a turn and alternate pressure between our big and little toes. A small, but strong, amount of dorsiflexion and pronation are definitely needed.

I tried to explain the above to my physio but was met with a completely blank face. I think I used too much skiing jargon. Before leaving, I asked, 'Do I still needed to wear this air boot?' and added, 'It's starting to affect my relationship.' He gave me a funny look and consented. 'Okay, you can stop wearing the boot but don't overdo it.' I left thinking we were talking about different 'its'.

When I got home I put my right walking-boot on. It was a bit of a struggle and I wondered just how difficult it was going to be to put a ski boot on the same foot, if indeed it would ever be possible.

'Maybe, I'll have to switch to snowboarding,' I thought,. 'After all my snowboarding jibes, it would be ironic if I turned into a 'grey on a tray'.

To celebrate my matching footwear, I had rather a lot of wine that evening. It was the first time I'd been, 'legless, since I'd been one leg less' – a joke I kept repeating until Debbie got sick of it.

The next day, I started making plans. I needed to be on top of my skiing game by December and there wouldn't be many snow-covered mountains available over the summer. I really needed to get back to Morzine and try skiing before the current season was out. But first I needed to be able to walk properly, then to drive again.

Week 4

Walking in shoes wasn't going well. I was suffering from what my physio called 'drop foot', which sounded like something a sheep might suffer from. I kept tripping over my right foot. I wasn't raising my toes high enough when I took a step and they kept catching on the ground. I tried to consciously exaggerate the correct dorsiflexion, which made me look like an extra from Monty Python's Ministry of Silly Walks.

At my next appointment, he gave me a foot suspender to cure the problem. The device attached my shoelaces to a strap around my calf with a small bungee cord and, according to Debbie, was not very sexy. It was a palaver to attach it but it worked and, literally, put the spring back in my step. Armed with my suspender I tried driving, at first only in an empty car park, but I was soon confident enough to head out onto the open road.

By Wednesday, I drove myself to my outpatient appointment with the surgeon. Dr Debs had agreed to meet me there and be my interpreter. I was keen to see him and compliment him on his excellent needlework but his registrar, a Spaniard, attended instead. The registrar examined my leg and made some encouraging noises. Debbie, worrying about my insurance status, asked if I was okay to drive. His answer was 'no'. Or more specifically it wasn't a 'yes'. Even Dr Debs found it hard to interpret his medical ramblings through his Spanish accent. This was worrying, having just left a vehicle in the hospital's car park.

I'm a great believer in the adage that, 'To ask permission is to seek denial'. I had assumed, maybe in ignorance, that I was driving legally. Now that I'd been told I couldn't by a doctor, I would be doing so in the knowledge my insurance was invalid. I was a little bit annoyed that Debbie had asked the question. I was better off with the assumption than the fact.

I stood up and hopped up and down on my bad leg, trying to prove to him it was fine. But I detected that he didn't want the responsibility of saying I could drive in case I had an accident and someone sued him. Luckily, while I was remonstrating, my surgeon showed up and seemed surprised to see me hopping around on a leg he had recently reattached. He took a more pragmatic approach to the driving issue. 'If you feel you can drive safely, then by all means drive,' was his opinion. It was a masterpiece of ambiguity, leaving neither him nor me liable for any resulting accident. His registrar listened and hopefully learned.

The following day I booked a flight back to Morzine. Seven weeks after leaving the place in an ambulance I would be returning, maybe not to ski but to resume chalet life for what was left of Season 8.

25. Bleeding Defenders

Only eight weeks after my accident, I limped down the stairs of an aeroplane at Geneva Airport. The doctors had suggested it might take ten or more weeks before I could walk properly but my sentence on Labrador Island had been commuted - I'd been let out early on parole.

I still had two weeks of Season 8 left before I had to vacate Chalet Benjamin. My probation officer (the physio) had told me to avoid skiing for the rest of the season but there were plenty of other things I could do in Morzine – run the chalet for example.

I did intend trying on my ski boots and maybe having a little skiing experiment to see if my comedy foot could control a ski. But I didn't intend to do anything that I'd class as skiing so I wouldn't be breaching the terms of my parole.

I'd also returned to Morzine on a mission to repatriate Landie. I intended, with the help of Sturmführer David, to drive her home myself. I'd tempted him with a week of skiing first but, seeing my plight, he had offered his services willingly.

Once in the arrivals hall, I bumped into a friend. He seemed surprised to see me standing on two legs. A rumour had been circulating around Morzine that I'd lost my leg in the accident! I assured him both my legs were still made of flesh and rolled my trousers up to prove it. He kindly offered me a ride to Morzine, which I accepted - grateful that I'd be spared the rigours of riding in a shared transfer van.

It's only just over an hour to Morzine from GVA, but being held captive in a small metal box with strangers for even an hour, can prove physically and mentally challenging. The physical challenges include: not throwing up, sitting in excessive heat or cold, being deprived of oxygen or being exposed to excessive g-forces. The mental challenges include: listening to the driver's music, listening to the puerile conversations of other passengers or being forced to contributed to them. Sometimes the biggest challenge is holding on to hope – hope that the driver doesn't actually have a death wish.

People always seem to talk to me when I don't want them to and ignore me when I fancy a chat. However, I have met some interesting people on my many journeys up and down mountains in small vans; unfortunately, I have also shared many a journey with idiots who seem to enjoy having a captive audience. I've also eavesdropped on new chalet staff (Pippa and her colleagues) setting out on their *gap-yer*, all bright-eyed and hopeful and others returning exhausted, depressed and fat – there is great comfort in tartiflette. For this reason 'Shortness of Transfer' is high on my list of Ski Resort Top Trumps.

En route to Chalet Benjamin, we popped into the Rhodos for a cheeky one. My leg might have been fixed, but I still couldn't make it walk past a bar. It was 'Open Mic Night', which was always a highlight of the social week. Staged every Monday by local musicians, anyone who can play an instrument or simply feels like singing can take over the stage. A tourist was singing 'I will survive' when I walked in, which seemed appropriate. As suspected, most of my old Avoriaz ski-club crew were assembled around their usual table.

I call them the 'Snow Geese'. Mostly retired, they migrated to their chalets and apartments each winter. Most are older than me but all are fit and active. They remind me that the key to retirement is to do it while your body still works. Their philosophy is simple, to 'ski, drink, eat and repeat' all winter. One, clearly worried he might forget, had the instructions written on his tee shirt. I was always a little jealous that, unlike me, they had no toil in Morzine. I joked that they weren't 'living the dream', but 'living the tee shirt'.

Lots of handshakes and kisses later, I sat quietly absorbing the unmistakable sounds and smells of an après bar. It was like no time had passed. It was groundhog Monday at the Rhodes and I was happy to be reliving it once again.

Sensibly, before things got alcoholically out of control, I headed back to the chalet. On entering the familiar building I was confronted with the many staircases to the top floor. This time I would ascend them vertically facing forward, instead of backwards on my arse.

There were just three guests in residence: Ukulele Dave and a couple of his mates. I ran through my injury story for the umpteenth time that evening and felt like reverting back to the shark-attack story.

Dave was half way through the BASI-2 course I'd managed to dodge and I was interested in how he was getting on. He was finding the course hard going and wasn't optimistic that he would pass. I put this down either to his pessimism or the stiff lipped examiners not giving anything away. In my eyes, he was an excellent skier and certainly a better BASI skier than me. I had a few more glasses of red with Dave and went to bed relatively sober – or so I thought.

Gaining qualifications is often about assimilating a doctrine and demonstrating you can deploy it effectively enough to join a club. There are no exams and few objective tests in skiing - you essentially have to impress those who are already instructors. They decide if you are 'at the level'. Trying to become a ski instructor can therefore be a very inconsistent and frustrating experience.

I woke with the all too familiar red-wine sickness and a category 3 hangover. [10] My morning task was to wake Landie from her eight-week slumber under the snow and I wasn't looking forward to this. If she refused to start I'd return to a world of misery. The wine run was only two weeks away and I didn't want to spend my last two weeks in Morzine dealing with Land Rover issues, although it might

---

10 The Tomlinson hangover scale: 1) I feel a bit tired. 2) I've felt better. 3) I feel rough. 4) I feel dreadful. 5) I have the shakes. 6) I've lost my phone. 7) Where am I? 8) Who am I? 9) Never again. 10) Please kill me.

have been a fitting end to the eight-year saga of our mechanical love/hate relationship. I seriously could have done without the hangover while facing this moment of truth.

If you don't count a dodgy headlamp switch, Landie was in perfect working order when I left her. She had two fully charged batteries and a friend was on standby for a jumpstart. Even though the temperature had dropped below -18C while I'd been away, her tank was full of proper winter diesel. There was no good reason to suspect she wouldn't start – other than that she was a Land Rover Defender.

I opened the driver's door, climbed in and inhaled deeply. The primary diagnostic tool you use on a Defender is your nose. If you smell burnt electrics or get a whiff of brake fluid, you know the vehicle needs attention. But all smelt well with Landie.

I love the smell of my Land Rover in the morning. It smells like no other car or indeed any other Defender. It's a subtle bouquet of musty dampness, diesel fumes and essence of WD40.

The smell changes slightly depending on the time of year and whom I've been ferrying around the previous evening. In the ski season, the aromas of stale alcohol and cheap perfume are added to the heady mix; in the summer they are replaced with the smell of cut grass and sheep poo. Often there is an overriding aroma of wet labrador.

But I know the base smell of my Landie, like a baby knows the smell of its mother. When I return to her after a hard day's skiing, fell walking or ladder climbing, I feel like I'm returning to a womb – she is the mother ship from which most of my mountain adventures are launched. At the end of an expedition, usually exhausted, I climb into her and inhale the reassuring air – then hope she will start.

Landie started first time on the first battery. Unwilling to accept success, I hunted for problems. I checked the oil and coolant levels. I checked all the lights, wipers, washer jets and all were functioning. I checked the tyres and even crawled underneath her to see if anything was hanging off. I'd once arrived back in England missing an exhaust box. To this day I have no idea where or when it fell off.

I waited for the engine to warm up and once it was up to normal temperature, I waited for it to overheat – it didn't. I had to conclude that I had a fully functioning Land Rover. Now all that remained was to see if I could drive it with my comedy foot.

I rolled forward and pressed the brake pedal. Landie stopped, but something wasn't right. The pedal seemed a bit mushy, and the brakes didn't bite until the pedal was close to the floor. I couldn't decide if this was normal or not – it had been a while since I'd driven a Defender. Was it my foot that felt mushy or the brakes? Having more recently driven a normal car where the slightest dab on the brake pedal caused the bonnet to dip, perhaps I was expecting too much from Landie by comparison.

There are quite a few ancillary systems in any vehicle you can live without but the braking system isn't one of them. I spent the next twenty minutes carefully driving around the car park deciding if it was safe for me to venture onto the road. I decided it was (probably) and headed to the supermarket.

I tried a few unnecessary emergency stops to reassure myself en route but I wasn't convinced. Was Landie braking normally or had I forgotten what normal was? Was my foot the problem? Should I seek professional advice and from whom: a mechanic, a physiotherapist, or a psychologist? I decided to wait till David arrived in a couple of days. He was used to driving Landie and dealing with my mechanical neuroses and could offer a second opinion on both of us.

The next morning, after a bad dream where David and I had ploughed into the back of stationary traffic on a French motorway, I decide to take more positive action – I would test the brakes with my good foot. I got up to speed on an empty road knocked Landie into neutral and stamped on the brakes with my left foot but I couldn't get the bonnet to dip – there was definitely something wrong with the brakes, not my head or my right foot. This was partially reassuring but left me with the problem of having to fix an actual problem.

If I called the AA they would send the vultures from the garage in Le Biot and, if history repeated itself, they would keep Landie for a couple of weeks then replace several random but suitably expensive parts before returning her.

I went online and searched the Defender owners' forums for advice. I often do this when I think something is wrong with Landie. Unfortunately it's a bit like googling medical symptoms – you usually end up self-diagnosing a terminal illness. However, the general opinion was that water droplets in the brake fluid had frozen during the cold temperatures and all I needed to do was bleed them out of the brake pipes.

I wasn't equipped to do this myself so I rang 'Landy Andy' the ex-pat who had helped me the previous season – he was unavailable. So I called a local French mechanic who was reportedly good, spoke English and, most importantly, was likely to bleed my brakes without bleeding my wallet. He was called *'Da-vid,* which was encouraging. In my experience all the best mechanics are called 'Dave', so I called him.

After declaring he knew nothing about Defenders, *Dav-id* reluctantly agreed to help me. I was uneasy at letting this Defender debutant loose on Landie. On inspecting her, his first words were, *'Zee bleed nipples are corroded - zay might snap off ven I loosen zem'*, which was worrying. Often, with Defenders, when you try to fix one mechanical problem, you end up with a bigger one. So, while *Dav-id* fiddled with Landie's nipples, I paced around her like an expectant father.

Dav-id successfully bled the brakes without snapping anything and, better still, it fixed the problem – full braking ability was restored. I declared him my new best friend, gave him some cash and drove back to Morzine delighted.

Ski or not, I could now enjoy the last two weeks of Season 8. Over the seasons, I have had to deal with a lot of Land Rover problems. Most have involved getting Landie to move but this was the first time I'd had a problem getting her to stop.

26. Misery loves Company

Although I'd been advised against it, I knew the psychological benefit of skiing again before I left Morzine, however pathetically, would be immeasurable. If not, my next opportunity to ski on proper snow would be the following December (just before the Leaders Refresher course) and that would be an agonisingly long wait.

This would require getting my comedy foot into a ski boot first – which seemed like the harder of the two tasks.

Both tasks involved thinking about things I hadn't thought about since I was a beginner. When something becomes automatic, you forget how to actually do it. 'How do you put a ski boot on?' I asked myself. I turned to Google to find the answer. After watching a 'how to' YouTube video, I realised that I'd actually been putting my boots on wrongly for over thirty years. So, one morning after the guests had left, I sat in the living room and studiously followed the video demonstration.

My trousers were getting in the way, so I took them off but even after following all the steps, my BASI boots refused to yield. I removed the boot's foot-bed, still no joy; I tried a thinner sock and a more slippery sock, neither worked; I thought about trying no sock at all, and covering my foot with Vaseline but mercifully I couldn't find any. So, I decided to superheat the boot by leaving it on the radiator for a while.

Once the boot had gained the malleability of a Baby Bell wrapper, I tried again and my heel finally popped into the rear of the boot. The feeling of elation was soon superseded with one of alarm – the boot was burning my ankle. That in turn was replaced with a feeling of embarrassment, when a guest unexpectedly returned to find me hopping around the chalet in my underpants, yelping. 'So this is what you get up to when we go out!' she exclaimed. Worried that the boot might harden and I'd be stuck in my underpants all day, I quickly extracted my foot and put my trousers back on.

The next morning, David, being a Ski Nazi, had left the chalet at 8am to catch the first lift. Being late March, the morning conditions would be too icy for a born-again beginner like me so I arranged to meet him at the top of the Super Morzine (The Super M) bubble at lunchtime.

En route, I picked up some beginner skis from Gravier's ski shop. Michele was surprised to see me on two legs. He told me that the English community, who favoured his shop, had all been talking about my amputation. I told him it was only a rumour, while suspecting that I'd found the rumours' source. Hair dryer in hand, he helped me warm and put my boot on. I'd seen him diligently attend to beginners and ease them through their first encounter with ski boots but I'd never personally experienced his excellent boot-side manner myself.

Equipped and hobbled, I headed for the Super M, begrudgingly buying a lift pass on the way, knowing I wouldn't get much value out of it. I arrived at the rendezvous point twenty minutes early - I always arrive early for everything, I just can't help myself. Rather than wait for David, I decided to try and mount my skis and slide down to the first chairlift some twenty metres below.

With a familiar 'clunk, clunk', my boots snapped into the sloppy hire bindings and once again, I was ski-borne. Everything felt normal, so I launched myself down the moderate slope in the snowplough position. It was hard to tell if my injury had reduced the braking efficiency of my snowplough. It seemed to be working – rather well in fact! It wasn't inconceivable that having my leg rebuilt might have actually improved my skiing.

Feeling like a beginner, I went through the chairlift turnstile and furtively looked at the folks in the queue around me. I really wanted to get on a chair by myself, and definitely not on one with other beginners, who might bungle their dismount and take me down with them. Smelling my fear, they all looked back at me with a similar disdain and let me ride alone.

I'd forgotten that being surrounded by other debutants is the biggest problem a beginner skier faces. Imagine the carnage that would result if we put all learner drivers behind the wheel of unfamiliar cars then sent them down the same cul-de-sac having removed all their brake pedals first. Beginner slopes are equally dangerous cul-de-sacs.

In this respect, learning to ski is a Darwinian process. The fit and fast-learning individuals quickly move to the more advanced slopes and out of the danger zone. Once you're on the more difficult slopes, there are less people to crash into and less out-of-control people to crash into you – unless it's the French school holidays of course. You face more life-threatening dangers (higher speed collisions and wipeouts etc.) on a red run than a green one, but a lower risk of being involved in a game of human skittles.

I dismounted the chair without incident and glided down the blue run and my foot seemed to be working. I briefly looked around at the scenery and rejoiced at being surrounded by familiar mountains.

However, I soon came across a ski-school snake, slithering from one side of the piste to the other.

A common hazard on the beginner slopes, ski-school snakes are often formed of ten or more toddlers all diligently following their instructor in a line. Some instructors seem oblivious to the barrier they are forming. The length of the snake can be equal to twice the width of the pistes, so there is often no room to overtake without going off-piste. I normally put the last child in my crosshairs and wait for him to turn before pulling the trigger. You always face a double jeopardy when overtaking a beginner. They are prone to randomly altering their trajectory and, because you're overtaking them, they have the right of way.[11] So any contact is always your fault – even if it's not.

Instead of overtaking the snake I decided to join it. I tacked on behind the last child, who was laying down some impressively clean tracks. I decided to see if I could match him – turn for turn. Skiing slowly is always difficult, but my right foot seemed responsive and although he might not have been trying, the child couldn't shake me off his tail. By way of a victory roll, I peeled off the snake, passed the bemused instructor, grinning – I could still out ski a bunch of five-year-olds.

At the bottom of the run I paused and celebrated the success of my first postoperative descent. I was still early for the rendezvous, so I decided to repeat the exercise. Unfortunately, while lining up for the chair, another instructor asked if I could take one of his toddlers back up with me – his charges were all too small to ride a chairlift alone.

Being randomly put in charge of a stranger's child is one of the unique experiences that skiing offers. In any other circumstance, you'd need a CRB check, to have been on a government-approved child-safety course and have the direct permission of the parents, but in a ski resort anyone tall enough to look like an adult is trusted with the safety of a child in what is, let's face it, a very dangerous environment. Does an assumed ability to ski rule out an individual from having homicidal tendencies, mental illness or frequent bouts of misopedia?[12] Do paedophiles not go skiing? It can however, be quite enjoyable talking to a French child without the presence of their parents. You can practise your French without being embarrassed and teach the child a few useful English phrases – or swear words if you're in a mischievous mood.

---

11 Fédération Internationale de Ski (FIS) have a 'code of conduct' for recreational skiing. It is generally regarded as the Highway Code for skier's. It is seldom taught and less often obeyed. It states that it is the overtaking skier's responsibility to avoid a collision.

12 Misopedia is the hatred of children, especially one's own.

My charge safely dispatched intact, unmolested and repeating the word 'buggeration', I skied back to the top of Super M to meet David. I gave him the good news, 'I think I'm back in business,' I declared.

Congratulating me, he suggested we ski over to Lindarets, a south-facing area of Avoriaz were the snow would be softer. I agreed and we headed for the Proclou chairlift. At the top, we dismounted the chair into what seemed like a sea of machete-wielding maniacs. Boarders and skiers converged from every direction with lethal blades attached to their feet.

We set off and were soon descending the blue run that winds its way through the forest towards Lindarets. Kamikaze boarders seemed to be popping out of the woods, right left and centre, skiers bounced off moguls all around me, and everyone seemed oblivious to my presence. I'm usually one of the quickest people on a piste but this time I was the slowest.

Another major problem for beginners is that they are constantly being overtaken rather than doing the overtaking themselves. When overtaking you are the one in control. You can choose the speed and proximity of the flypast. After assessing your target's potential for random behaviour you can leave suitable margins for error. When you're the one being overtaken, these things are left to the discretion of others who may be more reckless than you – or drunk. Some speedsters seem to use beginner runs for slalom practice.

David patiently waited for me at the bottom. Over the years, he had done a lot of Girlfriend Skiing (with me and other beginners) and he masked his frustration perfectly - especially when I suggested a long lunch. We went to one of my favourite restaurants and the wine flowed. It was fabulous to be eating in the mountains again.

Those who take sandwiches skiing to save money and those who use self-service places to save time, are really missing one of the main points of skiing – to have a civilised lunch in a ludicrous location. My whole skiing day is centred round the location and quality of lunch. If you don't set out with a geographical objective in mind and have an itinerary (coffee, lunch, après) you're simply skiing around in circles all day. A decent lunch not only gives skiing a purpose, it also serves as its reward.

In an unusual act of generosity I bought David's lunch. Normally, it's David's credit card that takes the pounding but the roles had been reversed: he was the guide and I was the punter. So unusual was this transaction, he sent Val a text, 'There's still something wrong with Chris. He's just bought my lunch!' Happy and replete, I suggested we head home via a couple of blue runs. Like a beginner, I was desperate to get my boots off.

On returning to the chalet, I found Ukulele Dave crying into his metaphoric beer – he had failed the BASI-2 course. I could scarcely believe his news. I'd seen many worse skiers with BASI-2 badges hanging from their chests. My injury had really been fortuitous – if he hadn't made the grade, I'd have stood no chance of doing so.

He seemed philosophical about the verdict, but others who had failed, were apparently outraged and cast aspersions on the ability of those who had passed. Conspiracy theories were flying around but I think it was just sour grapes.

Dave's two weeks of BASI purgatory had resulted in no reward. I empathised with him and remembered how I felt when, on my first attempt to pass the Leaders' Course, I'd failed. He confessed to shedding actual tears in private, the previous week when he just couldn't master BASI's version of the short turn. I too had failed to hold back the tears halfway through my course, when it became clear I wasn't going to make the grade.

Later, while we were propping up a bar in town, Dave admitted that he had lost his love for skiing in the past two weeks. He suggested that BASI's motto should be – 'BASI, taking the joy out of skiing since 1963'. I spent the rest of the evening commiserating with him – misery does love company.

27. THE LAST OF THE SUMMER WINE

If it's true and 70% of all the Defenders ever made are still on the road, then we must assume the other 30% actually made it home. The ill-fated Season 8 was drawing to a close and all I needed now was for my Landie to get me home.

Apart from the small matter of her brakes failing, Landie's behaviour had been exemplary that season. She had distinguished herself well on Bacon Run 8, I'd got her fuelling strategy right and she had weathered the February cold spell admirably.

In that respect Wine Run 8, was unusual. The question was not really whether Landie would make it back, but would I be able to drive her 800 miles? My leg was working, but still very weak.

Luckily Sturmführer David had agreed to be my co-pilot - an act of friendship for which I was extremely grateful. I'd put him on Landie's insurance many seasons before which had often proved useful. He was an experienced and capable Defender driver although he had never driven one on a motorway before.

A significant amount of the clobber I needed to take back to England actually belonged to him and Val - two sets of skis, three pairs of boots and two suitcases larger than my own - but the baggage came with the man, so I wasn't complaining.

What I didn't know was that David not only had a penchant for importing chickens to Morzine, but also one for exporting duck to England. I always like to take a couple of tins of Confit de Canard home myself – it's one of my favourite French delicacies - but I was a little surprised when he brought back ten tins of the stuff from the supermarket. I reminded him we intended to pick up wine at Calais and I wanted to stick below the maximum recommended axle weight for a Defender. This was a Wine Run, not a Duck Run after all.

We packed the night before our departure, inserting tins of duck into every unused corner of the vehicle – I'm still occasionally finding them now. I was keen not to use the roof rack. Placing anything on the roof would compromise Landie's top speed and fuel efficiency.

That evening, I threw a dinner party to use up all the remaining food in the fridge – and whatever dregs remained in the drinks cabinet. 'The Last Supper' (as I call it) is a chalet tradition of mine and it's nice cooking for friends instead of guests. Whatever uncooked food is left after the Last Supper, I give to my diners by way of a parting gift. The remaining bacon is ceremoniously handed over to whomever I deem worthiest.

David, the duck and I set off early the next morning. After bidding Morzine *au revoir*, I drove Landie down the mountain wondering when, or if, I'd return. While heading to Cluses and the motorway, David and I conducted a post mortem on the season. Having spent most of it on crutches in Sutton Coldfield, the season couldn't really be declared a success but at least Season 8 had started well and having skied again since my accident, it had ended well too. I was going home on a high.

Landie was running well and got up to 70 mph on the motorway without issue. David, who had not been looking forward to the journey, declared, 'She's not as bad as you made out,' referring to Landie's performance at warp speed. I explained the many improvements I had made to her over the years with pride. Unlike most of my previous passengers, David seemed genuinely interested in Defenders – although concerned that I might talk about Landie for the whole eight-hundred-mile journey. He switched the subject to our intended overnight accommodation.

We planned to stop at the Chateau De Cocove, so I described the luxury and culinary delights that awaited us. He didn't seem impressed; it all sounded a little too romantic for him.

Having done the journey seven times before, the navigation was easy: west past Geneva, then at Bourg-en-Bresse turn north towards Dijon.

Once David and I had passed Dijon, the complaints from my right foot could no longer be ignored so we swapped drivers. David soon discovered that Landie could actually do 80mph (down hills, with a tail wind) and I discovered the latent Boy Racer inside him. I pleaded with him to stay below 70 mph, but every time my attention was turned he shifted gear and overtook whatever was in front of us.

I didn't think it was possible to get a speeding ticket in a Defender but David seemed keen to prove me wrong. I explained that Landie was actually an agricultural vehicle, not a sports car, and the trick was to sit behind the lorries and gain fuel efficiency from their slipstream - not use it for a slingshot overtaking manoeuvre.

Accepting we were going to beat my existing Wine Run time record, I tried to relax. We chatted and put the world to rights, but conversation above 60 mph was difficult, Landie having the loudest voice.

I knew the conversation was drying up, when we started discussing the dead insects on the windscreen. 'You don't see that anymore,' David said, pointing to the latest casualty. Apparently modern cars are so aerodynamic that the flies get blown over them. Landie's windscreen being flat and vertical was an old-fashioned insect-killing zone. With his bout of nostalgia over, David turned off his hearing aids and crept Landie back up to 80 mph hoping I wouldn't notice.

I was slightly jealous of his ability to turn his ears off and isolate himself from the world and whinging passengers. Unfortunately this made giving him navigational instructions difficult. Every time I wanted to speak to him, I had to tap him on the shoulder and shout.

We made it to the chateau in record time. With hindsight, I should have chosen a less fancy hotel, but I knew how to find the chateau and they had a room free that evening. Having failed on previous

Wine and Bacon runs, I didn't want to leave finding overnight accommodation to chance.

Unfortunately they had made our room up in a double bed configuration. I'd forgotten to mention, when booking, I wasn't bringing Debbie this time. David wasn't impressed. So I persuaded the housekeeper to convert the room back to a twin bed configuration while we had a drink at the bar. I knew the sleeping separation distance wouldn't be much better, but at least there would be no overnight quilt war or any accidental cuddling.

We walked into the bar and I recognised the barman. I asked him for a Negroni and a ginger beer then waited for his reaction. He looked sideways at me, as did David, then he smiled, recognising me too. 'How was your season, monsieur?' he asked. 'Painful,' I replied, not wanting to go into the details, then I quickly reordered two plain beers.

I always find it awkward sharing a room with less-intimate acquaintances, or friends come to that. My solution is to get drunk with them first. That way there are no goodnight wishes or pillow talk – you just collapse on the nearest bed fully clothed. The excessive alcohol might make you snore but it's always better to be the snorer than the snoree. In this instance, David and I being old friends, there was no need for anaesthetics – and driving a Defender is thirsty work.

During dinner, still a little deaf from the day's driving, I noticed I was still tapping David on the shoulder and shouting at him, despite the fact his hearing aids were now reengaged. The restaurant was full of couples trying to have a romantic meal, so I tried to moderate my volume.

I noticed we were the only male couple eating, so I tapped David's shoulder and jokingly whispered, 'Looks like we are the only gay couple in the hotel tonight'. He looked confused and replied, 'pardon?' So, just as the music dropped, I repeated my sentence, at full Land Rover volume, 'WE ARE THE ONLY GAY COUPLE HERE, DAVID'. Everyone stopped eating and looked round at us. I picked up the wine menu and hid behind it, leaving David to grin his way through the embarrassment I'd caused.

All transgressions forgiven, we headed to Majestic Wine in Calais the following morning. I had a category-3 hangover. David refused to admit he had any hangover at all, despite matching me glass for glass, the night before.

Usually people who claim they don't get hangovers are in self-denial. Maybe they always feel rubbish and think the way they feel the morning after the night before, is normal. In my serious drinking days, I always had a hangover, so I too couldn't really determine what was a normal morning feeling. Once I started having a few nights off, I discovered it is possible to wake up full of beans, enthusiastically looking forward to the day ahead. The downside is that good feeling wanes as the day progresses. At least, when you wake up with a hangover, you know your day can only get better.

It suited me to go along with David's claim of superhuman tolerance to alcohol, because, without a hangover, it made sense for him drive. We arrived at Majestic half an hour before it opened. I felt like a very deprived and desperate individual hanging around an off-licence with a hangover waiting for it to open. However, I knew I'd regret not taking home some high quality, inexpensive wine for the summer. Once it opened, we were the first customers through the door.

It's very difficult to choose wine when you have a Cat 2 hangover or greater. You wonder around blearily eyeing up the bottles and the thought of drinking any of their content makes you feel queasy. You certainly don't want to taste any of the samples –David tucked in.

I met him by the checkout with his trolley piled high. I reiterated the maximum axle weight allowed on a Defender but he dismissed it with the words, 'Oh, it will be fine'. After loading my modest selection into the back of Landie, I helped David load his many cases and watched the Landie's wheel arches slowly lower over her tyres.

We set off for the ferry. I decided to drive so I could nurse my cruelly laden beast through her ordeal. The crossing was uneventful, and Dover gave us its traditional welcome when we rolled off the boat – road works and potholes. First-time visitors to our country, who choose this point of entry, must wonder why we still call it *Great* Britain. After cruising along empty and well-maintained French motorways the previous day, the contrast was stark. Although I do appreciate our roads are free to use – if you don't count the road tax.

We headed to the car park, known as the M25. Constantly having to use Landie's heavy clutch in the start/stop traffic was painful and the aggressive nature of the other drivers reminded me that we were in the South of England.

Before heading to Birmingham, I had to drop David off at his house in the Cotswolds, so we were soon on more countrified roads. My leg was hurting so I suggested that David took over the driving. I also thought he might enjoy taking the chequered finishing flag. This was a mistake.

Now on his home circuit, he relished every bend and corner, seemingly oblivious to the heavy cargo. We had more words, none of which were heeded, so I gritted my teeth. That was until he had a fight with a Fiesta.

The Fiesta foolishly overtook us on a dual carriageway then slowed down. So David overtook it. Seemingly annoyed about this, the Fiesta driver repeated his manoeuvre – and so did David. Three times the two cars jockeyed for pole position until the Fiesta driver, seemingly defeated, turned off the road. I pleaded with David to slow down, but I think he had turned his hearing aid off again or couldn't hear me over the noise of Landie's complaining engine.

While praying to the Land Rover gods for deliverance, we flashed past a sign at 70 mph. I think it said, 'Warning sharp turn - Max 30mph', but it passed in a blur. Before I could say anything, David was hauling Landie into the hairpin the sign alluded to and Landie's inside wheels where lifting off the ground.

I leant out of the passenger window trying to weight the wheels back down and noticed a cyclist trying to cross the road, I yelled at David, 'This is why you never let *ANYONE* drive your Defender'. He looked bemused. Mercifully, the bend abated, the wheels re-engaged with the road and the remainder of the journey was conducted in silence.

When it comes to cars and driving, men never really grow up. Debbie's father, for instance, still pulls hand brake turns on gravel car parks and always gives it full throttle to impress the ladies - and he is over eighty. It is rather endearing that there is a lust for fun still alive in the old fella. At thirty, the boy racer in me was killed when I lost my license for accumulated speeding offences. I joke that being banned from driving turned me into an alcoholic – my wife always had to drive, so I never had to remain sober. Since swapping fast cars for a Defender, I've never had another speeding ticket. The only difference between men and boys is the price of their toys.

Once safely parked on David's drive, I broke the silence. I thanked him. 'I couldn't have got her home without you,' I admitted but couldn't resist adding, '… and in such record time'. While helping him to unloaded the duck and wine, I also admitted to being a nervous passenger and a little over protective of my old lady (Landie).

After bidding farewell, I pointed Landie towards Sutton Coldfield, thinking I'd turned into my mother. She regularly scolds my father, from the passenger seat, for driving too fast. But he is just another man who really wanted to be a racing driver.

After the usual warm welcome from Debbie and Oscar, I unloaded my share of the wine and, when finished, gave Landie a pat on the bonnet. She had got me home one final time. I told Debbie that Season 8 was my last and The Chalet Project was definitely over. She smiled and said, 'Yer – right, tell me again in October'.

For once I stuck to my words; they weren't just the usual end-of-season sentiment. Both Landie and I had grown too old for the chalet business. I now had to focus on passing the Leaders' refresher course. Having put all my skiing eggs in the one Ski Club basket, passing it was now imperative.

28. Fellowship of the Dome

It had been a hard day of climbing up and down ladders. Summer was in full swing and I was back on the power tools, working for Farhad's crew in the less salubrious parts of Birmingham. I hadn't realised it, but being a sparky would not only help me get fit, it would also help cure my vertigo.

I was shattered but it was a warm and pleasant evening and I was looking forward to opening a bottle of wine when I got home - then to sitting in the garden nursing it. Actually, the weather and the endeavour were irrelevant: 6pm was wine-o-clock every evening in the summer. Then I remembered it was a Thursday and I was faced with a dilemma – to go skiing or not to go skiing.

Thursday night was 'BASI training night' at the Tamworth Snow Dome. Andy Jerram runs a two-hour training session there most Thursday evenings (between May and October). BASI hopefuls, from all over the Midlands, converge on the Dome to benefit from his expert tuition – some driving thirty or forty miles. The session starts at 8pm, a time when, on any other day, I'd be facing another dilemma – whether to open a second bottle or not.

Not only did I need to get fit, I also needed to work on my skiing skills for the approaching refresher course. It loomed in the distance like a school exam and I constantly felt guilty for not revising.

Often I was away or Andy had other commitments, so if I was in the Midlands on a Thursday and he was running a session, it was foolish to miss it. The problem wasn't just the lateness of the session but my attitude to ski lessons. I have a short attention span and soon get bored - especially with the small repetitive nature of indoor skiing. After about an hour, I'd usually start glancing at my watch and look yearningly at the windows of the Dome's bar.

Unlike the ski instructor stereotype, those who attend are not all young, talented ski athletes. In fact, most of us are over forty and not especially fit or attractive. Many of us are missing a full head of hair, a deep tan, and a sexy French accent too.

Many have ambitions to pass a BASI course and some even want to be ski instructors, but quite a few are just there to improve their skiing. My stated objective for attending the training sessions that summer, was to improve my SCGB Leading grade. Although, given the physical state I was in, I would have been very happy to keep my current 'C' grade.

A leading grade (C, C+, B, B+, or A) is a measure of 'mountain craft' – the ability to sniff out fresh powder and, more importantly, return those that follow with smiling faces or at the very least still breathing. More importantly, my leading grade would determine which resorts I could lead in. C leaders get the 'Driving Miss Daisy' resorts and A graded leaders get sent to places with big mountains. Saas Fee, for instance is a 'C' resort, Avoriaz is a B, Chamonix is an A and the Tamworth Snow Dome is possibly an E.

Andy's sessions weren't really appropriate for my objective. I needed to be a good off-piste skier, not a BASI ballerina, but off-piste snow is hard to find in the UK mid-summer.

Like any sports club, the eclectic nature of those who attend proves entertaining in the bar afterwards. You sit round a table with a dozen or so people you'd otherwise never cross paths with. It's a bit like staying in a shared chalet in that respect. Young, old, posh, common, blue- and white-collar workers mix with a dusting of part-time instructors and skiing professionals. It's a shame everyone is driving because, unlike in a chalet, not enough alcohol is consumed to really get to know each other. That activity is saved for 'BASI curry night', where those more local to the Dome meet in a pub then eat curry while telling tales of their exploits from seasons past. I usually get a lot of literary material from these sessions – assuming I stay sober enough to remember the anecdotes.

The training sessions follow a familiar formula: everyone assembles at the top of the slope and Andy asks us to introduce ourselves and to state our skiing objective (pass a BASI-1, 2, 3 etc.). He then explains the skill he wants to work on (long turns, short turns, carving, snowplough etc.) He then describes a drill theoretically designed to hone that skill – but often I suspect it's designed to make us fall over. These drills usually involve turning on one ski only, or jumping mid-turn and occasionally he asks us to ski backwards. He then demonstrates the drill perfectly and stands at the bottom of the slope watching (and sometimes filming) us trying to imitate his descent.

A master of constructive criticism, Andy gives individual feedback when we pull up next to him at the bottom. Some of his comments are more humorous than others:

'Looking like you're back in action, Chris'

'That was better Chris, but you're still slouching'

'This drill is aimed at you Chris – do it once more with feeling'

'Weren't you there when I explained the drill at the top?'

'Your grip is too loose – you're holding a ski pole, not another man's penis'

'That was so good Chris, I thought I was watching someone else!'

'You're a pretty good all-mountain skier Chris, but . . .'

Andy and I had reached a bit of an impasse with my stance. He has never liked the way I stand on skis. He's spent most of the last five years trying to stop me slouching. I tell him, 'I can't help it. I've slouched since I was a child.' My maths teacher at school, a frighteningly large man called 'Mr Hess', had a similar issue with me. He used to propel a blackboard rubber at me whenever he caught me slouching over my desk. At least Andy has never bounced anything off my head although I can feel his exasperation in other ways. Basically, you can't teach old skiing dogs new tricks.

Andy always refers to his group of students as 'the team'. Other BASI trainers do this too so it's probably part of the BASI trainer's methodology. The BASS instructors in Morzine also tried to bond their students into a team and when I was training for my aborted BASI-2 this perplexed me. We were not practising synchronised skiing or entering a skiing relay race; we didn't intend to pass a baton or throw a ball between us while skiing; we would all pass or fail the course individually.

I never understood why the British Olympic team is called a 'team' either. Is an athlete going to jump higher or run faster for his team than for himself? Maybe I'm just not a 'team player'; maybe some people are and feel skiing is lacking in this respect. But, try as some may, piste skiing is just not a team sport. Unless you're a ski racer, skiing isn't a sport at all. Conversely, there *is* a team aspect to skiing off-piste, which cannot be done safely alone and progress is made at the pace of the slowest skier - and success can only be declared if everyone gets home uninjured. However, I would like to point out that there may be no 'I' in 'team', but there are definitely two in 'skiing'.

We might not have been a team but there was a fellowship in the Morzine pre-BASI-2 training camp. Our goal in common, to have a life on skis or just a need for validation, created that fellowship. The observations, suggestions and empathy of the other hopefuls was useful. The same fellowship exists at the Dome. Most of us are middle-aged men with a mutual wish to have spent our youth less wisely, all aspiring to a life we should have chosen, rather than the one we did. Of course some might just like skiing on a Thursday night in the middle of summer.

Although I'd given up on progressing up the BASI ladder, I did need to practise my skiing skills. My comedy foot was still a little insubordinate and I needed to show it that I was still the Boss. Skiing at the crowded Dome also helped me in defeating the Snowboard Demon - I'd developed an irrational fear of snowboards, or more specifically their edges. Thanks to my accident I was getting the collywobbles every time a snowboarder came close to me. This only happened on the piste, I hasten to add - I had no problems standing next to one in a bar.

The Dome was often full of beginners, the young and the reckless, so there were often uncomfortably close encounters with snowboards, which inadvertently provided me with flooding therapy.

That evening, after an alcohol-free après session, I left the Dome at 11pm feeling very self-righteous. I was pleased that I'd opted for skiing, not wine, although I did intend to have some later. Still dressed in my ski gear, I chucked my skis into the back of Landie and headed home. I was the only vehicle on the back roads to Sutton and my mind was wandering. It wasn't until I came to my first roundabout that I noticed I was on the wrong side of the road!

To my horror, I realised that I'd been driving on the wrong side of the road since I'd left the Dome - some distance back. I'd been skiing, I was in Landie and my head was in the Alps. My automatic pilot had assumed I was still in France.

Folks often ask me if I find it difficult driving on the right side of the road but, once I land at Calais or indeed when I return to Dover, I seem to automatically make the switch. Remembering to drive on the correct side is clearly easier if other cars are about, assuming other absent-minded Brits are not driving them - which is always a possibility in Morzine.

One problem I do have when driving in France, is remembering which way to swerve. What happens if a Frenchman and an Englishman find themselves heading for a collision? (That's not the start of a pub joke - it's a serious question). The Frenchman's natural reaction will be to swerve right and the Englishman's to swerve left. This can turn what might have been a close miss, into a head-on collision. This is probably what happened when Max and I collided in Les Crosets - the Swiss drive on the 'wrong' side of the road too.

Having reset my autopilot back to UK mode, my thoughts returned to the Alps. Just practising at the Dome wasn't really going to cut it; if I wanted to pass the refresher course I needed to practise in some deep off-piste powder. I also needed to acclimatise, not just to the altitude but also to the general environment. The back-country skiing in Tignes is bleak and intimidating - especially in poor visibility on a freezing December day.

All mountains are intimidating until you get to know them. Once you become familiar with what's round most of their corners, the ski demons are less likely to jump out on you. It had been five years since I'd skied in the Espace[13] Killy and I needed to re-familiarise myself with it - I needed to go on a recce. Fortunately, the Ski Club provided me with the perfect solution. They were holding their annual Premier Party in Val-d'Isère the week before the course.

The Party is a hotel-based, off-piste skiing holiday with local guides included in the price. Some sixty or so crusty hardcore members usually attend, along with many off-duty Leaders. Morzine Mary usually went so I knew the skiing would be suitably hardcore. It's a Ski Nazi's dream holiday - first-lift/last-lift skiing with little or no lunch.

The next day, I rang up the Club and booked myself a place at the party. Unfortunately, they had no single rooms left, so reluctantly

---

13 The combined ski areas of Tignes and Val d'Isère were formally known as the Espace Killy. The area is accessed via the Tarentaise Valley in the Savoie department of the French Alps. Jean-Claude Killy, was a famous French skier who was raised here. He must have recently fallen out of favour, because the ski area has rather boringly, been rebranded as 'Tinges- Val d'Isère'.

I agreed to share a room with a stranger. I winced when they asked me, 'How would you like to pay?' I wanted to say, 'begrudgingly' - it had been a while since I'd paid for a skiing holiday.

I continued to throw money at the ski demons. I knew the avalanche risk in the Espace Killy seldom fell below four in December. So in order to placate my morbid fear of avalanches, I decided to buy an airbag – which was a considerable investment.

In my mind, Tignes has a disproportionate number of avalanche deaths each year. There is little official collation between resorts (reporting avalanche deaths is bad for business) so I've drawn this conclusion myself. However, early season snow is often unstable and Tignes is a mecca for off-piste powder hounds - and a lot of them are ill equipped, untrained and generally a bit gung-ho. It probably doesn't help that I've witnessed an avalanche death there too.

An airbag system, when incorporated into a backpack, will inflate a large balloon around the wearer's head if they pull on its ripcord. This theoretically makes the person larger and less dense so they naturally rise to the surface of the tumbling snow. The main issues with the system are:

1. Remembering to pull the cord when caught in an avalanche, not being able to reach it or forgetting which shoulder it's located on.

2. Preventing accidental deployment in small spaces, or deliberate deployment by drunken mates.

3. There is little statistical proof that they actually work. Although, it must be said that people report 'died' more often than they do 'didn't die' –if an airbag saves a life, it's unlikely to be report to officialdom.

Now I was all set. The only thing left to do was to get fit. I vowed that every other morning, between now and the Premier

Party, I'd go for a run if I wasn't working – a promise that I would renege on within two weeks.

29. Return to The Fells

It wasn't long after returning to Birmingham that I started to get severe mountain-withdrawal symptoms. Surrounded by urban ugliness, pollution and flat-land people, I needed to get a fix - the Snow Dome was a very poor methadone. I decided it was time to go walkabout. I configured Landie into Campervan mode and headed north to the Lakes.

I always feel good when heading north. It feels like I'm going home. It's always with reluctance I head south - unless I'm heading for the Alps of course. But then I regard that as heading 'up' not 'south'. It must be a hang-up from when I first left Hull to seek my fortune in London. I call it the 'Dick Whittington effect'.

Climbing a Lakeland fell was also on my list of recovery sub-challenges. I needed to prove my right leg and comedy foot could still bag me a Wainwright summit. My leg was more or less fully functioning (I could ski) but could it sustain a day of fell walking?

En route I intended to visit my Liverpool friends, Shiv, Morzine Mary, Westy et-al. I'd missed Scouse Week in Morzine that winter, thanks to my injury, so I'd missed them. Even though they no longer stayed with me, I still enjoyed skiing and drinking with them. Possibly even more, now I was not responsible for getting them home at 3am.

Historically held in March, Scouse Week has always been the highlight of my après season. Although, strictly speaking, not all who stayed in the chalet that week of the year were from Liverpool. It usually involved a small amount of girlfriend skiing followed by a mammoth amount of après skiing – if drinking and eating from 2pm to 2am can still be called après. It would always involve spending a lot of time in Morzine's infamous Buddha Bar.

Officially now called the Tibetan Café, the Buddha Bar was the scene
of many an après alien abduction during the early years of the Chalet
Project – large parts of which, I have no recollection. Each evening
the bar goes through phases. In the early evening, it seems like just
any other après bar with a dodgy band belting out sing-along rock
classics; later on (after midnight), the DJ increases the tempo and all
manner of Alpine life forms materialise. It's dark, steamy and hot.
As the toffee vodkas go down, the hedonism goes up. Middle-aged
holidaymakers dance with seasonaires and French locals. Like the
Hotel California, once in the throng, suitably lubricated, I found it
almost impossible to leave - until the lights went up at 2am and I'd
realise the Lithuanian supermodel I'd been throwing shapes with was
really 'Audrey', a mother of two, from Birkenhead. Well, that's how
it used to be. Now, like Phil Collins, I don't dance.

Memories of previous Scouse Weeks filled my head, as I drove north. I
cringed at some of my behaviour and vowed not to get blind drunk in
Liverpool. It was Shiv's birthday and a large night out was inevitable.
We met in town and, like in any northern city, people were dressed
up on a Friday for a big night out. It was unusual to see my friends
all dolled up - I rarely see them in anything other than ski gear. I
wore my middle-aged man uniform – chinos and a collared shirt.

After a posh meal we ended up in an underground gin bar with
a 'speak-easy' feel. The ladies danced to retro music and I played
the 'my leg hurts' card so found a table and nursed my gin. I could
have been in the Buddha Bar in Morzine, only the bar was full
of women, not men, and the occasional waft of BO was missing.
Generally the clientele looked better groomed and more attractive.
Several obvious cougars stalked the establishment, making it feel like
Morzine in March.

I remained on the sober side of the group in order to restore my
reputation – or rather undo the one I got in my early life as a chalet

host. However, when we got back to Shiv's, I celebrated my newly demonstrated sobriety by drinking half a bottle of gin. I woke with what I initially thought was a category 3 hangover, then I noticed I still had my socks on, so I upgraded it to a category 4. I can tell how bad a hangover is going to be by my state of dress when I wake up. The removal of socks seems to be an unnecessarily difficult task when drunk. If I still have my socks on when I wake up I know it's going to be a difficult day.

Then the agents of entropy struck, as they tend to do when you're at your weakest – I couldn't find the keys to Landie. 'This could be a very short walk-about,' I thought.

After a strong coffee, I remembered that I had a spare set hidden inside Landie, so I set about breaking into my own car using a coat hanger. I'd seen it done in TV crime dramas and, given that there is a large gap around Landie's passenger door, I thought I'd give it a go. It worked! In broad daylight, on a street in Liverpool, I'd learnt a new skill – how to break into a Land Rover.

I bid farewell to Shiv and headed north again. The usual nightmare traffic on the M6 presented itself, and a 50mph speed limit through endless road works. In a normal car, it's very difficult to stay at that low speed, on a motorway - not to mention frustrating. However, in Landie 50mph is a comfortable cruising speed.

I finally turned off the M6 and headed to my secret beach on the banks of Ullswater. I was intending to do some real wild camper vanning this trip - but still wanted to be near a pub.

Once again, I found myself sitting by a lake, watching the sun go down over the magnificent Cumbrian Mountains, enjoying the solitude. I got a brew on and watched two great-crested grebes rub necks on the water - part of their mating ritual. The noise of the previous night was still pulsing through my head, amplified by the peaceful tranquillity I now found myself in. It seemed impossible that only twenty-four hours ago, I was drinking gin watching humanity cavorting and now I was watching waterfowl do the same.

I was a bit apprehensive about heading up onto the fells alone in the morning. The weather forecast wasn't good, and I was also worried my leg would let me down. I planned a small walk, but mountains always need respect, no matter how small or friendly they appear.

After the sunset, I walked to a local pub and had some food along with the prerequisite number of pints needed to sleep in the back of a Land Rover which, from experience, I knew was three.

In the morning, I woke up to the forecasted rain and the fells looked angry. Their peaks were shrouded in dark menacing clouds but not wanting to waste a precious day in the Lakes, I set off anyway. Soon I found myself climbing a staircase made of stone.

I'm often in awe of the Lakeland paths. When I travel up or down sections made from skilfully laid stones, I think about the toil of their creators – and how much greater it must have been than my own. Ancient shepherds, drovers and Roman soldiers used many of the routes. Although their journeys had purpose and mine are pointless, I'm literally following in the steps of much hardier mortals. While labouring up their paths, I feel connected to them and the mountains they too tried to tame. Undoubtedly, the Alps have a similar human history, but you can't make that connection when skiing down its pistes.

My plan was to summit Sheffield Pike and return via Glenridding Dodd, a modest and relatively low-altitude walk. The lower slopes were relatively easy and would have made for great off-piste skiing. I often think that if only it snowed more in Cumbria the Lakes would make a fine ski resort.

My views were soon obscured by mist and all I could see was the insides of a cloud. I pressed up the path into the heather. Sweat was dripping off my brow and I was blowing like an old steam train. My lack of aerobic fitness was worrying me and I had to keep stopping. At least, I was now training at altitude, I thought. Towards the summit the heather thinned and a rocky landscape unfolded. The visibility was now so bad that navigation was a matter of spotting the next cairn and heading towards it. I thanked those who created the piles of stones that mark my way, across the centuries that separated us. I always try to add one stone to each cairn I pass.

The whiteout demons don't exclusively operate in the Alps. Spotting the next cairn in the mist is a similar game to finding the next piste marker-pole in a whiteout. There is the same fear of getting lost and falling off a cliff. However, with fell walking, you can always go backwards and retrace your steps.

Being lost in the mist on a fell seems less life-threatening than being lost on an alp. There is often the sound of a lamenting ewe calling for her missing lamb, which does give mist-cover fells a more sinister feel. You also have more features to guide you (rivers, walls, fences, sheepfolds). I also have a GPS location system on my phone with a detailed digital OS map – which is cheating I know. It's actually very difficult to get lost on the fells if you have a charged iPhone - unless you are especially talented.

Just short of the summit, I propped myself against a cairn trying to catch my breath. I noticed an apparition approaching through the mist. It had the curvy shape of a tall woman with loose long black hair streaming down to the small of her back. I hadn't seen another living thing, apart from sheep, that morning and I wondered – what new demon was this?   She paused and, looking in my direction, revealed an ashen yet beautiful face with jet-black lips and matching eyebrows - she looked every bit like a vampire. She set off again, altered direction circumventing my cairn well out of fell-banter reach. I just sat there, panting and watching the vampire glide back into the mist.

I pushed on to the summit wondering if the encounter had only taken place in my mind. When I got to the top, I took a selfie with the summit cairn, and congratulated my foot, my leg and my lungs.

Instead of pressing on to the Dodd, I decide that 'a summit in hand, was worth two in the mist' and headed directly down to the Helvellyn Youth Hostel for a cup of tea. The descent was easy and, a couple of hours later, I walked into the hostel triumphantly, only to find my Transylvanian beauty serving behind the counter.

I asked if she had been on the fells that morning. She said 'yes' and that there had been a creepy old man slumped over a cairn 'sweating like a rapist in court'! So she had given him a wide berth. I remained incognito. That encounter meant I'd never forget my return to the fells after injury – and why I've added a cross and some garlic to my list of survival gear.

The weather improved for the rest of my trip and several more summits were ticked off my list. I returned to Sutton Coldfield physically exhausted but mentally refreshed. My ability to continue my summer passion had been restored – I was back in the peak bagging business.

30. Party in Val d'Isère

December had finally arrived and, despite my personal grudge against the Espace Killy, I was glad to be heading there. It meant no more forcing myself out of bed and into Lycra. There would be no more running nor guilt about not running, no more BASI sessions at the Dome nor guilt about missing them either. There would be no more dieting or guilt about eating cake either. The Leader's Refresher Course was just a week away and my body was either ready or it wasn't. All I had to do now was to reintroduce it to off-piste skiing.

I was attending the Ski Club's Premier party in Val d'Isère but I didn't intend to do any partying. I wanted to use the holiday to practise my powder skiing and reacquaint myself with the cols, couloirs and glaciers of Tignes, where most of my ski demons where born. This was my third trip to the demons' home turf and the score was currently one-all. It had been five years since I'd equalised the score and finally passed the Leader Course. I wanted to practise on the actual match pitch.

The last few months of summer 2017 had been unusual, not least because I'd embarked on a fitness campaign. Normally I spend October and November worrying about chalet bookings, Landie problems and generally preparing for a season of hosting in Morzine. But there would be no Season 9 for the Chalet Project; I was no longer a 'chalet host' but simply a 'Ski Club of GB Leader', or at least I was for one more week - if things didn't go well in Tignes, that tenure would also run out.

I waited with anxiety for my skis to arrive in the baggage hall at GVA. If EasyJet had lost my S3's, my campaign would have been off to a terrible start. My skis finally turned up and I wheeled my baggage into the arrivals' hall hoping to find my transfer driver. This isn't always an easy task at GVA on a weekend in the winter, when thousands of skiers try to find hundreds of drivers in a mêlée of skis, bags and message boards.

Some of the larger and more reputable transfer companies make finding their drivers easy. Some have stands emblazoned with their logos, some equip their drivers with large boards on which to display passenger names and some make their drivers wear sombreros! Others rely on the initiative of their passengers. I once spent a frantic hour finding a coach driver, who was asleep in his cab (with his phone turned off) while twenty Club members sat on their suitcases tutting. One driver I found was sat in the café with 'Mr Olinkson' written on the back of a fag packet propped up against his coffee cup. I sometimes think it's a miracle everybody ends up in the right resort.

One of the problems I have with the Espace Killy is that it's a painfully long way from an airport. You're lucky if a transfer there takes less than four hours. The roads are prone to avalanche blockages and traffic jams. One year, hundreds of Christmas holidaymakers got stuck on the road between two avalanches and had to find refuge in a local church hall. I guess this is the risk you take if you want great early-season skiing. You need to be at the top of some really high mountains for guaranteed snow and it's always going to be a long and hazardous journey getting to them.

I found my driver with relative ease, although his other passengers were obscuring his bit of paper with my name on. They had been waiting a while so I apologised and explained that my skis had taken ages to come through.

My traveling companions where a couple of debutant seasonaires, heading to 'Val D' as they called it, a sporty looking couple and a bunch of gobby Northern lads who were heading to Tignes (typical of Tignes clientele in December). Once we'd loaded our cases into the boot, the lads took the back seat, the couple sat in the front with the driver and I sat in the middle row with the seasonaires.

Once underway, the couple started to ask the driver the usual transfer driver questions:

'What's the snow like?'

'How long have you lived in Val?'

'Are you a skier or a boarder?'

There was also a lot of macho bragging and skiing one-upmanship going on in the back so I tuned into the seasonaires' conversation.

Naomi and Finn (classic *gap-yer* names) were, coincidentally, heading to jobs in the same chalet hotel (which was just 'awesomely amazing'). They had never met before and I think Finn took a shine to Naomi – and so did I; she was gorgeous. I think he thought his winter was off to a great start and that the seasonaire life would deliver all it had promised.

Finn's chat-up technique involved painting himself as an international free spirit. He had just spent the summer kite surfing in Mexico (which was 'awesome'). Naomi was from Faversham and had just finished 'uni' at Bristol (which was 'amazing') and her dad was something big in the City. After two hours of listening to this courtship and getting a little irritated with the word 'like' being used as punctuation, we hit a traffic jam caused by a gilets jaunes protest.[14]

I know the French are the masters of revolution but I don't know why holding up tourists helps to put pressure on a government. One protester held up a sign saying 'FREXIT'. Presumably, feeling the French were missing out on the constitutional fun we were having in the UK or that leaving the EU would somehow improve the lives of the disenfranchised.

On seeing the sign, the couple in the front foolishly started talking to the driver about BREXIT. The driver was well informed and gave

---

14 In 2018 French protestors all took to wearing high visibility yellow vests (gilets jaunes). I assume, they were worn as a symbol of solidarity against the policies of the Macron government rather than for safety reasons.

an articulate summary of the referendum result and concluded that the majority of leave voters had been misled. Then a bombastic voice came from the darkness at the back of the van, 'I voted to leave and I knew exactly what I was voting for, mate'.

It's always important to know your audience when offering opinions on politics, religion or snowboarding – the driver had made a big mistake. Now with new input, the BREXIT debate continued with ferocity. After an excruciating two hours of listening to the bulldog in the back argue with the spaniels in the front, I had to interject. 'Guys, there are some spaces that are just too small for politics – and the inside of a transfer van is one of them.' Silence ensued.

Once we reached the Brévières Dam, the Tignes contingent were offloaded into another van and the pro-Europeans continued to Val D. After dropping off the couple and the lovebirds, the driver gave up on finding my hotel and dumped me in its general vicinity.

I stumbled around in the deep snow trying to find my hotel. The directions I'd been given proved to be entirely inaccurate. It was hidden behind a group of other buildings and had no obvious means of entry. I found a door that, unexpectedly, opened into the hotel's bar - I think it was a fire exit. Still burdened with my skis, luggage and airbag, I burst through the door straight into a room of rowdy drinkers. A flurry of snow entered with me to further dramatise my entrance. I had arrived at the Premier Party.

Having made few friends in the transfer van, it was good to see some familiar faces. A Leader I'd qualified with, a guide I'd followed in Les Arcs and a member I'd skied with the previous season - all seemed pleased to see me. The bar buzzed with the loud conversations of hard core skiers – 'I've fallen into a nest of Ski Nazis', I thought to myself.

I had a couple of unavoidable beers with the familiar faces then went to reception to check-in and find out who my roommate would be. Mike was his first name, but I didn't recognise his surname.

I spent the rest of the evening unsuccessfully trying to avoid drinking. I finally found and introduced myself to Mike, who turned out to be a forty year-old Scotsman. Not wanting to sleep with him sober, we propped up the bar together and were the last to leave the party.

I was pleased we had a large room with a significant amount of separation between the beds. I soon fell unconscious on mine having failed to remove my socks. I was woken an hour later by a loud ungodly noise. It could only be describe as the snort of a wild boar followed by the whinny of a stallion - or the snoring of a drunken Scotsman. I suspect that I had been snoring too, but I'd been significantly out gunned.

Day 1

In the morning, having spent most of the night harbouring homicidal thoughts, I went to breakfast shattered hoping some food and coffee would help cure my Cat 5 hangover - it didn't. Luckily, thanks to high winds, all skiing was cancelled. I'd spent a fortune for six days of precious training and I'd just lost one, but I didn't care because it meant I could spend the day sleeping. However, the guides had other ideas and decided that we would spend the day avalanche rescue training.

On my request, I'd been put in the silver group. Most of the skiers on the holiday had purple or gold off-piste skiing grades, but I didn't want to risk being a tail-end-Charlie all week, so I opted for the slower and allegedly, less competent group. I put this choice down to 'recovering from injury' when asked why an existing Leader wanted to go in a silver group. Later that week, I congratulated myself on this decision having discovered my fellow 'team members' were great company, not just great skiers. We had been allocated a young local French guide called Fred. He was a delight too – and proved good at his job.

That night, I hoped Mike might not drink so much and that the previous night had been an aberration but I was treated to a similar performance of animal farm. Worryingly, I noticed he actually stopped breathing for about two minutes between snorts. I suspected he suffered from sleep apnoea – not just alcoholism.

Day 2

In the morning, I gave Mike my diagnosis. But his condition wasn't news to him. He admitted the bloke he'd shared with last year had checked out after two nights. In a bout of emotional honesty, he then told me his last girlfriend had just left him – I didn't ask why, I knew. My training week seemed in tatters.

At least the wind had abated (or at least outside it had) and the lifts were likely to open, so we headed to our 8:30am rendezvous with Fred, at the bottom of the Olympic Télécabine, a bus ride away. Breakfast was a bit of a fiasco. I put this down to teething problems with the new intake of staff. This is always a risk when you book the first week of a season – the staff are often learning on the job. It didn't help that 60 Ski Nazis were all trying to have breakfast at once.

Once at the top of the Olympic, the weather in the Espace Killy did what it mostly does in December – create the perfect conditions for the ski demons to surface. An icy cold wind gusted from the west and driving snow on the summits alternated with floating fog in the valleys to keep visibility permanently limited. Given the conditions, Fred sensibly stayed on or near the pistes and we practised some skiing drills under his instruction.

We skied a couple of black runs, which were essentially off-piste mogul fields and apart from needing to stop after every couple of turns, my leg, my comedy foot and my mind didn't let me down. I think I was too tired to tolerate any nonsense.

209

In the afternoon, I left the group early, intent on securing a single occupancy room for the night. However, the hotel didn't have any empty rooms. So, I walked over to the posh hotel opposite and booked a luxury room for the rest of my stay in Val D and effectively chucked another €850 into my requalification pot. I was intent on getting a good night's sleep at any cost.

My new hotel was elegant and full of sophisticated French folks who helped to remind me that I was actually on a holiday in France. It irritated me that I had paid twice for my week's accommodation. It was even more irritating to know that Mike, once again, had secured a single room without paying a supplement. I grabbed some takeaway food then went to bed early.

Day 3

I woke up in luxury, refreshed and without a hangover (Cat 0). The weather forecast was promising but the avalanche risk was high (4). I rendezvoused with the others, who were discussing the 'shocking' dinner they'd endured at the Club's hotel the previous evening. 'The food was disgusting' and 'the portions were mean' – I suggested the latter was a positive, given the former complaint.

A waitress had even burst into tears after an angry complaint. I felt for her, and irritated that some moron had shouted at a debutant seasonaire – I guess her season wasn't shaping up quite as well as Finn's.

Fred decided to take us over to Tignes, which was good for me because there lay the off-piste I most needed to conquer. Tignes was deserted and generally, throughout the week, we seemed to have the mountains to ourselves. Fred had a good nose for easy powder (powder on slopes less than 30 degrees) and deep power too, which proved exhausting, but great practise.

I had trouble linking my turns and getting my powder bounce going. He kept shouting at me through my *'talkie-walkie'* (a French walkie-talkie), *'wiggle zee ass, wiggle zee ass, wiggle zee ass'*, which made for a rather surreal sound track.

After lunch, Fred took us to the famous/infamous Chardonnay Bowl. After reaching its lip and squeezing between two lumps of exposed rock, a wide expanse of untracked powder presented itself. Although initially steep, the snow was kind and for a moment, I remembered why I liked backcountry skiing. That all ended, when I discovered there would be an hour of side stepping needed to climb out at the bottom – I guess the clue was in the word 'bowl'.

That evening, not wanting to be antisocial, I returned to the party hotel for dinner. It was unlikely I'd get a refund, so I thought I'd get some value out of my original booking. The food wasn't that bad, if a little slow in coming. I discovered a lurgy was going round the party. Many of the partygoers had developed a barking cough. I speculated that they might all be suffering from high altitude pulmonary oedema, having spent too much time above 2500 metres – but concluded they just had a chest infection.

Day 4

The avalanche risk had dropped to 3, which was still considerable. However, I was starting to trust Fred not to get me into something too tricky or buried alive, so I was almost looking forward to the day's skiing.

I was a bit worried when Fred ducked under an orange barrier, a no-no when I'm leading. But we all followed him, assuming he knew what he was doing and that warning barriers didn't apply to guides. He suggested we attached our skis to our rucksacks (never a good sign) then he marched us up 500 metres of a steep piste basher track – which tested my fitness to its limit.

After an all too short breather we remounted our skis, then poled over a plateau, to find yet another expanse of easy untracked powder. I was relieved to see a piste lay at its terminus – so no walkout would be needed. Being in sight of a piste is of great psychological benefit to me. It means, should something bad happen, I know in which direction to crawl.

We all whooped our way down to the piste. There were a few spectacular wipeouts, but mercifully none that involved me, which grew my confidence. Unless you're close enough to help find and recover his skis, one man's wipeout is another man's rest period.

On the way back to Val D, Fred decided to use a deep gully (to the side of the Bellevarde piste). It looked like the world's deepest terrain trap. If the snow had slipped off either side we would have been buried metres deep. Fred assured me that it was safe – but I wasn't convinced. Fred was young for a guide, and hadn't got what I call 'proof of age'. There are old guides and bold guides, but no old, bold ski guides.

Skiing gullies is always great fun. To lose speed you simply head up one side until you almost stop, then you flip round and head back up the other side - which makes you feel like a half-pipe champion.

Trying to impress the imaginary judges with my version of a backside-one-eighty, I soon forgot about all the snow above my head. Seeing the end of the gully approaching I straightened up and planned a high-speed exit from the imaginary pipe – the finale to my trick routine. Now in a tuck position, I heard the flapping of canvas behind me. Initially I thought my airbag had accidentally deployed, but before I could stop and check, a pair of skis whistled passed my ears – a ski borne paraglider[15] had flown over my head.

He had recklessly flown (literally) down the same gully not expecting to see a skier blocking its exit. I shouted at the human bird, but he was long gone before he'd heard all my creative adjectives.

Day 5

I woke to a rather misty day. After an early start and in my case, a civilised breakfast, we all set off again for Tignes. We ducked under the same warning barrier and repeated the previous day's hike. This

15 Ski paragliding, also known as "Ski Gliding" This is an extreme sport that amounts to pa-ra-gliding off a mountain while skiing. Technically speaking, it's ski-launched paragliding. The primary difference is that Ski Paragliding usually involves flying, while paraskiers remain mostly on the terra firma.

time we turned left instead of right at the end of the plateau and continued some distance further before halting at what appeared to be a sheer drop into a white abyss.

It had been three days since the last snowfall and I think Fred was struggling to find us easy to access fresh powder. Guides pride themselves on finding their clients un-skied slopes. This causes them to go deeper and deeper into the backcountry in order to find them. Three days after a dump, the snow is often more stable and less likely to avalanche. So you're more likely to die from exhaustion trying to reach pristine powder, than suffocating under it.

It was impossible to make out what lay below us. The light was so bad and the snow so featureless, it was hard to determine the contours of the valley beneath. 'Surely we're not going down there?' I thought. In dropped Fred.

Fred disappeared into the whiteout and like the vapour trail from a missing aeroplane, his tracks were the only sign that he had once existed. His tracks gave the valley definition, and judging by the deep scar his first turn had made, the snow was several metres deep. A couple of the group dropped in ahead of me, complying with avalanche protocol – one at a time, leaving a large gap. Their tracks added more definition, but waiting for them to get safely ahead was agonising. Finally it was my turn and with heart now firmly in mouth, I dropped in too.

I landed my first turn successfully, throwing snow up into my goggles – but this didn't matter because the next few turns were always going to be conducted purely on feel. After a few exhausting turns, I stopped to wipe my goggles revealing an animated Fred eulogising about the snow in front of me.

The valley soon flattened and the visibility improved. I noticed Fred was now following a single set of ski tracks – we weren't the first down the valley since it had last snowed after all. Which was disappointing for Fred but a relief for me.

Seeing tracks ahead can provide false comfort and following them can be a mistake. They do confirm that at least one person has already ventured where you are about to go. If they are the tracks of a single skier you might assume their creator had good local knowledge and therefore the route you're on is viable. However, if you follow them into the unknown you are gambling that the tracks will lead to safety not to a frozen body.

Worse, if the tracks you are following suddenly stop (and there is no corpse), you won't know if you have been following a paraskier towards a cliff or if wolves had taken the body away. If you haven't brought your parachute, both these scenarios will trouble you when following a single skier's tracks.

Once you start following a set of single tracks, you'll start to wonder about their creator and if your skiing ability is equal to theirs? They may be heading towards some extreme terrain, where no sane skier would want to follow, which would explain why they were skiing alone.

In this instance, the tracks confirmed Fred wasn't pioneering a new route. After a couple of kilometres, the tracks turned up a hill. Judging by the disturbed snow, their creator had stopped to put skins on his skis. We followed, but without skins progress was painful - particularly for me. My twin tipped skis offered no backward resistance. My poles didn't have very big baskets either, and they kept disappearing into the snow if I pushed too hard on them. None of us were equipped for ski touring or 'uphill skiing' as I call it.

Once over the hill the tracks headed downwards and gravity, once again, provided propulsion. Thinking the slog was over I relaxed, and admired a fleeting glimpse through the clouds of the Brévières Dam below – which helped me get a fix on our location.

The sun was forcing its way through the clouds too and the temperature was rising. I started stripping off layers trying to cool down after all my exertion. It always amazes me how quickly I can switch from being mildly hypothermic to mildly hyperthermic when skiing – the latter is probably due to poor aerobic fitness.

The tracks took us towards a wooded area where they joined what must have been a goat path during the summer. The path consisted of many little schusses, between closely grouped trees. We followed the path which traversed around into the next valley.

Before leaving the trees, the path narrowed and dipped round the lip of a deep ravine. With a steep rocky face on one side and the ravine on the other, the path had effectively turned into a shelf. The edge of the shelf was showing signs of erosion and had partly crumbled into the ravine, leaving barely enough room at its narrowest for two parallel skis.

The ski demons quick spotted the shelf section of the path and declared it a 'no fall zone' – an area where falling would be fatal. So they decided to have a party of their own in my head.

It was essential to attack this section at high speed in order to get up the other side of the dip. The exit slope being only two feet at its widest, side stepping or herringboning up it wasn't an option. Fred made it look easy, but by the time it was my turn to make the do-or-die manoeuvre, the ski demon party was in full swing.

I set off trying to fully commit myself to gravity, but I ran out of momentum a couple of metres short of safety and started sliding back down the path towards the open mouth of the ravine. I frantically grabbed at a bush above me and used it to claw my way to the others waiting at the top – who seemed to find my predicament amusing. After calming down, I thanked a god I didn't believe in, for growing the bush.

Next, we found ourselves in a clearing with small saplings sticking up through the snow, which concerned me. A swathe of small saplings surrounded by fully-grown trees is a sign of recent avalanche activity.[16]

The saplings got bigger and more densely packed. They gave me physiological comfort, but caused havoc in the ranks. Every time someone hooked a ski around one and fell, they disappeared from view and were only locatable by skiing towards the post wipeout laughter.

While wondering if this was *really* Fred's intended exit route I noticed he had his mobile phone to his ear. Had his wife called him about a domestic matter? Was he booking a restaurant for lunch? In my pessimistic mind, I concluded he was calling for advice on how to get out of the forest.

Finally we came across a piste – it was closed, but it meant civilisation was close. When I sidestepped onto what turned out to be a red run, I promptly fell over on its icy surface. While lying bemused, staring at the sky, I noticed a huge raptor circling above me – it was almost certainly a Bearded Vulture.[17] Worried I was looking too much like carrion, I quickly got up and followed Fred down the piste into Brévières - where Fred had indeed, just booked at table.

Instead of being lunch, I ate lunch with the others. None of the Brévières lifts were open, it was too early in the season, so after lunch we caught a taxi back to Val D and another great adventure was in the bag.

---

16 Avalanches often cut swathes through forests and saplings grow in place of the felled trees. The size (and therefore the age) of the saplings indicated how long ago the original trees were knocked down. Small saplings might indicate that avalanches frequently pass through that section of the forest. Of course, the forest might just be managed and the trees cut down by humans.

17 The Bearded Vulture, also know as the Lammergeyer, was thought to pray on lambs and small children, so it was hunted to extinction in the early 19th century. After proving that its diet consisted almost exclusively of skeletal remains conservationists successfully reintroduced it into the Southern Alps in 1987. It has a wingspan of 2.5m, with a beak and talons to match and you wouldn't want a close encounter with one.

That evening, after a little après, I joined my new comrades at a fancy restaurant in town. They had given up on the catering at the party hotel. An exquisite, if expensive, meal was enjoyed all served with fine French wine and a lot of ski banter – finally I was at an actual party in Val d'Isère.

Day 6

I woke up with self-diagnosed pulmonary oedema. It's always hard to tell if you're ill or just hung-over, when you've enjoyed yourself the night before. When you're over fifty, you feel pretty lousy most mornings, irrespective of your nocturnal activities, so it gets really difficult to tell. However, I was coughing like an old coalminer, who smoked twenty Bensons a day. So I concluded I'd caught the Premier Party lurgy.

'Bloody typical', I thought, 'the one week I need to be well and I'm ill!' I cursed the bush-growing god. I decided to abandon skiing for the day, and rest. I would spend my last day wandering around Val D then enjoy my last night in single room luxury. I suspected my room in Tignes would be primitive and, knowing my luck, I'd have to share it with another Neanderthal.

31. Loneliness Versus Irritation

Assuming one is not an unpopular person (let's also assume the author has friends) then going on holiday by oneself might seem a bit sad. It's one thing to go on a skiing holiday to ski with other single skiers, but another to go into the mountains alone.

People often engage in solo activities because they don't have anyone to do them with. I'm blessed with a lot of free time in the summer and my friends (imaginary or otherwise) are cursed with full time employment. But that's not the main reason I often go fell walking on my own.

When I walk alone, I cross paths with many other solo walkers and most stop for a chat. They are usually pleasant and affable, which suggests that they too might have friends, so why have we chosen to walk alone?

However easy going you think a holiday companion might be, when you are held in close confines with anyone for a period of time, they inevitably become irritating. Simply agreeing the day's itinerary or choosing where to eat and drink can lead to disagreement. I find that those who say, 'I'll just go with the flow' are usually the most problematic. When you holiday alone, you can simply please yourself.

After a season of chalet hosting, and constantly being in the company of people (often strangers), it's refreshing to live, albeit in the back of a Land Rover, alone – at least for a few days. It also gives me a break from the irritations of family life in the summer. Living with teenagers is always tough – especially if they are not your own.

After a season leading skiers, it's pleasant to engage in an activity without any concern for others. I don't have to worry that I'm going too fast, too slow or that I've chosen a walk that is too long, too difficult or too scary for anyone other than myself. Nobody else will suffer the consequences of my navigational mistakes. The only person that I'm going to get lost or damaged is myself. It is possible to go on a skiing holiday alone, but not so easy to find solitude on a ski slope.

The main disadvantage with walking on your own is motivation. When I wake, tired from the previous day's exploits, I often think, 'Can I *really* be bothered?' I find it hard to get out of my sleeping bag. It's easy to find an excuse for not getting up, roll over and go back to sleep. You can convince yourself, the weather looks 'iffy' or that some minor injury needs resting and there is nobody around to give you a boot.

Once I've given myself a little pep talk, I usually crawl out of Landie and set off. I soon start enjoying the environment and find it hard to believe I harboured thoughts of packing up and driving Landie home. Then, when the going gets tough, the self-gratification is replaced with the reality of the lonely task ahead.

When the slopes steepen and sweat starts pouring, I start to wonder. 'What on earth am I doing this for?' Then I look up at my intended summit, which seems impossibly high and far away, I think, 'Only masochistic pleasure can be gained from this day', then I harbour thoughts of turning back.

It's much harder to halt an ascent when you're walking with fellow masochists. They can be strong when you are feeling weak, and vice versa. They can also convince you the prize is worth winning, because they desire it themselves.

When walking in company conversation can be a welcome distraction. A joke is often offered to boost morale, 'It looked much flatter on the map'. Words of encouragement are uttered, 'We are nearly halfway' or 'I have a pork pie we can share at the top'. I often utter such sentiments to boost my own morale more than that of my companions.

Once there are more contour lines on the map below than above me, thoughts of turning back are replaced with summit fever. I think,

'Whatever happens, I'm getting to the top of this bloody mountain'. I don't want to waste the effort already invested by failing to capture my prize – the summit selfie. I also know, if I did turn back, I'd have to start from the bottom again on another day. I'm driven upwards by a desire to tick another mountain off my Wainwright list.

Avalanche avoidance experts would call this mentality, 'over commitment to a goal'. Sticking to a planned off-piste route, no matter what snow conditions are encountered, is common. If a group of skiers has spent hours hiking to the top of a famous couloir, then pretty much nothing is going to stop them from skiing down it. All wisdom is forgotten and any signs of impending avalanche the mountain has provided are ignored. The group's attitude is often, 'Let's just do it', when 'Let's just *not* do it' is often the best suggestion.

The biggest disadvantage of climbing a fell alone is there is nobody to celebrate with when you reach the top or indeed take the important summit photographs. There is nobody to salivate with over the approaching beer when you descend and nobody to relive the adventure with, when you finally get that pint in your hand.

Allegedly no fan of humanity, Wainwright preferred to walk the fells alone. However, he chose to document his routes and share his thoughts in his guidebooks. While making notes up on the fells, he must have felt the imaginary company of his future readers. I like to think that, even though I hadn't been born, I was walking with him in spirit. When I retrace his steps, he is effectively walking with me, especially if I've read his guide to the fell the night before (which I invariably do). In my head, I often hold conversations with him. When I catch myself doing this (wandering the fells talking to an imaginary old man), I question my sanity – too much loneliness can send a person insane.

However, when walking solo my fortitude is tested on the way up, my self-esteem is nourished at the top and my inner survivalist is fed on the way down - then my ego is watered in the pub. I enjoy the scenery, the fresh air and the challenge. I might feel lonely, but I enjoy convening with nature and visiting bleak places high up, although I never hang around for long on summits when I'm on my own. If I'm honest, I enjoy visiting them more with other people. The human mind wasn't really designed to be on its own.

I do enjoy the selfish aspect of my solo trips. Some seek solace in solitude but I use it as an antidote to months in the crowded Alps and the irritation of others. But I prefer irritation to loneliness most of the time. However, it's good to occasionally choose loneliness – especially if, like me, you're not keen on sharing your pork pies.

32. Strictly Come Dancing on Snow

It was a short taxi ride from Val D to Tignes Le Lac, where the Ski Club had booked a chalet hotel for the Refresher Course. None of the rooms were ready, so I went for a wander down to the frozen lake and the shops, bars and restaurants surrounding it.

I couldn't believe five years had elapsed since I'd last seen the place. The memories of triumph and defeat were still vivid. I looked up at the surrounding mountains, and remembered how exhausted, overwhelmed and frightened they had once made me feel. But it was a mild, sunny day and they looked benign. It helped that I'd already spent a week flushing the demons out of them. 'Those mountains are now my friends', I murmured to myself, not really believing my own voice. I reflected on my journey – not the taxi ride from Val D, that had been uneventful, but the metaphysical road I'd taken to Tignes.

Everyone seems to have been on a 'journey' these days – nobody ever seems to just travel anymore. I know it's a term for the tribulations faced on the route to success, or indeed failure, but the metaphor grates. If, the motivational poster is right, and 'life is a journey not a destination' then death must be the destination it refers to. So it doesn't really matter what path we choose for our journey – possibly the longest one is best. I also yawn when people say, 'You only live once'. Apart from ignoring the promise of most major religions, it's a statement of the obvious offered to justify doing something stupid that might end that singular life – 'And you only die once' is my usual reply.

My 'journey' to Tignes hadn't started in Val D, but in a helicopter in Switzerland nine months earlier. I'd travelled via the hospitals in

Thonon and Birmingham, and then I'd been marooned on Labrador Island for a while. I'd returned to Morzine triumphantly and driven Landie back across France – very fast. I'd summited a Lakeland fell or two and been up and down a ladder with a screwdriver in my mouth a countless number of times. I'd ascended and descended the slope at the Snow Dome more than a few times too. I'd run in circles around the streets of Wylde Green, on many a cold morning, trying to get fit. Tignes had been my ultimate destination and now I had arrived. I'd battled with my foot to get there and now the real battle was afoot.

I tried to put the next four days into perspective; I told myself, 'nothing of magnitude is actually at stake – just five more years of subsidised skiing'. But, being a Ski Club Leader was important to my existential subconscious, and I felt like an athlete who had just arrived at the Olympics.

I wasn't after gold, but I needed a podium finish. I needed to improve or at least keep, my purple grade (two down from gold), both on and off piste, if I were to keep my blue jacket. I also harboured ambitions of improving my Leading grade, (from a C to a B) so that I might be sent to more famous resorts.

On returning to the hotel I discovered my roommate would be Duncan, a mild mannered Leader who often attended BASI nights at the Dome. I was pleased, assuming his sleeping habits would be far removed from those of the drunken Scotsman – I was more likely to disturb his sleep with my coughing.

After entering our room, and discovering that the beds were a mere six inches apart, I looked out of the window. I had a clear view of Trolles, the black run I'd spent a harrowing morning probing avalanche debris for a body seven years earlier. It would be a grim reminder for the next three days of how dangerous Tignes could be in December.

Before dinner we meet the 'training team', our guides and judges for the course. There were some familiar faces in the line-up. Cathy and Roland, who had given me the thumbs down, on my first attempt to pass the Leader Course. Shep's face was missing. He had given me the thumbs up two years later, but he had since retired. A new face, Bruce, was now the Ski Club Chief Safety Officer. I hoped that I would be in Cathy's, or indeed Bruce's, group, but flinched at the thought of skiing with Roland.

The only Frenchman amongst them, Roland had a reputation for fast, relentless skiing. We had become better acquainted, since our first snowy encounter. He had stayed with me in Morzine during Season 6 – and proved not to be the skiing ogre of club legend, but a friendly and entertaining man. I had a chat with him first.

I told him about my injury and being no lover of snowboarding, he sympathised, '*zee problem with boarders iz you can't tell which way zay are about to turn*' – which could equally be true of some skiers. He had been under the knife too. Both knees had been replaced, making him bionic.

After a welcome chat from Bruce, I went to the noticeboards to discover my fate. I had been assigned to Cathy's group on the first day, Bruce's on the second and Richard's (a guide unknown to me) for my third day of the course. I also discovered who my 'team mates' would be: George (recently voted 'Leader of the Year'), Suzie (soon to become teacher's pet), another Chris (which would prove confusing), Bob (a dour Brummie) and Zoe who was a snowboarder!

It is completely possible to lead a bunch of skiers on a snowboard. There are even a few advantages to using a snowboard – none of which spring to mind. But speed isn't one of them. She would keep the group at a steady pace, but my newfound phobia of snowboard edges played on my mind.

The course itself would involve first-lift/last-lift skiing, bracketed by early morning and evening mountain safety lectures. They would include videos of real incidents and fatalities. We would basically be shown the many ways you can die on a snow-covered mountain, then be expected to follow our guides into avalanche territory.

Dinner was a sober affair, or at least it was for me. It had the feel of a school reunion, most leaders refreshing for the first time since passing the Leaders' course together. Like any school reunion, some pupils had grown gregarious, some boastful, some liked to play the fools. Some leaders were interesting; others were just loud and irritating. There would be no opportunity for loneliness in the small packed hotel for the next few days. All present were bound by their experiences in a blue jacket. We all had one thing in common – a uniform fetish. I went to bed early to get a head start on the snoring.

Day 1

After a restless night of snoring and coughing, I woke up with a feeling of dread. The weather had taken a turn for the worse. It was snowing and the mountains were draped in low cloud. It would be a cold day of skiing in poor visibility. My cough had got worse and I apologised to Duncan for keeping him awake most of the night with my whooping.

After a morbid 8am lecture, I headed to the boot room to saddle up. Unfortunately the heated boot rack hadn't been turned on. After an exhausting thirty minute fight with my frozen right boot, I finally got it on. I vowed to sleep with my ski boots on the following night.

I met Cathy and the others by the lifts. Everyone was on their best behaviour, and trying to sound knowledgeable, while Cathy went through the day's briefing. The poor visibility meant the off-piste skiing would be limited, which was good news for me - there would be no aerobically challenging backcountry skiing.

We took it in turns to lead under Cathy's gaze, which was a matter of spotting the next piste marker through the pea soup. Cathy repeatedly kept losing her rucksack in the snow and imploring us to find it quickly. We had to pretend the rucksack was an avalanche victim with only 15mins of life expectancy if they remained under the snow. Luckily she had left a transceiver in her rucksack and, more importantly, she had remembered to turn it on.

It is surprising how difficult it is to use a transceiver in search mode. Each model operates slightly differently, and it becomes difficult to interpret the beeps and arrows they try to communicate with. You can often follow their directions round in a circle if you're not familiar with a specific device. That is why it's always best to buy and regularly play with, a transceiver of your own.

Over lunch Cathy shared her own avalanche horror story, when she alone saw a couple buried under a mountain of snow. On arriving at the scene, Cathy had picked up the wife's transceiver signal first and dug until the victim's airway was clear. Then Cathy set about finding the husband. Unfortunately, he was buried in an inverted position and by the time further help arrived to help dig down to his head, he had died. Luck had saved the wife. Had Cathy locked on to the husband's transceiver first, probably neither would have survived. It was a sober and sobering lunch.

In the afternoon we met two of the other groups and to our surprise, all the guides lost their rucksacks simultaneously. With so many Leaders trying to take charge (and impress the judges), chaos ensued. Cathy played the distressed friend of one of the buried rucksacks. She tried to mislead us about how many people were supposedly missing and where they were last seen – the point being confused eyewitnesses should never be trusted.

I was on the scene when the first rucksack was dug out. To save me from further personal exhaustion, I declared that 'the victim wasn't breathing', so I gave the rucksack CPR, while the others continued to stumble around in the snow trying to find the other rucksacks.

My fear of being responsible for a rescue is almost equal to that of being a victim. Should I not be successful I'd be haunted by thoughts of what I might have done differently. To perform a successful rescue quick thinking and a cool head are needed or, failing that, an ingrained procedure to automatically follow. This was the real purpose of the repetitive training – to engrain that procedure. Moving around in deep snow, never mind frantically digging, is exhausting. Even if I did start digging in the right place, it worries me that someone's life might depend on my fitness.

Thanks largely to Cathy's misinformation, the last rucksack was taking ages to find. By now the light was fading and the lifts were closing so the guides started to help find it – I think its owner had accidentally left his wallet inside. Once it was exhumed, there was a cavalry charge in the dim light down a mogul field. All the horses had tired legs, and there were many fallers.

Once back at Le Lac, Cathy concluded we had all done well and I concluded that Day 1 had been a success. We'd spent more of it digging than skiing, but we'd all proven to be effective at finding lost property. After another chilling lecture and a little wine, I went to bed early and cuddled my ski boots.

Day 2

The next morning we set off with Bruce. The weather hadn't improved so, once again, we couldn't stray far from the pistes. He also let each of us lead in turn, all were keen to prove they could find powder to the side of the pistes. It was hard to determine the contours of the terrain, and frankly foolhardy to leave the piste without intimate knowledge of what lay beside it. Avalanches weren't the risk, but getting stuck in a dip between pistes would have proven exhausting to walk out of – not to mention embarrassing.

The visibility improved towards lunchtime and a few decent pitches of fresh powder were found, all of which I survived. Bruce was intent on finding the perfect place to dig a snow pit.

The purpose of a snow pit is to expose the historic layers of snow in order to establish the snow pack stability. On a steep-ish slope, using an ice saw, a section of snow is removed all the way down to the soil. A skilled eye can determine how easily one layer of snow will slide over another thus predicting the likelihood of an avalanche in that vicinity. The science is fascinating but the practicality of digging a pit at the top of every slope before you ski it is questionable – so is carrying a saw around with you all day. But, perhaps, doing it at the beginning of a trip would prove useful, if only to learn what might be lurking under your skis for the next few days.

We all dug our own snow pits, making the scene reminiscent of sandcastle building competition. Bruce pointing out several worrying weaknesses in the snowpack he had spotted in his pit - weaknesses that I'd been obliviously skiing on top of for most of the previous week.

It soon became my turn to lead again and I spotted a pitch to the left of the piste I knew was safe. It wasn't exactly untracked but the powder was fluffy and deep and it looked safe. I set off, making large sweeping turns to save energy. The pitch was very wide and the whole group spread out behind me.

Halfway down, I noticed George and I were on a collision course, him sweeping in from the right and me sweeping in from the left. I adjusted upwards, tightening my turn – so did George. I adjusted down – so did George. It was a complete replay of my collision with Max (the Swiss snowboard assassin), only this time we were traveling fast and off piste.

I braced myself for a head on collision thinking, 'Oh no - not again!' Images from Labrador Island and the Queen Elizabeth Hospital flashed through my head. Luckily, in the last second of opportunity, we both swerved left and avoided a head on collision (we were both English after all). We did clip shoulders though, sending both of us flying.

After an injury self-assessment, and finding no blood on my trousers or in the snow around me, I asked George if he was okay. But he was struggling to get up - something to do with his dodgy knee. With Bruce's help he finally got remounted, but was clearly not a happy man. I think he thought the collision was my fault and I'd put his course result in jeopardy. Although clearly in pain, he did manage to ski on.

That evening a rumour was circulating around the hotel that I'd 'taken George out'. I was keen to point out that I'd started the descent before him and he was technically overtaking me and therefore it was his responsibility to avoid hitting me. I did feel sorry for George, a popular and extremely pleasant man, but it was just bad luck we had collided and he had come off worst. The last person I'd collided with had walked away and I'd ended up in a hospital. Collisions just happen when you ski in proximity to others, no matter how diligent the participants think they are being.

Day 3

Finally, on the last day the sun came out and thankfully George seemed to have forgiven me and was skiing well. The purpose of the day was to see if we could plan and execute a day of fun, yet safe, off-piste skiing. Much discussion, but little consensus, had taken place the previous evening; although we had agreed to ski over to Val D and the order in which we would lead. We set off with the new guide Richard in tow, not knowing anything about him.

We skied down the icy La face de Bellevarde, Val D's signature black run which proved a bit tricky on powder skis and onto the Solaise area. Richard derided us a little for ignoring what he thought were great, and eminently skiable off piste pitches we had failed to spot on the journey.

When it was my turn to lead, I could see potential danger in just about every piece of snow that wasn't laying on a piste. I'm not sure too much knowledge can be a bad thing, but after three days of avalanche avoidance training, I'd subconsciously decided the only safe thing to do was stay on pistes. I think Richard got a little frustrated with me regurgitating information from the lectures to justify not skiing down what he thought were safe slopes.

At one stage he tried to persuade me to take everyone beyond a line of cliff warning signs, because the snow there was untracked. Assuming this was some sort of test, I flatly refused. I found out later he had been serious. The cliff was actually quite a long way from the warning signs but he had that local knowledge and I did not.

On the way back, I hesitated when Richard suggested we skied down the Bellevarde gully. I explained my reluctance. It was a massive terrain trap and although it looked like hundreds of skiers had been down it already their tracks were no guarantee that it was safe - he hadn't considered the potential for an airborne assault from paragliders either!

He complimented me for being studious then suggested we all skied down it anyway, because it would be great fun – it was.

Bob chose the final pitch of the day. Access was via a long traverse, which was especially painful for me with my dodgy right foot, and no doubt equally torturous for George with his dodgy knee. I was resentful that Bob had decided on such a difficult pitch so late in the day, but I guess it was his time to shine and he wanted to impress.

I peeled off early then found myself isolated in a gully that was two metres deep in churned up powder – I think it was a closed black run. I started to panic, 'one fall here and I'm toast', I thought. I knew only twenty successful turns would be needed to reach the lift below, but my head was suddenly filled with demons and I fell.

I spent the next thirty minutes flaying around in the snow trying to find my skis, all alone with nobody to help me. Being out of sight, nobody even knew I'd gone down. 'Typical', I thought, 'after all I've been through– this is how it ends'. Finally I found both my skis, remounted them and skied to the lift. I kept the incident quiet. 'If nobody sees you fall – it doesn't count as a fall,' I reminded myself.

Before dinner that night I reflected on the course. It had been much easier than I'd expected. The collision aside, I'd only fallen over once and importantly nobody had seen that. The skiing I'd done with Fred the previous week had taken me much deeper into the backcountry and further out of my comfort zone. If passing it hadn't been so important to me, the course would have been an enjoyable three days of mostly pleasant skiing.

Just before dinner, the guides took us individually aside for a debrief and the unceremonious handing over of our new grades. I was relieved to find I was still rated as a purple/purple skier and delighted my leading grade had increased to a B.

Dinner would have been a riotous affair, had everyone not been shattered. But a good effort was made at the bar afterwards. Most folks were celebrating but a few were disappointed with their grades and bemoaned the injustice of those awarded to others. Judging skiing ability is a very subjective business.

A few leaders had been downgraded, but nobody had lost their right to wear the blue jacket. Nobody was standing alone, the only failure in a room of success, as I had done seven years earlier.

I woke up early with my socks still on and therefore knew a category 5 hangover awaited me. I was coughing like an elephant seal with bronchitis but in between hacks I was chuckling silently. I was still on a high from my triumph over injury and ski demons – most of all I was relieved that I didn't have to go skiing that day. All I had to do was sit on a coach to GVA, fly home and then sleep for a week.

Unfortunately the transfer coach didn't turn up. After waiting for an hour, it was looking like I'd miss my flight. So I flagged down a cab and, with five other leaders in a similar predicament, I persuaded the driver to take us to GVA. It would be expensive, but we were all past caring.

It was a high speed and painful journey. It was a painful journey for me, because the bloke behind talked about his pump manufacturing business for three hours without pause. It was painful for everyone else too, because I coughed the whole way to Geneva – but at least no one mentioned BREXIT.

Thanks to some spirited driving, we made it to GVA in time – for my flight at least. With hindsight, that journey was probably the most dangerous part of my ten-day adventure.

I flew home, looking forward to getting fat and unfit over Christmas. I was physically broken, but I had secured my prize. I had five more years of subsidised skiing in the bag, five more years of skiing at the front and five more years of skiing in blue – or so I thought.

33. THE END OF AN ERA

After Tignes there was the small matter of surviving Christmas, then Debbie and I flew to Morzine for New Year. For once, we were not hosting New Year's Eve in a chalet but would be guests in someone else's.

It felt very decadent, flying to Morzine, although I did feel guilty about leaving Landie behind. But she was surplus to requirements. No bacon needed importing, no guests needed ferrying around and sadly no wine or duck needed bringing home - Season 9 would be a Land Rover free season.

Not having a vehicle in the Alps was occasionally problematic but it was less inconvenient than having a problematic vehicle. I did miss hacking around the Alps in a classic Defender. Without Landie by my side, I looked like just another tourist.

Seemingly disappointed that the Project was over, the Ski Nazis started their own mini chalet project and rented a place in Morzine for January and March. I spent several weeks with them and also went on Scouse Week that season, which was a reminiscent blast - although my liver regretted it.

That season, The Club also sent me to Saas Fee and Méribel. I fell in love with Saas Fee, but not so much with Méribel, my visit having overlapped with the school holidays. In total, I spent nine weeks in the Alps that season. I spent far more time actually skiing in Season 9 than any previous season – and cooked significantly fewer eggs.

I missed seeing and skiing with my regular guests and I tried to keep in touch with some of them. I was buoyed by the news that Ukulele Dave retook and passed his Level-2 and was back in love with skiing once again.

Some might conclude that if you live a dream, then stop, it wasn't a successful venture. Others would say, 'all good things come to an end'. But really, dreams don't end, they evolve. I was still living a winter dream - to spend my winters in the Alps - the dream had just become peripatetic. The Chalet Project wasn't really over - it just needed re-branding.

My summers had evolved nicely too. I had a proper job and thanks to my Landie Van, I could spend most of my free time in the Lake District. Being self-employed meant I could choose when I worked and that wasn't very often. However, just being an electrician was an effective existential tonic. I didn't need to do much *actual* work to prove my value to society.

I was all set to repeat Season 9, the following winter (2019/20). The Club had already allocated me two weeks of leading in Saas Fee and another back marking in Les Deux Alpes, a place I've always wanted to visit. The Ski Nazis had rebooked their Morzine chalet, so my Morzine fix was assured. I looked all set for the season and indeed for three winters beyond it - and no skier over fifty needs to plan further ahead than that.

Then the agents of entropy stuck, this time masquerading as lawyers. In July (2019), The Club unexpectedly announced the end of its leading service!

The Club had removed its leaders in France a few years back, after one was arrested for allegedly teaching without the necessary qualifications. A long and expensive legal battle ensued between the Club and the ESF.[18] The Club's lawyers unsuccessfully tried to point out that Leaders were unpaid volunteers and we simply skied at the front, like the most experienced skier would do with his friends. The argument and case were ultimately lost. In the eyes of the judge, because we had our expenses paid, we were receiving remuneration,

---

18 Along with a fine tradition of skiing excellence, the Ecole du Ski Français (The ESF) have a reputation for vigorously defending their livelihood and their mountains from invading foreign instructors. Unlike other Alpine countries, an English instructor needs to be qualified to BASI Level-4, before the ESF will accept he is competent enough to teach on their mountains.

so we *were* acting as professionals (not volunteers) and therefore under French law, we needed to have the prerequisite qualifications.

Officials at the Club became increasing worried that what happened in France would happen in other countries, even though other nationalities are not quite so good at running a closed shop.

A debate raged about who would be responsible if someone got injured or died while following a Leader - possibly the Leader, possibly the directors of the Club. So the Club sought legal advice. It was postulated that the most experienced skier in any group of friends, would be responsible for the safety of all who skied with them and legally accountable for any mishaps. Basically, nobody could ski with anyone of lesser ability, without the risk of being sued.

Sadly, we live in an age where everyone looks to blame someone else for their own misfortune – and get compensation. Perhaps I missed an opportunity to cash-in on my own injury? Max was a professional instructor and must have had liability insurance. But not once did I think of suing him. Having published this book declaring my injury wasn't really his fault, I think that window of opportunity has now passed.

On a recent first-aid refresher course, I was advised to keep medical interventions to a minimum, while I waited for qualified paramedics to arrive. I would be liable for any action I took, however well intended, if it exacerbated an injury. It seemed to me that the safest option was to let the casualty die. If this suing culture doesn't abate, or laws are not changed, we will soon be at a stage were nobody dares to do anything for anyone.

I don't blame the Club for seeking further legal advice; a precedent had been set by the French judge and if another case came to court, the Club wouldn't have a leg to stand on (no skiing pun intended). However, 'to seek permission, is to court denial' and that's especially true if you seek it from a lawyer. They too, are worried about being sued for giving incorrect advice. It's less risky for them to say 'no' than 'yes' and both answers have the same billable value.

The upshot of all this was, after a hundred and seventeen years of facilitating safe social skiing, the Skiing Club of GB was now too worried about being sued to provide any on-snow services - it was the end of an era.

Surprisingly, the Club still intended sending me to Saas Fee for two weeks the following season. But I wasn't allowed to ski with members – or at least not in any official capacity or indeed in my blue jacket. I would now be called a 'Rep' and my duties would involve organising social activates and the hiring of professional guides – if enough members wanted to stump up for one.

I was initially horrified that I would be called a 'Rep'. It would be a massive existential downgrade from being called a 'Leader'.

I was also outraged that now anyone could become a Ski Club Rep – no skiing prowess was needed. It felt like a proud military regiment had been disbanded and the ceremonial uniforms were being handed out to any Tom, Finn or Tarquin. I felt sad that there would no longer be a Leaders' *esprit de corps*. [19]

I felt cheated out of my hard-earned five years of skiing at the front. I felt sorry for the debutant Leaders who had just passed the gruelling (and expensive) Leaders' course only six months earlier - their blue jackets would never see action - I realised it also meant I would need to buy a new ski jacket.

Actually I needed to replace a lot of my skiing kit. My helmet had cracked, my goggles were scratched, my ski boots had become painful again, my transceiver needed updating and my S3's had started to delaminate – I needed new powder skis. I thought, 'Maybe this is a good time to give up skiing before it needs another round of

---

19 Subsequently, the Club decided that 'Reps' would still need to take the 'Leaders' course, re-fresh every five years and be a purple/purple graded skier. I'm writing this in a time of flux - so don't take my words here as Ski Club gospel.

investment? Maybe I should use the money to buy a set of golf clubs instead?'

After a couple of weeks I remembered that I didn't like golf and it was seldom played in the mountains. So I started to think more positively. Being a Rep would make my life easier. I'd still get all the perks of being a leader; I'd still have my skiing subsidised; but I wouldn't have the responsibility for looking after members on the snow. I'd just have to drink with them and I was good at that. I was undisputedly a 'gold' standard après skier.

Perhaps the Club would soon grade its resorts for après action and indeed a Rep's ability to handle it. Morzine would obviously be an 'A' class après resort. Laax (darling) would, like most of the Swiss resorts, be a 'C'. St Anton would be an 'A+'. I'd begrudgingly give Val D a 'B', for being the home of the Folie Douce brand of après bars. Although I prefer establishments where the dancing on tables is spontaneous and frowned upon by their proprietors, rather than actively encouraged.

I did worry that membership of the Club would drop without offering a free leading service. I postulated that it wouldn't be long before even Reps would be surplus to the Club's requirements. Ending the leading service might be the death of the Club.

I resigned myself to being a Rep and hoped none of the above would come true. At least being a Rep meant I'd never have to take another refresher or first aid course again – or return to Tignes. But I couldn't escape the fact that attending the refresher course had been a pointless and expensive exercise. Once again, I'd stressed and worried about something that turned out to be inconsequential. One thing at least, the looming course had motivated me to make a speedy recovery from injury – it had provided me with a goal and a deadline. 'What endeavour in life is not ultimately pointless?' I asked myself.

Having passed the refresher course I could at least declare that my leg and foot were now fully operational. I have, however, still not regained the fine motors skill need to control subtle movements of my right foot. This makes the smooth driving of modern cars (with their sharp brakes and delicate pedals) very difficult – my ability to drive a Defender in wellies hasn't been affected.

34. Skiing Without Demons

After writing three books on the subject, you might have thought there was nothing left to say about skiing or about life, limbs and a Land Rover - but I'm going to give it one last chapter.

You might have thought that, after nine years of fighting imaginary demons, I'd grown tired of skiing. My eulogies about fell walking in this last missive might lead you to think that I intended to swap white mountains for green ones - but you'd be wrong. I still want to spend most of my winters in the Alps and still consider Morzine to be my winter home.

You might have thought that after eight years of being a chalet slave, and three volumes of whinging about it, I'd have grown sick of the chalet business - and you'd be right. The only thing I regret about ending the Chalet Project is that, if I'd managed a ninth season this book might have been called 'Neuf is Enough' - which would have been a much better title.

I'll admit that, irritating as they are, I will miss having a stream of new people entering my life, even though I feel my study of posh people on holiday is now complete. For some, the purpose of any endeavour is to meet new people. The older I get, the less tolerant I have become and the more I enjoy being on my own – if I'm honest, I wasn't that tolerant when I was young.

If the purpose of life is to meet new people, I can recommend driving a Defender. Wherever you go in the world, you'll meet other Defender drivers. You also meet lots of nice men who drive breakdown trucks and you make friends with salt-of-the-earth mechanics. You build relationships with those who sell you parts and give you advice and sympathy. You're never really alone, or at least not for very long, when you drive a Defender.

You might have thought that I'd backed the wrong horse by betting that I'd get more skiing gigs from the Ski Club – only time will tell if you are right. It does look like I've been forced to retire from skiing at the front and I'm not entirely unhappy about that.

I can now ski within my own limits, immune to the ski demons, the expectations of others and the responsibility of getting them home. At my age I'm told 'I shouldn't have to do anything I don't want to do', although perversely I'll miss being challenged. I no longer need the validation of wearing a blue jacket - I'm over my uniform fetish; I can now say, 'I *was* a good skier and I *was* a good guide', and no doubt, the older I get, the better at both I will have been.

I've learnt a lot from my time in blue. I've learnt how not to look lost when I am lost and to hide my self-doubt from others. I've learnt how to panic and not let it show or let the ski demons affect my judgment. I've also learnt a lot about mountain safety. I've learnt that many fools ski where angels dare not tread and I now know not to follow them blindly – the fools that is.

You may have thought that being badly injured could have put me off skiing and that it was the snowboard demon that finally got me, but I've learnt that we are more often frightened by our demons than actually hurt - we suffer more from our imagination than from reality. When skiing we play in the lap of nature, which is often a dangerous place to muck about in. But I think it's worth taking a few calculated risks, to get an adrenaline fix and that going skiing is a great way to challenge fear and conquer our demons.

You may conclude that most of the predicaments discussed in these books were of my own making and ask why would someone, with so many ski demons, keep putting himself in their reach? However, in between the incidents of jeopardy and stress described in my books, I've had hundreds of hours of pleasurable skiing. I didn't documented most of them – primarily because describing happiness isn't very funny.

Without consultation, our parents dump us in the big predicament called 'life', usually for selfish reasons. We are born with no way of escaping death. At least with skiing we are responsible for our own predicaments. When we do find ourselves stuck between a rock and a hard place on skis, the solution is always to ski into the hard place. We can't go backwards so it's pointless wishing we'd chosen a better route. Skiing mirrors life in that respect – there is no going back in life and regret is a pointless emotion. When skiing we often move from one snowy predicament straight into another. To enjoy skiing and indeed life, you need to accept the predicament you are currently in and be an existentialist.

From reading my books you may conclude that owning a Defender is not for you. It's often said that the day someone buys a Defender and the day they sell it, are the happiest two days of their lives – but that's not true in my case.

Landie has bought me joy on many a day – usually on days when it wasn't imperative that she started. Every time I turn her ignition key I tingle with excitement because every journey we make together is an adventure. Every time I drive Landie I feel like I'm going on an expedition – even if I'm just driving up the M6 to the Lake District or on a hunter-gatherer mission to ASDA.

Foolishly, Land Rover has just launched a new Defender (to go on sale in 2020). Unless they stuck to the original design brief, I'm sure Defender stalwarts won't like it.

It needs to be able to carry four sheep or eight soldiers in the back, with the option of hosing it out in-between. It needs to work submerged and be self-draining. The engine, at a push, needs to run on old chip pan oil and, if only one wheel has traction, it still needs to move forward. It doesn't need airbags, but a chassis made of girders, to utilise whatever it hits as a crumple zone. It needs to use aluminium body panels to hide structural rust, which can be knocked back into approximate shape with a lump hammer. And finally, it must look better when it's been stuffed through a hedge or two and is covered in mud.

I suspect Land Rover will have failed to meet these criteria. What they will have forgotten is that Defenders are primarily loved because they haven't been spoilt by progress.

My last words must go to the mountains - no doubt you knew they would. Skiing would not appeal to me if it weren't for the landscape it is done in. It's impossible to be in the company of mountains without being in awe of their grandeur. Created by forces we cannot imagine, on a timescale beyond our comprehension, they have a bewildering magic that spellbinds curious humans. It's impossible to stand on top of one, without wondering what's behind the one next to it – and whether it's possible to climb up it or ski down it.

While we try to capture their summits, mountains liberate us from the strife we face in the flat places between them. When in the mountains, just being alive and staying that way, is all that matters. When we ascend them we move in the direction of heaven and all our problems melt away. If you find me in trouble, take me to the mountains so I can wash my soul – just keep me out of the Buddha Bar in case I accidentally drown it.

Everything now having been said, that needed to be said, I will sign off and hope our paths intersect in Morzine one winter soon – although not on the piste. I'm looking forward to Season 10 and to skiing without demons. Now I must go and buy a new ski jacket – any colour but blue will do.

Printed in Great Britain
by Amazon

81365744R00149